Food For Our Grandmothers

Related Titles from South End Press

The Last Generation : Poetry and Prose by Cherríe Moraga

Sisters of the Yam : Black Women and Self-Recovery by bell hooks

State of Asian America : Activism and Resistance in the 1990s
edited by Karin Aguilar-San Juan

State of Native America : Genocide, Colonization, and Resistance
edited by M. Annette Jaimes

*Race, Gender and Work : A Multicultural Economic History of Women in
the United States* by Teresa Amott and Julie Mathei

*Reproductive Rights and Wrongs : The Global Politics of
Population Control* by Betsy Hartmann

The Battle of Beirut : Why Israel Invaded Lebanon by Michael Jansen

The Fateful Triangle : The United States, Israel, and the Palestinians
by Noam Chomsky

Intifada : The Palestinian Uprising Against Israeli Occupation
edited by Zachary Lockman and Joel Beinin

My War Diary : Lebanon, June 5-July 1, 1982 by Dov Yermiya

*Punishing a Nation : Israeli Human Rights Violations During the Pales-
tinian Uprising* by AL-HAQ/Law in the Service of Man

Food For Our Grandmothers

Writings by Arab-American and Arab-Canadian Feminists

Edited by

JOANNA KADI

South End Press – Boston, MA

Cover illustration and design © 1994 by Linda Dalal Sawaya. Painting is based on photo of her great grandmother Mariam Ganamey, Douma, Lebanon c. 1930.

Images on pp. 142-145 taken from a Palestinian Red Crescent Society poster.

Text design and production by the South End Press collective

Printed in the U.S.A.

Library of Congress Cataloging-in-Publication Data

Kadi, Joanna.
    Food For Our Grandmothers : Writings by Arab-American and Arab-Canadian Feminists / edited by Joanna Kadi.
        p.   cm.
    Includes bibliographical references (p?) and index.
    ISBN 0-89608-490-6 : $40.00. — ISBN 0-89608-489-2 (pbk.)

    1. Feminism—United States—literary collections. 2. American literature—Arab American authors. 3. Women—United States—Literary collections. 4. Arabs—United States-Literary collections. 5. Feminism—Canada—Literary collections. 6.Women—Canada-Literary collections. 7. Arabs—Canada—Literary literature—Women authors 10. Canadian literature—Arab authors. I. Kadi, Joanna.
    PS509.F44F66 1994
    810.8'09287'089927—dc20 94-27043
    CIP

To my grandmothers

To our grandmothers

Contents

Acknowledgments

Special thanks to Jan Binder. I would not be where I am today without her incredible love, support, and encouragement. This book is much better because of the help she provided with the day-to-day work involved in such a project.

I am very grateful for the work of my editor at South End Press, Dionne Brooks, and the South End collective in general. I also want to acknowledge my appreciation of the initial support of this project that came from Barbara Smith and Kitchen Table: Women of Color Press.

Throughout the process of editing this book, I've received so much emotional support and sustenance, as well as help with political and artistic decisions. Thanks to all of these wonderful people: Lisa Albrecht, Marti Farha Ammar, Sue Baker, Lisa Bergin, Katy Gray Brown, Katie Cannon, Elizabeth Clare, Becky Conekin, Andrea Densham, Jim Fairhart, Gio Guzzi, Sheri Hostetler, Marjorie Huebner, Myke Johnson, Judith Katz, J.A. Khawaja, Karen Luks, Lisa Suhair Majaj, Dan McMullin, Charlotte and Joseph Michael, Jeff Nygaard, Juliana Pegues, Elissa Raffa, Susan Raffo, Merri Rose, Linda Simon, Linda Suzuki, Joann Vasconcellos, Lynne Whitney, and Beth Zemsky.

A Note About Arabic Terms

Many Arabic words are used throughout this book. By and large, I have left the transliteration the way the authors wrote it. All of us grew up hearing Arabic very differently, because of our countries of origin, our class and regional backgrounds, and the time period our families immigrated. It seemed more appropriate to leave these words and terms mostly as they are, rather than having them conform to one standard, formal transliteration.

Similarly, it seems we all cook with a certain flair and a certain lack of restrictions. The recipes marking each section all came with remarks of this sort: "I never measure it out, they'll have to taste as they go." We all grew up believing that one part of cooking was eating every step of the way, figuring out what worked and what did not. It worked well for us. Try it.

Introduction

JOANNA KADI

I sat in a wooden desk, its top scarred by the pens and knives of students who had gone before me, and stared at the map of the world hanging over the blackboard. "This represents the earth," Mrs. Gallagher said emphatically as my feet swung a few inches above the floor. "North is at the top, south at the bottom. You need to know how to read maps, so that you know where you are."

I could not challenge my teacher, but I didn't know what to make of all this. For one thing, the way I perceived towns and cities, countries and continents did not match the neat, concise way they appeared on maps. For another, even when I learned Mrs. Gallagher's basic map-reading formula, I often did not know where I was. Her formula did not answer my questions. My grandmother told me that Syria and Lebanon hadn't been separate countries when she was growing up, but Mrs. Gallagher spoke adamantly about clear boundaries between them, past and present.

Confused, I dangled my feet in silence.

My dictionary tells me a map is a representation of the earth's surface showing both physical and political features. This definition fits with what I now believe about maps: they exist in many forms, some are complicated and contradictory, and north is not always at the top. Different maps also provide us with new information about where we are. Creating a map is a powerful experience. *Food For Our Grandmothers* can also be understood as a map, representing both physical and political features of the earth's surface. Complicated and contradictory, north is not always at the top. It provides new information about where and how we locate ourselves in the world. Finally, creating this book has empowered, and hopefully will continue to empower many of us.

Maps appear in different forms. Mrs. Gallagher never explained that, but I've figured it out myself. It's true that some maps are on flat

*paper with straight lines, and it's also true that some are twisting
and winding. Braided.*

*I remember standing in that small bathroom watching what
my Gram did with her beautiful hair. It fell past her waist. Dark grey
with light silver threads and a few dark brown ones remaining. She
divided it into three even strands—no easy task.*

*Take those three pieces and weave, curve, twist. Do not pull so
tightly that it hurts your scalp; do not weave so loosely that the hairs
separate. It's hard to find that balance.*

*There are things I once took for granted whose beauty, endur-
ance, and usefulness now astound me.*

I once took my grandmother, my Sittee, whom we called
Gram, for granted. Everything I remember about her I once took
for granted. Today, I am puzzled by and ashamed of this.

Gram had a loving voice, a ready laugh, a soothing touch. Her
green thumb allowed her to grow any plant under any conditions.
She survived poverty in her homeland only to have it follow her
halfway around the world. She loved poker and never lost at cards.

Gram had small, strong, gnarled hands. Work-worn hands,
busy hands. I watched them kneading dough for Syrian bread. I
watched them wrap a new bowl of laban in several towels to sit
overnight. I watched them roll out spinach pies. I watched them
cut freshly-baked kibbeh into diamond-shaped pieces.

I watched those hands braid hair. Beautifully. Daily.

*I know it is possible and I believe it is necessary to create maps
that are alive, many-layered, multi-dimensional, open-ended, and
braided. I watched Gram combing that long hair, dividing it into
three equal parts, twisting and turning and curving the pieces.
Braiding tightly enough so that each hair stays in place, but not so
tightly that it hurts. It is difficult finding that balance.*

*It is difficult finding that balance. Take three strands—one that
is Gram, one that is me, one that is the force of history— twist, turn,
and curve; do not pull so tightly that it hurts; do not weave so loosely
that strands escape. It is difficult finding that balance.*

My grandmother's life began in the Lebanese mountains in the early years of this century. Twenty years ago an aunt told me the name of the village; Aduba Qozhaya. She only told me once. I never forgot it. I carried it with me, a small seed in my left hand. I looked on maps but never found it. It is too small for most map makers to notice.

Gram emigrated to Canada as a young girl—part of a large family looking for a better life. She married a man who had come from Beirut and he died young, decades before my birth. I think pneumonia was the cause. I think poverty was the cause.

So Gram raised five children alone. They had little money. "But she always had food to share," my father said to me once as we drove to the shopping center. He rarely mentioned his childhood. So this story was a most unexpected gift. "All the hobos passing through on the trains during the Depression stopped at our house for dinner, and she always fed them. I thought there must have been a mark on our door, telling them to come in."

These days I am able to appreciate my grandmother's very remarkable and very ordinary beauty. I do wish I could talk to her, I have so many questions. Do transplants ever find home? Are we weakened by the ever-present feeling of not belonging in the west or the east, of having a foot in both worlds but no solid roots in either? Or are we stronger, more innovative and creative, able to make home in odd sites, able to survive in small, hard places, plants growing out of rocks? Perhaps this is our advantage, perhaps this is what we bring to the world. Find home wherever you can make it. Make home so you can find it wherever.

There are things I once took for granted whose beauty, endurance, and usefulness now astound me.

Lebanon is east of here. I am sure of this fact. After all, its location is the Middle East. An appropriate name only if one is a colonizer standing west and invading east. The Middle East. What's in a name? Quite a lot, actually.

Lebanon. I grew up tasting Lebanon and hearing its music, but not speaking and only rarely hearing its language. Often I listened to English spoken by a tongue that had first learned Arabic, a tongue that hissed the s's and rolled the r's. And now when I hear "broken English" it edges its way into my heart.

Lebanese. Not Black. Not white. Never quite fitting in. Always on the edge.

There are things I once took for granted whose ugliness, endurance, and uselessness now astound me.

Dig out a map of my old high school. Try to re-trace those corridors, try to re-cast those sound waves echoing off walls lined with yellow lockers. "Oil slick." "Arab whore." "Greasy Arab."

Jokes I once laughed at, tried desperately to see the humor in. Kevin O'Reilly brazenly skipped school for a whole day; a daring act in 1973. The year of the oil embargo. Arab enemy. Kevin presented his own note to the homeroom teacher next day. "Had to go fight the Arabs and get our oil back." Laughter.

Words of a prophet. Eighteen years later it happened. Although "fight" is not the word I would use.

As Arabs, like other people of color in this racist society, our race is simultaneously emphasized and ignored. For long periods of time no one can remember that Arabs even exist. This is the case no matter how many times non-Arabs are reminded of our presence. Of course, this forgetfulness changes once there is another "crisis" in the Middle East. Crisis: A by-product of past and current colonialism. During crises, Arabs can be reassured we exist as a distinct racial group. We will remember it, in the dark of night and the light of day. We will feel the effects of the social construction of "the Arabs" that has cast us as enemy, other, fanatical terrorist, crazy Muslim. If we are women we can add to that list veiled Woman and exotic whore.

I cannot remember the last time I saw a newspaper headline that did not link Palestinians and terrorism, Islam and fanaticism. Some people are surprised to learn I rarely read newspapers.

I desperately needed a map during the massacre known as the Gulf War. All Arab-Canadian and Arab-American activists—and even those who tried to stay hidden—did. Avoid that street; Arab-

bashers are lurking. Don't go to that demo; too many FBI cameras. Accept this speaking engagement, but not that one. Leave your khaffiya at home tonight. Wear that button. Don't display your grief so openly—it's not the time or the place. Lock the grief inside those brown eyes and hold it there for however long it takes. Don't talk about what you know.

We can talk about what we know, we can work for radical change, we can create maps that chart new ground. I hope this collection of essays and poems offers landmarks, signposts, names, and directions not only for Arab-American and Arab-Canadian communities but for other communities of color and our allies.

Books such as this one have functioned and continue to function in those ways: I am thinking of *This Bridge Called My Back: Writings by Radical Women of Color*, edited by Gloria Anzaldúa and Cherríe Moraga, *Home Girls: A Black Feminist Anthology*, edited by Barbara Smith; *Making Waves: An Anthology of Writings By and About Asian American Women*, edited by Asian Women United of California; *A Gathering of Spirit: A Collection by North American Indian Women*, edited by Beth Brant. Books such as these help record a community's history and spirit. They are valuable maps in our struggle for liberation, offering the hope and information, sustenance and analysis, education and challenges that we need so desperately.

This book is a new map, created by writers, activists, artists, poets, teachers, a mother and daughter team, and two (blood) sisters. We are lesbians, bisexuals, and heterosexuals; of different generations; working class, middle class, upper-middle class; women born in the Arab world and women born here. Even with all this diversity, *Food For Our Grandmothers* is not complete, because many of our experiences and histories are still to be explored. I hope many anthologies follow this one. I believe that this collection is a good beginning, however. I believe it provides a helpful map for women and men in our community who are struggling with issues of culture, identity, history, and activism.

Editing this book raised many political questions. One question I grappled with long and hard was the book's title, and in particular, the phrase "Writings by Arab-American and Arab-Canadian Feminists." Arabs are Semitic people who originated on the

Arabian Peninsula. The nineteen Arab countries on the west part of the Asian continent and the northern part of the African continent are: Lebanon, Palestine, Jordan, Syria, Kuwait, Saudi Arabia, Yemen, Oman, Bahrain, Tunisia, Algeria, Egypt, Sudan, Qatar, Mauritania, Iraq, Libya, Morocco, and the United Arab Emirates. Those countries, along with the non-Arab nations of Turkey, Armenia, and Iran, are often referred to as the Middle East. In some contexts, Somalia and Djibouti are also considered part of the Middle East.

Three contributors to this anthology are of Middle Eastern, but not Arab, descent: two Armenian-Americans and one Iranian-American. These women share a great many things with Arab women. It made sense to include them as contributors and offer them a chance to give voice to their experiences. Yet the title I came up with does not include them.

I tried to find a title that included all contributors to this anthology, and I did not. But as I searched, I gained a new perspective on the power of names and the effects they have on our psyches. Names are critical for a personal and communal sense of affirmation. Choosing our names and thinking through their implications, rather than accepting those given to us by the dominant culture, is an empowering act. I've come up with three possibilities for naming ourselves as a community—Arab-American/Arab-Canadian, people of Middle Eastern/North African descent, and West Asian/North African.

The term "Arab-American/Arab-Canadian" appeals to me. It allows us to reclaim the word Arab, to force people to hear and say a word that has become synonymous with "crazy Muslim terrorists." It affirms our identity and links us to our brothers and sisters in Arab countries. However, there are two problems with this phrase. It does not link us to larger groups of people of color, that is, Asians and Africans, but rather sets us apart and in isolation. This problematic dynamic already exists, because few other groups of people of color know much about or care much about Arabs. It feels important to me to disrupt and change that pattern. Second, "Arab" excludes those three countries with whom we share so much—Armenia, Turkey, and Iran.

If we use the term "people of Middle Eastern/North African heritage," then Iranians, Armenians, and Turks would be included. However we would then have a new consideration, one that I consider an unresolvable political problem concerning the term "Middle Eastern." That term was given to the Arab world by Western (European) colonizers who named the region only as it related to their particular worldview. It's a term that could only make sense to white colonizers so certain their existence and homelands were the center of everything that they actually named huge regions of the world in relation to themselves. It is offensive to me, and not at all affirming, to use such a term to describe my identity. Using the term "Middle Eastern" feels very much like I am adopting the oppressor's language.

The third possibility, "people of West Asian/North African descent," does not feel like the oppressor's language. Further, it does include Arabs and Middle Eastern peoples. Because some Arabs now living in various European countries, such as England and France, identify as West Asian, it may increase visibility for all of us if we use the same term. It would also help forge a strong connection to other people of color, particularly South Asians, whose cultural, religious, and political heritage is similar to ours. However, it is not a perfect solution. I fear that using the term "West Asian/North African" will once again make Arabs invisible. I can safely say that in the United States and Canada people do not think of Arabs as being included with Asians or Africans. Of course, that may change in time. A few years ago, no one considered people of Indian and Pakistani descent South Asians. Now they do. Other Asians acknowledge their existence. It is entirely conceivable that this may happen with Arabs—we may become more visible, and may be perceived as part of a larger group.

One reason it's hard to find an accurate name has to do with our invisibility. It's tough to name a group when most people aren't aware the group exists. I constantly meet people who can't comprehend what I mean when I identify as Arab. "What?" they repeatedly ask, even though I've spoken clearly. That's why, after one particularly bad day, I coined this phrase for our community: The Most Invisible of the Invisibles. Not only did it make me feel better, I realized it might make people stop and think about what I mean. It raises questions about who the other invisibles are, and whether Arabs really are the most invisible. I believe we are. In the United States and Canada, it is not only white people who refuse to see us, it is other people of color—Latinos, Africans, Asians, Natives—who do not acknowledge our existence.

In reflecting on this book's title, I am aware that the subtitle is far from perfect, and that its ambiguity reflects the current complexity and messiness we live with. By contrast, the main title, "Food for our Grandmothers," came to me easily and cleanly in the early days of putting this book together. Reading through a pile of manuscripts that had recently arrived in the mail, I was struck by the incredible number of them centering around our grandmothers and what they had given us. I began to conceive of the book as a way to give something back to our grandmothers and to our community. *Food For Our Grandmothers* made sense as a title, both because the book is an offering back to our grandmothers/our community, and because it offers *appropriate* food for our grandmothers—the Arabic food that many of them made daily. The theme of food is woven through the book. A common Arabic food is used to embody the themes connecting each section, and a recipe using that common food accompanies each section.

There are things I once took for granted whose beauty, endurance, and usefulness now astound me. Thankfully I am at a point in my life where I did not take the following stories for granted. I marvelled at their beauty. I cried over their endurance. I absorbed them in my bones so their usefulness could be with me always. I offer these stories—beautiful, enduring, and useful—to our grandmothers, to ourselves, and to the generations after us.

Food For Our Grandmothers

I

Olives

Our Roots Go Deep:
Where We Came From

Olives

Olive trees in various parts of the Arab world date back thousands of years, and many still bear fruit. This is a fitting image for a discussion of our history. Olive trees represent our long connection to our land and culture. Thus, one of the violations committed by the Israeli army/government upon the Palestinian people, the uprooting of centuries-old olive trees, is horrific. Those trees represent Palestinian connection to the land, as well as their livelihood and culture.

✍ Tomato Salad ✍

3-4 large tomatoes
1-2 cucumbers
3-4 green onions
1 bunch mint
salt and pepper
olive oil

Cut the tomatoes and cucumbers into chunks. Mince green onions and mint. Mix together. Add salt and pepper to taste. Pour olive oil over salad. Let it marinate for at least one hour. Taste again, in case you need to add more salt or oil.

Tomatoes fresh out of the garden are best. Also, extra virgin olive oil makes a big difference. Eat with Syrian bread.

The simplicity of this salad—flavored mostly with the taste of olive oil—makes it special.

✍ Source: Joanna Kadi

Recognized Futures

LISA SUHAIR MAJAJ

Turning to you, my name—
this necklace of gold, these letters
in script I cannot read,
this part of myself I long
to recognize—falls forward
into my mouth.

You call my daily name, *Lisa*,
the name I've finally declared
my own, claiming a heritage
half mine: cornfields golden
in ripening haze, green music
of crickets, summer light sloping
to dusk on the Iowa farm.

This other name fills my mouth,
a taste faintly metallic, blunt
edges around which my tongue
moves tentatively: *Suhair,*
an old-fashioned name, *little star
in the night.* The second girl,
small light on a distanced horizon.

Throughout childhood this rending split:
continents moving slowly apart,
rift widening beneath taut limbs.
A contested name, a constant

longing, evening star rising mute
through the Palestine night.
Tongue cleft by impossible languages,
fragments of narrative fractured
to loss, homelands splintered
beyond bridgeless rivers,
oceans of salt.

From these fragments I feel
a stirring, almost imperceptible.
In the morning light these torn
lives merge: a name on your lips,
on mine, softly murmured,
mutely scripted, both real
and familiar, till I cannot
distinguish between your voice
and my silence, my words
and this wordless knowledge,
morning star rising
through lightening sky,
some music I can't quite
hear, a distant melody,
flute-like, *nai* * through
the olives, a cardinal calling,
some possible language
all our tongues can sing.

* *Nai:* Arabic flute

Sittee (or Phantom Appearances of a Lebanese Grandmother)

THERESE SALIBA

I know that whenever a group of women are gathered together, the grandmother always makes a phantom appearance, hovering above them.

—*Angela Carter*

When you kill the ancestor, you kill yourself.

—*Toni Morrison*

My grandmother's passport is written in French. At the time she took to travel she was twenty-four and Lebanon and Syria were under French mandate. The year was *mil neuf cent vingt et un*, 1921. This document, issued by the *Haut Commissariat de la Republique Française* in Beirut, grants Mlle. Victoria Brahim Simon, born in Lebanon (Liban) in 1897 in Douma, died in____, permission to visit Los Angeles, California, U.S.A. to be reunited with her mother and brothers. It describes every detail of her anatomy:

age - 24	mouth - small
size - 160 cm	beard - n/a
health - good	mustache - n/a
hair - chestnut	body-round
eyebrows - "	face - "
forehead - ordinary	complextion - white
eyes - green	

But the accompanying picture of my grandmother in three-quarter profile is more telling. She stands straight, her chestnut hair drawn back from her face and tied up in a black velvet bow covering the side of her head. Her eyebrows form a sculpted arch above her eyes, which stare obliquely beyond the camera. Her round face is stern. Her arms envelop her wide body, her hands in a tight clasp over her belly. At twenty-four in Lebanon she is a veritable old maid.

According to her 1929 naturalization papers, I see that she is thirty years old, two years younger than she would be according to her passport. The paper bears no picture of her, but states that her complexion, hair, and eyes are now brown, dark brown even. Maybe, I think, this is part of the process of naturalization, the loss of years, the gaining in darkness, the irony of a procedure that as it naturalizes an alien, making her "as if a native," defines her as darker, as Other. The loss of years must have been an act of self-invention, a little lie on my grandmother's part, for the story was told that she had lost her birth certificate back in Lebanon and no one ever knew her age. But the darkness, the dark of her complexion, the brown of her eyes, and the dark brown of her hair on this paper could only be attributed to some *trompe l'oeil,* or the monochromatic vision of the naturalization clerk. As long as I knew my grandmother, her skin was fair and her eyes were green, though in later years they were clouded by age.

She came from the Old Country, a place I imagined where everything was dusted and worn, so she was old to me and her ancient air was enchanting. Hers were an enduring people from a nomadic tribe who some generations ago had settled on fertile hillside in the mountains north of Beirut. It was a comfortable place in peacetime, I was told, but the city had known little peace for longer than she could remember. Sometime between the two great wars, fleeing famine and plague, she and her brother ventured to the New World.

My grandmother spoke little of her old way of life, but it bled through into everything she did. Her speech was thick and heavy, scattered with unfamiliar words; her cooking, seasoned with foreign flavors. Her cooking was the source of her pride and was revealed in the dimensions of her round body. Her full face rested atop her shoulders, her jowls jiggling with delight as she uttered her favorite words, "Suhtein! Suhtein!" (Eat! Eat!). Her nose was peculiarly large, a bulbous mass that spread from cheek to cheek with a slight indentation at the tip. In keeping with Arabic tradition, I called her "Sittee," thinking it was her name, but later learned that it meant "my grandmother" in that foreign tongue she so often spoke.

"Sittee, I hope my nose isn't as big as yours when I get old," I giggled.

"Hmph! Well, when you stop growing, your nose doesn't, and when you've lived as long as I have, you end up with this." She chuckled, touching the tip of her nose with her red-painted fingernail.

Sittee had spent most of her life eluding years and the fragmented history of her homeland. She took from time freely, handfuls of years she felt had been stolen from her. She disguised her age as best she could, dying her hair rusty red, painting her lips with ruby gloss. And as her sight grew dim, I would sit beside her on the couch while she held a cosmetic mirror out in front of her, her jowls expanded in the magnified image of the glass. "There's one," she'd say, pointing out the uncomely whiskers that sprouted from her double chin, then I plucked them out, wincing more at the pain than she. In my eyes, she was ancient from the day I was born.

On weekdays I lived in an American world. But on weekends, I lived in a world of foreign foods, strange language, incense, ritual, bazaar and bizarre. Sittee embodied this difference. She was a widow, a bitter woman who maintained notions of her nobility from her Lebanese village even as she rolled grapeleaves in the tiny kitchen of her Hollywood apartment. As a child, I was enchanted by her scent of lemon jasmine, her dyed red hair, her painted nails, her bureau full of sampler gift items (she would let us choose one gift every week, gifts she got at luncheons, whatever they were). And when she came to visit, she came bearing *fistu* (pistachio nuts), pomegranates, *kibbee* (pressed lamb), Syrian bread, and holy bread. There was something sacred and human in this culture that let you take holy bread home, bread that was thick and full, unlike the stale wafers of the Catholic church where my mother often took us on Sunday mornings. I looked forward to the monthly bazaars at the Orthodox church where I could wander from table to table, tasting honeyed pastries, trying on bracelets and bangles, holding tightly to my grandmother's hand. "*Ya 'albee inte*," she would say to me, as she spread her fingers across my chest. "You are my heart."

If a woman could be a land, then Sittee was Lebanon to me. If a person could be colonized as a country, then Sittee still bore the scars of French colonization. Once while I explored the relics in her apartment—pointed gold slippers with braided straps, chiseled brass plates, pastel-colored glass trays holding *fistu*—I found a stash of letters scrawled with words I couldn't recognize. I was learning to read and had taken to reading anything I could get my hands on. I pressed the thin paper to my nose. Everything, when held close enough, smelled of lemon jasmine and Jean Naté. Sittee saw me trying to decipher the letter, pried it from my hands, and began reading aloud in a strange, melodic sound that I knew was not her native Arabic. I stood staring up at her, my eyes fixed on her mouth, the ruby lipstick faded from the edges of her lips which formed round "o"s and purring "r"s. She looked down at me and drew me to her. "French," she said. "Isn't it a beauuuu-tiful language? Beauuu-tiful." I nodded. "I learned it in school," she said, "and when you are old enough, you must study French, too." Years later, I did. And though she never told me to learn Arabic, I studied that as well, but never learned to speak it as fluently.

That day, while I was thinking about the beauty of the French language and distant lands where everything was either beautiful or old, I escaped into Sittee's bathroom and locked the door. I took the mirror from her counter, a mirror encased in platinum with the initials "VSS" engraved on the back in a delicate hand. Victoria Simon Saliba. I knew Victoria had been a queen of some place, and that Sittee was named after her. Sittee always kept that mirror on her bathroom counter beside a matching platinum brush that was as big as my head and had soft natural bristles. But I never understood why she would need a mirror when she had that giant mirror before her on the wall, so I looked at these relics from the Old Country as merely ornamental, as signs of nobility, and I would lock myself in the bathroom for long hours, pretending to have problems with my bowels, only to play with that mirror and brush, to gaze at my small face in the broad face of the mirror, to run the heavy brush through my fine hair, to imagine myself a queen of sorts in her queenly toiletry. Sometimes I would let my younger sister in, but she of course would have to be the servant who would brush my hair while I uttered commands in a newly discovered language, my make-believe French.

Years later at a downtown bookstore, I heard Lebanese writer Etel Adnan explain how the nuns at the French colonial schools told the students that they must not speak Arabic, that it was an irrational, illogical language, and that French alone was the language of rational thought. I'm not sure if Sittee believed this. By that time she was not around and so many of her stories had been buried with her. But like so many of the Lebanese who chose to think of themselves as more European than Arab, tracing their descendants to the ancient Phoenicians and the wonders of the conqueror rather than the conquered, she seemed to relish excessively the French language and Jean Naté perfume.

The lemon jasmine was from Lebanon and the Jean Naté from France, and as she stood over me in the kitchen while I pulled the tips and strings from the green beans and washed them, Sittee's fragrance swam around me in the steam from the chicken boiling on the stove. The loose skin on her upper arms jiggled as she kneaded dough, and then rolled it out before my sister and me. We stood with glasses in hand arguing over who would cut the round forms for the meat pies, and who had to fill the forms with lamb and pine nuts, then fold the edges up and press them into perfect triangles. As I was ten and my sister only eight, I would have won these arguments had Sittee not insisted that we share the tasks. And while the meat pies baked, Sittee stuffed *koosah* (zucchini) with lamb and rice while my sister cut tomatoes for *tabouleh,* and I chewed on the pine nuts spilled across the kitchen counter. Sittee never told me I would ruin my appetite—this was all part of the process of tasting and testing. In Arabic tradition, it is said that you eat as much as you love the cook. Every seed, every appetizer counted as part of this love, and we always ate well.

As we stood in the steamy Saturday afternoon kitchen kneading dough and pinching meat pies, I asked Sittee, "Was Lebanon beautiful?"

"Yeeee!" she said, then lapsed into memories and ramblings in Arabic, the only language that could express her country's beauty. Every time I wanted to experience Lebanon, she lapsed into sounds I could not decipher, as if a country cannot be translated to any other language except that which is native to it. It didn't seem to matter to Sittee that I missed the details of her yearnings in the rise and fall of her voice, but I did understand that this country was beautiful—not in the way the French language was beautiful, but in the way a lone cedar growing out of jagged rock is beautiful. Sittee's clouded eyes watered as she spoke of Lebanon. Something awful, some great apocalypse had destroyed her country. But the way she described the cedars and their dark branches in the evening breeze from the verandah of her mountain villa, I thought surely our family was among the ancient Egyptian pharaohs. We had lost much in coming to this country, but I imagined that Cedars Sinai hospital, which stood in the heart of Los Angeles, was a modest commemoration to my family and the cedar trees that brought Sittee to tears.

When Sittee's sister Genvieve came from Douma to Los Angeles to visit, her burnt leather face told once again how Lebanon made everything old. I had never before seen a face so creviced and dried to that prunelike quality of things left too long in the sun. Her gray hair was pulled back from her face and tied in a knot behind her head. Genvieve, though several years younger than Sittee with fair skin and dyed red hair, looked like her sister's mother. As the sisters sat beside each other on the sofa, it was clear that they inhabited different worlds, though they were both born and raised in Douma. Genvieve still lived in this mountain village, but moved between Douma and Paris when the civil war got troublesome. She had ten children, and when one of her grown sons was shot in the head and killed while crossing the street in Beirut to buy some milk, she came to visit her sister in Los Angeles. But she would return again to Douma. The root of the word "Douma" in Arabic means persistence, continuity, perseverance. They were the three best words I could find to define the women in our family, as Sittee and Genvieve sat on the couch in the evenings, telling stories in Arabic and running green thread through their leathered fingers, around a crochet hook, the half-made blankets falling over their knees.

Saliba, my grandfather's name, comes from the Orthodox tradition and means "bearers of the cross," a distinctly Christian name. My grandfather was from a not-so-distant mountain village to the south of Douma, and I imagine my grandparents looked on similar cedar trees in the dry evenings, rustling with cicadas' wings.

They met in this country after an exchange of photographs brought them to their wedding day. Sittee was almost forty by then, and my mother insists that her photograph had been finely touched up, particularly around the nose and jowls. But whatever the arranged exchange entailed, I'm sure Sittee felt fortuitous to have such a handsome groom.

My grandfather was photogenic, after all. I knew him only in pictures that Sittee kept by her bedside or stored away in old shoe boxes, but the way Sittee spoke of him, I knew he too was from that noble line of Phoenician kings of Old Country fame, long before the cedars of Lebanon were transformed to neon in Los Angeles. Samuel Saliba's ancestors had traveled to China to bring silkworms to the mountains of Lebanon, and these centuries of silk spinning and fine fabrics were handed down in the New World to a traveling garment salesman, specializing in children's clothes. Sittee said she had never remarried because she did not want to give up the Saliba name. When she said this, she pressed her folded hands to her heart, and wove long stories about my great-great-grandfather Saliba who was mayor of the village, and who, during the plague went about burying the dead among his people, until he too caught the disease and died, and how another great-uncle was archbishop of this diocese, and how another was a famous doctor named Moses who invented a cure for a disease I couldn't pronounce.

All this history is written in a book. The introduction to the book says, "History is only a biography on a larger and more exhaustive scale." The book traces the Saliba history back to the 5th century B.C. in ancient Sparta. I studied Sparta in the fourth grade, and we learned that the Spartans were a warlike, fighting people who couldn't defend themselves against the peace-loving and rational Athenians. We are always on the wrong side of history. Except that the Salibas were Christians from the earliest days after Christ, not converts from the Crusades, and this seemed to give us some advantage over pagans and Jews and Muslims, at least according to this book, which claims to contain "no aberrations." After centuries of battles and defending the cross against Judaism and Islam, after spreading Christianity throughout Syria, Palestine, and Lebanon, and after the brothers of a particular line begat sons, and more males begat more males, the Saliba line of the story ends: "Samuel, the fifth son of Moses, begat Ronald (my father) and

Gilbert. The said Samuel died in California in 1949." The story tells only the history of men.

ᵃᵗᵇ

I knew Sittee's history only in the confused and convoluted ways of a child. By the time I was old enough to understand her Old World ways and decipher the language of her movements when I couldn't understand her speech, I was a teenager. Because I wanted to forget my Arabness and to be like everyone else, I didn't have much time for Sittee. Besides, we had moved to Seattle, and our Saturday afternoons together diminished to brief visits in summertime. I remember how on each visit, she sat on her sofa dressed in black (another friend had passed away, another death of memory) beneath a painting of a shepherd boy leading his flock along a dusty road. It was a picture of an Italian landscape, but Sittee said she bought the painting because it reminded her of home. When she said "home," she always meant Lebanon, a Lebanon her memory had fixed in a pastoral painting. I sat beside her beneath that painting playing with the nap of her olive velvet couch, rubbing it the dark way, then the light, as I had done as a child. Back then, when she noticed me staring at the painting, trying to place her in this landscape of orange rock and olive trees, amongst the sheep crossing a small stone bridge, she pointed up at the one black sheep in the flock, and said, "See, this little black one is you." Then she pulled me to her, and kissed me loudly on the ear with a force that left my ear ringing.

Sittee died when I was twenty. I was attending the university when I heard she was sick and drove 1,000 miles to see her. Her air of antiquity that had once left me in awe had decayed. Her gray skin hung loosely on her shrunken frame. The red dye gone, her white wisps of hair faded into the colorless sheets. I sat beside her for hours, clinging to her withered hand as she moved between wakefulness and sleep, between Los Angeles and Lebanon, while I spun remembrances of Saturday afternoons in the kitchen with her, as if all my talk could keep her with me. And as if in the kitchen ten years ago, I asked again, "What was Lebanon like when you were my age?"

Even Sittee's Arabic lay silent within her as some memory floated past her clouded vision. I wondered what she saw in her faraway thoughts—the cedar branches in the evening wind, her mother kneading dough in the kitchen, mountains rising up out of the Mediterranean on summer days at the beach.

At last she spoke. "Your life isn't worth anything," she confessed to me. "Life isn't worth a thing."

᠊ᢦ᠊

Sometimes I think if I tell these stories enough, I'll understand Sittee's last words to me. When I told my brother what she said about the worthlessness of life, he thought for sure she had said that because I was a woman, because Arab culture rides the value of masculinity with reckless bravado, and that even Sittee had bought into it. He should know since he was the sole male grandchild and the recipient of all these benefits—as a boy, coffee cans full of pistachio nuts, boxes of color-coated almonds, and in later years, thousands of dollars. But I find his interpretation too simple, because Sittee was a strong woman, and not likely to be beaten down by virtue of her gender no matter what tradition said. I think for her this conclusion may have come from the slow accumulation of loss—of homeland, of husband, of heart.

Sittee trusted too much in the promise of America while living with nostalgia for Lebanon. She believed what she read in the morning paper as she ate sour yogurt. She believed in the nobility of the past, and though she was from a family of endurers, she had a tendency to misjudge her enemies. To her French was beautiful, red hair and white skin were beautiful, and she always told me to stay out of the sun because my olive skin had grown dark as a coffee bean. The Palestinians, she said, had destroyed her homeland. And though I only knew Lebanon from textbooks, I knew that Britain and France had taken control of and carved up the Middle East, and then had given Palestine to the Jews, who drove the Palestinians into Southern Lebanon and neighboring Arab states. So if the Palestine Liberation Organization had a hand in Lebanon's destruction, Israel, Western Europe, and the United States all had at least two hands in Lebanon's civil war which had ripped Sittee's country into shredded memories of mountain villas and quiet summer evenings on the verandah.

Sittee had returned to Lebanon for a visit in 1958. Arab nationalism was at its height, and President Eisenhower, concerned with protecting U.S. interests in the region, landed 15,000 Marines in Beirut. Lebanon's President Chamoun tried to align Lebanon with the West against the Arab states, and Sittee joined in this alliance. She baked sheets of cookies, drove down to the port in Beirut, and distributed them to the U.S. marines. I imagine her with her boxes of *ba'laywab* moving among the blue-suited men, in what she considered a patriotic gesture to her new country, with no sense of contradiction or conflict as she drove back up the hills toward Douma.

In 1991, I decided to travel to Lebanon, so my father sent me Sittee's passport and naturalization papers. Because U.S. hostages were being held in Lebanon, the United States still had a ban on its citizens traveling there. But if I could prove I was of Lebanese heritage and purchase a plane ticket through Amman or Cairo, I could somehow circumvent the restrictions. I had filed for a Syrian visa, because although the civil war had ended, Lebanon was now under Syrian control. But my cousins, who lived in my grandfather's village of Bteghreen in the mountains above Beirut, were having problems with various factions who resented the United States turning the other way as Syria took control of Lebanon. They feared the anti-American sentiment in the wake of the Gulf War might cause problems in my travel plans. "Do not come," they insisted. "Wait until things have settled down here. We can't be responsible for you."

I thought then that I would never see Lebanon, that it would disappear before I had the chance to return. I looked down at Sittee's passport. Too many borders seemed closed. And though I spent the summer instead in the West Bank, just miles from Lebanon, I couldn't enter Sittee's country because Southern Lebanon was under siege from Israel and the borders were closed.

The mountains in northern Palestine must look something like Sittee's village, I thought, staring out from another verandah upon a hillside of olive trees, listening to cicadas rustling in the heat of midday. I waited with my husband in the dust of the road for a taxi to Jerusalem. When I got in beside an old man, his burnt leather face framed by a black and white *kaffiyeh*, he smiled pleasantly, sensing our foreignness. "Hello," my husband said in Arabic, "We're from America." The man turned to me and, noticing my Arabness (brown face, dark hair, and dark eyes), raised his eyebrows as if to say, "You too?" "I speak a little Arabic," I said, as I prefaced everything on this trip, "My grandparents are from Lebanon." "*Yee, Lubnan,*" he said, pressing his leathered hand to my cheek. "*Lubnan, Lubnan,*" he shook his head as his eyes began to water. We sat staring into each other's faces in silent recognition of loss, as we drove past the corrugated steel of the refugee camps, past the Israeli military camps, and I had a sense then why Sittee's eyes always watered when she spoke of Lebanon.

When I got my first job teaching high school in the inner-city, my mother took me to a local department store and bought me several outfits to wear. When I returned home, I spread them out before my father for his approval. He looked up at me over the top of his wire-rimmed glasses and said, "You're young. What do you want to wear all these dark clothes for? You'll look like those old ladies from the Old Country."

I gathered up the clothes, draped them over my arm, and stood before my father, thinking of my aunts and great-aunts who gathered in Sittee's kitchen to roll grapeleaves as their Arabic words bounced back and forth across the table, their fingers as busy as their mouths. Their dark clothes had not struck me then, but I think now, perhaps I had inherited a history of mourning.

Sittee appears to me now at night standing beneath a lamp-post, her shadow spreading up the stairs of my apartment building. I walk down the steps toward her, calling her name. She motions to me to follow and together we glide along the sidewalk, my fingers reaching for the fringes of her crocheted shawl fluttering in the night wind. She is taking me somewhere, I don't know where. As we wind our way through the deserted alleyways of the bazaar, past tables of jewelry, perfume, and ceramics, past shops without vendors, I reach for her hand and we stand together beneath the domed archway of the night, speaking Arabic, her language I have come to know.

Great-Grandma Michael

TRISHA F. HARPER

for Lisa Majaj and Naomi Shihab Nye

Window drapes in her death room
Heavy yellowed lace, thicker
than a shield, than the bayou's heat
swamped at her
porch steps

I am pinched
in patent leather, knees locked
under a velvet green dress
collared by lace. I breathe
slow-rot odor of the dying

My own mother grips my shoulder
steers me at the pillow. My panic
grows hysterically
silently, breathes my great-grandmother's
last oxygen

One of her daughters
fluffs the pillow, knots
a noose of Arabic
under my lace
straightens the bedclothes

I think in pieces

                           She smells like she's 400
                           When she's dead no one will call us

Mikhail anymore
Grandma will make baklava

I lean my neck into the noose
gulp for air too dark
for me, mortally wounded
My own grandmother clicks pine rosary
beads in the living room, prays for her
mother's American salvation
...Thy will
be done, on earth as it is...
I think to cry but can't, am nowhere
near it

I am closer to peeling off my new
shoes, to rending my laced collar, tightening
the noose
My mouth gapes to wail songs
of the dead in a language I don't know

to suck my great-grandmother's
fingers
into my mouth
clamp them steady
with my teeth

As if her fingerprints on my tongue
will teach it what it doesn't know
As if they will pull from my stunned heart
prayers in a language it sings
in a language she understands

My mother jostles me
Say something to your great-grandma

I step back, shrug
I am four
I do none of those

things

Longing for Winter

ADELE NE JAME

for my grandmother

How she would work late winter afternoons
in the parlor, the Singapore lamps burning
dark yellow, all the colors in that room
reflecting each other, Veronese green
into ocher, ocher into flaming sienna
and in that light, the outline of her body
seemed as dark and harmonious as the bitumen
of an early Cézanne canvas. Her hands
resting on my shoulders held up the muslin
as she imagined a pattern for the velvet
so lavishly chosen, a bolt of luminous
blond silk unfurled on the sofa,
the lining, she had said, to be worn
against a young woman's bare flesh.

Standing there, in the hypnotic light of
that room, hardly aware of her fingers
fitting the seams, how often I would hear,
diri daharik, "turn your back"
in Arabic, the imperative,
that would call me out from among
the alembics, the firelight of
the heart where every loss is known
in advance, where betrayal,
however distilled,

is never coolly burned away.

She, who lived, and married
not the one chosen for her—*the lunatic*
whose house should fall into ruin, she would say—
but Wadia from the Shuf mountains,
the one she tenderly called cousin
all her life. She who believed in dreams
predicting the future, who on high holy days,
whether in Beirut or Bay Ridge, had walked
barefoot to church, had once offered the long
hair of her first son to Saint Fena,
matching the weight of it with gold.
She, who would recite
the love story of Boaz and Ruth to me,
eighty verses in French or Arabic,
who was dishonored by a husband's
betrayal with other women,
was abandoned in the late years
by his dying first.
Finally, it was she who sat alone
on the steps, crying in the perishing
afternoon light.

In the end, no one is saved, the poet says,
and no one is wiser. On this warm and
starless night, lying here with you,
astonished still
by the slow extravagance of your body
over mine, your eyes are
dissonant with desire and remorse.
And as soon as you dress to leave,

dark and silent and not for me, really,
the night's song, an unguarded sound,
that particular knowledge of mouth and palm
as if tucked inside a pocket
with what little evidence
there is of love or repair—
all become for you an affirmation
of disbelief, a sad kind of praising
to fill the welcoming night air.

And how these gorgeous unmoving trees
are a burden. How completely
a life is altered by a gesture
of restraint, the thing not
offered, the unspoken imperative that,
acquiescing, I take up,
and with the turning back, this
terrific longing for winter and the deadly calm
music of an indifferent heart.

Battling Nationalisms
to Salvage Her History

L. J. MAHOUL

Although I have gone through numerous stages in thinking about what to call myself—Lebanese, Lebanese-American, white American (my immediate family being light-skinned), Semitic, third generation Lebanese-American, Lebanese...with altered voice...Christian, you know, Maronite, Phalange, Fascist—Arab has never come to mind. Sometimes it has depended on the company. My family would be aghast if I said Arab, so might other Arabs who never have had occasion to question their Arab identity. West Africans or Brazilians might think of me as not only American, but of Lebanese Maronite descent, those merchants and shopkeepers of ill repute. At each point along the way, I have thought I had settled upon a satisfactory answer to the question of nationality. But it has become more complicated as I have related the history I grew up with to the history viewed from the alternative places these names signify.

Only during the Gulf War did I finally think of myself as an Arab-American. Arab protesters were sought after to voice opposition to the war, but I refused to preface my remarks with a flag to this identity. To most people I have a Scottish surname, changed by my father's father, but more important, my family history never translated into an Arab nationalism borne out of U.S.-style racism or out of anti-Arab harassment by agents of the U.S. government. I passively accepted that Arab-Americans were not considered a minority group like other racial-ethnic groups protected by anti-discrimination civil rights laws. Although I knew better, I never systematically challenged the mythology of assimilation that "we" are white, Christian, hard-working, and non-political; not Muslim, Arab, colored, or fanatical. It was the Gulf War that opened my eyes to the reality of Christian Lebanese organized as *Arab*-Americans for radical causes even though I knew of no one in my extended family or our Lebanese community who shared my political beliefs. Indeed, the viciousness of anti-Arab sentiment in my family made it nearly impossible to cut through the lies of Lebanese nationalism. My mother recalls growing up in the 1950s and being asked about her nationality. She stumbled through a list of answers looking for one that might gain a nod of affirmation. Although she contends that she was never subjected to "overt" racism, she had to say Syrian (or Italian, or Greek...) since nobody had ever heard of Lebanon. When her father learned of this, he berated her for associating the family with Syrians, whom he considered Muslims. The idea that we spoke Lebanese and not Arabic probably originated with her father as well, who thought it important that the children learn how to speak only English. As a result, my parents' generation understands but cannot speak Arabic.

I am now learning Arabic and it has enabled me to break through to another submerged history: my grandmother's. Not too long ago, when earnestly helping me to learn Arabic, she asked for some *quid pro quo* in the form of English lessons. She communicates mostly in Arabic but had an unexpressed yet longstanding desire to learn English. My sister and I worked together trying to satisfy her top two requests—writing her children's names in English and writing checks. My sister took charge of the checkwriting lessons by printing some numbers, months, and dates. I demonstrated how to write my aunts' and uncles' names and then wrote out a translation of the Arabic alphabet to the Roman alphabet. Even though we soon realized that checkwriting involves so much more than we could offer, the joy she displayed in first learning how to write her children's names in English and then the anticipation of writing a check was nothing short of remarkable. The fact is that nobody had tried to teach her how to issue her own money in sixty years, while she endured her husband's constant orders not to spend it.

My grandmother was opening herself up in these new ways only because of the freedom she felt during one unusual visit to my family's home some distance away from the one she shares with her only son. Although travelling and changing her daily routine set her health back, the radical improvement in her disposition made her illness hardly noticeable. She never looked better than when she recounted her autobiographical stories to me. She chose to share two incidents: the first time her parents arranged a marriage for her and a time when she gathered water alone on a river bank and thought she might be abducted by two men on horseback.

Describing her husband as simple and from a very mean family, Sittee resented her mother for forcing her into marriage and what it meant at that time: leaving her mother to go to the United States in 1930 at age sixteen (for which her mother apologized when she migrated three decades later). Sittee faults her mother for not giving her away to the first caller, even though Sittee was embarrassed and disgusted with the entire process. A man from the Lebanese village of Hamana had been to Venezuela and brought back a bundle of money. Passing through the village of Aitaneet, he feasted his eyes upon my Sittee with her long auburn hair. At the age of fourteen, she remembers herself as shy, covering her face when other girls did not. Soon he came visiting. Although some family members approved the match, especially an important uncle of hers, Sittee hated his nasty glances at her body and eventually became physically ill. In retrospect, Sittee thinks of how his older age and wealth might have meant proper schooling for her, yet she does not acknowledge the role her induced sickness played in foreclosing this option.

Unlike Sittee's father, her mother believed she was not feigning illness and also believed the story about the men who set out to steal her. Her father took her out to the grape fields where he worked and asked her to fetch water a long distance away. At the riverside below an embankment she heard the voices of men plotting above. She escaped by crossing the river and heading home. Refusing to work in the fields ever again, she avoided the danger of encountering moneylenders and steamship agents who commonly marauded the Mount Lebanon area in the early 1900s. Ottomans began to conscript Christians after 1908, so they exerted a heavy interventionist presence as well. Sittee's father apparently made frequent trips to the United States, so he must have been aware of this treacherous environment. Even though her father returned home with a small fortune, Sittee only wishes that he would have never returned. Recalling hunger so severe that she would collapse, she insists that during her early years it was her mother who frequently went searching from village to village for food. Probably this took place during World War I, when massive starvation struck as the British, French, and their local agents choked off the area from food supplies. In contrast to the pervasive paradigms of nationalistic Lebanese history that I grew up with, it's been unbelievably *hard* to learn even this much about the life of my grandparents. My Sittee's newest expression is a stinger, coming now at the age of 80. "Ah...what a life...what can you do," she says with a cadence that each day brings her closer to death. When she saw me writing down these fragments of her life, she asked, "Why?" "Because you're a very important person, Sittee," I told her. "Only you think so," she responded. And that is true. She is a timeless, beloved entity whose history is not known. By all her daughters' accounts, and her own, she did not want to come to the United States nor marry my grandfather. As a result, I know more about her first years in the Old Country than I suspect I will ever know about her life here.

Not everyone in my family supports my attempts to get close to my grandmother. As part of my uncle's need to gain her exclusive attention (and money), he hoped to sever the bond between us by emphasizing my irreverence for some of the family's most deeply held beliefs about religion, race, and sexuality. I found out later that the week before my visit with them he accused me of believing that the "Blessed Virgin Mary" had four children, something he considers utter blasphemy. To put his comment in perspective, in the Maronite fascist party's * 1970s war against the Palestinians, who are mostly Sunni Muslims, party members recruited Catholics by warning that the Blessed Virgin Mary could become virtually extinct. And because of my Sittee's strong identification with the Mother of the Church, this is no small matter to her. But this is not all. To round out the attack, my uncle told my grandmother that I am a lesbian. Although I am not, it certainly has not been uncommon for homophobic family members (which is all of them) to associate my feminist beliefs with a lesbian sexual orientation. My mother found this accusation so reprehensible that she could hardly bring herself to tell me about it.

---

* The Kataeb Party was born in the 1930s and drew inspiration from the Hitler Youth, Franco's Falange, and a traditional grouping around the Gemayel family. It became the strongest Maronite Christian party because of its wide base of support among the Maronite petite bourgeoisie.

During my visit, my uncle manipulated us even further. By drawing me into an argument over the 1992 uprising in Los Angeles, he set me up as a fanatical abeed lover in Sittee's presence. Blacks have become the Arab Muslims of America and therefore are considered terrorists at best and pitifully barbaric at worst. This latest encounter with my uncle and Sittee so clearly exposes all the contradictory pressures and deep ambivalences I feel toward my family. I derived my anti-racist consciousness in reaction to my family and not in response to anti-Arab sentiment directed at me or even other family members, who were proud of their Lebanese heritage and lamented only the embarrassment of being labeled a member of a "lesser race"—Chicano, Filipino, or Black.

Our rigid internal hierarchies are those of class, skin color, gender, and sexuality. Yet in spite of them, I had to figure out how to maintain family, and especially this relationship with my Sittee. Numbed by the overwhelming conservatism of everyone I knew as my family, I nevertheless needed to break through the fear and hate so ingrained in the experience of the first two "family loving" generations and find some explanations and another history. Like bringing the Freudian unconscious to consciousness, there's no telling what lurks behind that innocent question about one's personal history. Since the grandmother I mention here is my only living grandparent, she has been the focus of this treacherous probing, often unwilling to confront her past. She is now hemmed in by her only son (who lives with her) and freedom has yet to come her way.

Sometimes I wonder, though, how she too has been a solid defender of the mythology. There is no question that my mother's family represented the ideal Lebanese immigrant experience writ large to create the impression that it was naturally so. My uneducated grandfather owned a restaurant with his brother, and their wives never worked outside the home. My mother still insists that most Lebanese made their living by owning small businesses despite the evidence that 75 percent of Arab immigrants (both men and women) were peddlers, craftsmen, or unskilled workers, and that several of her aunts and uncles worked in factories at some point in their lives. My mother also denied the experience of my father whose parents were Lebanese Maronite immigrants. Growing up poor in North Carolina, the son of a travelling truck driver, my father embodies the struggling immigrant's will to work hard and uplift the next generation. But the momentum of class mobility silences his history too, a result of being both poor and from the south. Although I've tried to understand my Sittee's life and her generation's beliefs about national identity, I need to understand my own political upbringing and the politics that still haunt and feed my extended family. Even though most of the revised history of Lebanon is now uncontroversial and acknowledged today by historians who helped in the myth-making, such as Kamal Salibi, it still remains threatening. It took the Gulf War, which my family supported, to finally push me toward a direct confrontation with the familiar history that had disturbed me ever since I can remember. Not too long ago, though, I glimpsed the other side of the coin: the silence surrounding my grandmother's life. Why do we know so little about her life or even what she thought about her memorable experience—especially those from her childhood and early adult years? The silence does not reflect lack of interest, but lack of an appreciation of history and a preoccupation with current events in the family (like the control wielded by my uncle now that my grandfather is dead). Much of the silence must no doubt be attributed to the fear of confronting the past and challenging comfortable myths about our histories.

For My Son Shaadi

MARTI FARHA AMMAR

In a third-floor ballroom
from the 1920s I watch a ten-year-old
use hardwood floors, vaulted ceilings
for a basketball court. Hair dripping
he moves from athletics to music,
a steel drum, a palette of sounds.
But his blood runs to America
from the Arab World not the Caribbean.

Dressed in black pants,
white shirt, tasseled loafers,
he waits for his first gig.
Blotches of red appear
on his translucent face.
"I wish my skin were dark
like yours, mom," even though his blood
runs to America from the Arab World.

One thick bar of brow rests
over eyes, irises black.
In the mirror, his straight hair
refuses to hold. He says,
"Mom, why can't I have curly hair
like you or Emaka?"
Emaka's blood runs to America
from Africa.

My brother, older by two years
as dark and swarthy as me.
The first son, the patriarch's
namesake. His hair
never straightened,
his skin never bleached.
His Hittite nose never broken,
reset or re-formed.

In the mirror I recognize
my nose reworked.
I see my brown skin
burned by bleach.
I remember facial hair
removed by wax, ripped
from the surface. I know
those eyes, irises of black
with indistinguishable pupils.

Crossing Over to the Other Side

MARTHA ANI BOUDAKIAN

My great aunt Tsainig refused to change her name when she came to the United States from Western Armenia in the 1930s. Her older brother, my grandfather, anglicized the family name Hampartsoumian when he came to the United States several years earlier. He shortened it to Hampar and all other members followed suit. With her fighting spirit, Tsainig, whose name actually means "little voice" (which she has anything but) insisted on keeping her name as Hampartsoumian. She would not compromise something as precious to her Armenian identity as her name.

Two generations later, my life is a different story. As an adolescent I wanted desperately to get rid of any attributes that marked my Armenian identity. I tried to remove all of my body hair, plotted the date of my nose job and breast reduction surgery, and imagined how I would neutralize my name. I wanted nothing more than to mold the telltale signs of my Armenianness into something that just didn't stand out—into something "normal." My grand transformation also included failed attempts to starve myself and to control my volatile Armenian spirit, in short, to make myself as little an aberration as possible from WASP culture. I believed that despite my attempts to attain normality, I would never be good enough, because I was not made of the right stuff.

What does "normal" mean anyway? Calling something a cultural "norm" usually means following the ways of those with the most political and material resources in any society. They define and impose their experience of normality for everyone. The concept of cultural norms in multicultural societies is historically enmeshed in power, colonialism, and control. In the United States, norms are defined and imposed by white, upper-class men, as they are in much of the world. Any way of life that differs from that elite patriarchal norm is marginalized until it is conveniently co-opted by the dominant culture; even then it remains marginal. "Passing" for normal means trying to emulate the dominant culture, in order to survive in it. To break this oppressive cycle, we can refuse assimilation and choose what black feminist scholar and activist bell hooks calls power on the margin. She cites the margin as a place of resistance where oppressed people can take what is useful from the dominant culture without adopting its ways. She clearly designates a difference between being a marginal object, forced to the edge of a society, and a marginal subject, finding power to resist from the home space of the margin.*

Armenians have lived on the margin, both as marginal subjects and marginal objects. Having been dominated for so long by other peoples, Armenian communities worldwide are known for their insular cohesiveness. However, many Armenians in the United States have managed to "pass" as best they can in the dominant culture and still remain centrally involved with the Armenian community. On the whole, Armenians in the United States have not suffered intensive economic oppression. To survive, we have shifted our value systems to accommodate capitalist, industrial society by becoming literate in the language of the oppressor.

More reflective of what I understand to be authentic Armenian values is the ethic of valuing people over money and material possessions. Armenian culture also encourages the well-being of the collective rather than Western individualism. My people have an ancient and expressive literary, spiritual and artistic tradition, connected to other Near Eastern cultures, yet very much its own. We are a lively, strong, generous and loving people, deeply connected to our native, mountainous land.

A critical event in recent Armenian history was the Genocide of 1915 to 1923. During that time, the Ottoman Turks decimated the population of Western Armenia (the eastern half of modern Turkey). They killed 1.5 million Armenians and deported many others to the Syrian desert via forced exodus. The genocide was masterminded by the Young Turks, the latter-day dictators of Ottoman Turkey. They massacred my people because we maintained our Christian faith, managed economic prosperity, and presented an obstacle to the Young Turks' attempt to revive a dying empire.

My family and hundreds of thousands of other Armenian families endured horrors as obscene as those of any genocide—

* bell hooks, *Yearning* (Boston: South End Press, 1990), 145-53.

summary executions, deportations, rape, and torture. My own grandmother, orphaned at age eleven, shaved her head to disguise herself as a boy and escape sexual assault by Turkish soldiers. She then spent the rest of her childhood at an American mission orphanage.

The Genocide left a permanent imprint on the psyche of the Armenian people, one that is reflected in the insularity and inflexibility of our communities in diaspora today. The United States appeared to Armenians, as to many other immigrants, as a promised land, relatively free from oppression and full of opportunities for economic prosperity—a promise which has become a reality for many Armenians here.

Most of us refer to Armenia and other places in our Middle Eastern diaspora as the "other side." This reference is particularly apropos in the case of Western Armenia, a life and place destroyed during the Genocide. As a child listening to relatives refer to the other side, I thought of it as an old, backward way of living; a place that smelled and tasted like basterma (garlic-cured beef), onions, dill, and strong cognac, where everyone knew everyone else's business, where old women would persistently try to marry me off to the right family. I bought the arrogant and racist myth that they had reached the light by coming to the United States. In reality, for those who came here, crossing over from the other side was like leaving one life behind for the next—a spiritual passage. The other side then became a homeland of the mind and soul that Armenians in diaspora have strived to preserve.

I am an Armenian woman, born and raised in the United States; an American-Armenian woman. I live a hyphenated existence—two poles coexisting. Where does one end and the other begin? I function in two worlds, and I am on the margin in both of them. Within me exists the interface of those two worlds, yet they are very separate. Within me exists a place that is both of those worlds, merged and discrete, and a place that is neither of them. It is a place called home. It is a radical place called the other side.

A few years ago, a friend asked if my childhood sense of alienation came from being Middle Eastern in a white, Anglo town. I thought about it briefly and said no. Little did I know I had begun a journey I will continue for the rest of my life, a journey that has brought me home to the maze of being a bicultural diasporal

Armenian feminist. It's a labyrinth that has a center I'll always be going toward, though I've already arrived there. The center of this labyrinth is the other side.

In the beginning was the womb of Armenian family and community. Ample aunties hugging, feeding, adoring me, pinching my cheeks, and giving me big wet kisses. Huge family gatherings, with lots of noise, arguing, joy, people, and, of course, food—simply the warm and unconditionally accepting space of home. I knew nothing of dissonance, assimilation, biculturalism, racism, or even sexism.

My parents chose not to speak Armenian to me or my siblings. I question if it was an active choice or deference to internalized oppression. I do not envy the position of my parents. The children of Armenian immigrants, they grew up in the 1930s and 1940s. At that time, non-European ethnicity was definitely not "in." Even the masked racist trend of idolizing "exoticism" that we see today did not work in their favor fifty years ago. My parents lived with parameters defining a good American that were even stricter than I have. Radical identity reclamation was probably the last thing on their minds.

A generation later, I am vocally resisting what I call cultural bleach—I have the privilege of being able to reclaim a radical identity. Cultural bleach is a force in white supremacist U.S. mainstream culture, wherein light-skinned people of color are urged to consider ourselves physically, historically, and ideologically white. Resisting cultural bleach is a refusal to participate in this kind of assimilation and instead to affirm who we are.

From age six, I became conscious of our difference. I felt proud of my Armenian identity and carried a feeling of coming from and belonging to a place I couldn't touch. But on the surface, that translated to just feeling weird and out of place. The sense of marginalization and displacement grew throughout my teen years. I felt a sense of otherness, yet it was amorphous, elusive. I knew where my family had originated, yet I didn't make a connection to what that meant geopolitically.

Through high school, college, and many different adult experiences, being Armenian remained a side dish in my consciousness; until I was in my mid-twenties and studying feminist theology. I knew by then that an ethnic/political/sexual/spiritual identity storm was brewing inside. And sure enough, it erupted that year. While enrolled at the Women's Theological Center for a year of study, my sense of displacement became more acute than ever.

By that time, I felt out of place with white women, more at home with women of color, and generally confused by this identity business. I began to question if I was "of color." Then one day at an anti-racism workshop my classmates and I divided into our usual groups of white women and women of color. Until that point we had all assumed I would go to the white women's group. I told my peers with some trepidation that I didn't know where I belonged. I then made a decision that changed my life. On that day, in the midst of the Gulf War, I came out to myself and the world as an Armenian feminist, as a Middle Easterner, as a woman of color.

I am clear about this identity, though I struggle with it. The self-hating judge inside taunts me. She says, "What do you think you're doing? You're a rich white girl from the suburbs. You are a fake, projecting your disillusionment all over the place." And many white women seem threatened by my process and treat me as a wannabe. It is as if I have defected from their camp, when I was never really an accepted member, nor did I belong there in the first place. From women of color, I receive unequivocal support.

Yet I know my identity has not come out of a void, nor is it a phase or a whim. This process is historically and experientially based. It's my way of dispelling the myth that Armenians/Middle Easterners are white Europeans. In the United States, we are socialized to believe that Middle Eastern identity is nebulous and liminal, or a European subculture. In actuality the "Middle East" represents a group of ancient West Asian cultures.

My political, social, and spiritual outlook on life and the world has shifted in a dramatic and true way. I am even more committed to challenging my own racism and that of the world, and I know my responsibility to acknowledge the privilege I have. This process has transformed my colonially inspired self-hatred into self-love and pride. And it has paved the way for me to come home, to cross over to the other side.

Shifting from a feminist to an Armenian feminist identity also represents a profound change in the way I interact in the women's community. Armenian and feminist are two sides of the coin that is myself. I now deem myself primarily accountable to women of color. Speaking and acting as an Armenian feminist, I am no longer a sympathetic and wistful outsider to women of color struggles, groups, and gatherings, but a participant. Engaging in movements to bring about local and global justice with other women of color is a way of creating the other side in the present world. I honor my wise grandmothers. I honor my sisters. I honor my daughters yet to come.

I must also ask myself the specific question: "What does it mean to be an Armenian feminist in the United States, in the Western industrial diaspora, on the eve of the twenty-first century?" To me it means, among other things, choosing power on the margin with other Armenian feminists. The Armenian women's community is still diffuse—Armenian feminists in the United States have only just begun to gather among ourselves to discuss our experiences, how we want to organize ourselves, and to process, process, process! But again it is a difficult decision to reclaim and recast the margin. Armenian feminists must make space, home for ourselves—the mainstream Armenian community will not make it for us.

I have made the choice to carry forth the sense of Armenian, of Middle Eastern home, and do new, wild and creative things with it. I am an Armenian—as strong and committed to my community of origin as I am innovative, rebellious, and daring. Such liberation has made me even more delightfully uppity. I no longer feel obligated to explain myself to the dominant culture or to receive validation from it, nor do I apologize for or explain my body. I no longer want to be plastic and hairless with conical tits; I refuse to try to manipulate my body to conform to Wonder Bread standards of beauty. I feel accountable to the forces that matter; white mainstream culture is not one of them.

In the summer of 1991, I went to Armenia, my political motherland.* There, I spent time building houses with a community of Armenian refugees from Azerbaijan; they were forced to flee their ancestral homeland in Azerbaijan due to the war between Armenia

---

* My actual motherland is Western (Turkish) Armenia, destroyed by the Genocide mentioned earlier in this essay. Our homeland has been usurped and repopulated by Turks. What is now the Republic of Armenia, formerly a Soviet Republic, is Eastern, or Russian Armenia.

and Azerbaijan over the Armenian enclave of Nagorno-Karabakh. What moved me most about Armenia was being in a place where the ethnic norm was my norm—I was in the majority for the first time in my life. I found that Armenians there did not expect the crux of their Armenian identity to be some monolithic and archaic representation of "the Old Country." Rather, it was diverse and alive. Being Armenian was not the source of painful inferiority complexes. It just was. And yet Armenia was not the other side for me—it did not feel like home. I will not resolve my issues by boarding a plane to Yerevan. The other side is here and now.

The Queen, Carcasses, and Other Things

J. A. KHAWAJA

1.

Whenever I travel back to my original home in the Caribbean I go and sit by the big salt pond near the beach. It looks calm and thoughtful like it always did, that is if a salt pond can look that way. And I think of the cow everyone said walked too far out into the pond. It drowned slowly trying to get back to the safety of the shore. The bottom of the pond was quicksand. As a six-year-old child I couldn't imagine how something so thoughtful would do that to a cow. Why doesn't someone get a bulldozer and pull the cow out of the quicksand I wondered. Whose cow is it anyway I asked. If it belonged to a white person something would have been done I'm sure. I said to my mother who spoke French. She learned it in Quebec. My mother who spoke English. She learned it in a Canadian school. My mother who spoke Arabic. She learned it from her mother. My mother the immigrant whose dutiful silence I had decided made her an accomplice in the death of a cow. My mother who is a woman.

And so I committed myself to try to imagine where the bulldozer and crane could have positioned themselves so that they could rescue the dead cow or any other cow or even person who might meet the same fate. I went over the circumference of the salt pond each Sunday that we went to the beach but could not find a spot or place that would have made its rescue possible. And even my father who was born there and who likes cows. My father who could have saved the cow didn't. My father who speaks English he learned in the Caribbean. My father who doesn't speak Arabic. My father who is a West Indian Arab. My father who is a colonizer. My father who paid no mind to the death of the cow.

It came to be that on all the Sundays of my life I would search
the still heavy surface that covered the cow's remains and think
about how things did not seem to be what they were. Like the
concealed bed of quicksand under thoughtful water. Like my
mother's mother who spoke French in Quebec. She learned it in
Beirut. Like my mother's mother who spoke English. She learned
it in Canada. Like my mother's mother who spoke Arabic she
learned in Syria. Like my mother's mother who was colonized.
My Canadian grandmother a woman who is dead.

Soon after a sign was put up next to the salt pond. It said quite
simply "Be Careful." So you would only know it was quicksand
if you tested it out for yourself as I had done. Or if someone had
told you so. And maybe not even then unless you were in the
habit of believing that person. If you were a certain kind of child
that would have been a difficult thing to do. Older people lied.
There was no sense in hoping them to do anything different
because they didn't know how. Or who they were. If you've met
people like that you would know what I mean

like the cow their carcasses wait for full exposure. I can see
them just below teasing the surface I always thought. Tilted just
so or so or so. Protruding just so or so. Like under my father's
mother who speaks English. My father's mother who never
learned Arabic. Like my father's mother who is a West Indian
Arab. My father's mother who speaks West Indian english. My
father's mother who is colonized. My father's mother who
colonizes. My grandmother who is an old woman

abandoned testimonials of a time. Identities gathered up into
single words. Multiplicity into singularity. Father. Mother. Grand-
mothers. Me. Privileged Arab ethnic. Caribbean Arab immigrant
outsider. Identity constructed contrived reconstituted on the
battle ground of visions closing in. The carcass of a dead cow.
What remains in the mind of a child.

2.

When my father's mother was sixteen she still loved school. The woman who taught her and her sister up the alleyway told her she was good. She was a bright girl. In 1930 she was a bright girl she loved school and she was to ask her parents and Miss Rawley if they could find the money to send her away to school because she loved her lessons so. Me nah nah. Wack. Do you think you live in a village. Repeat after me. Me nah nah. Me no no. I do not know. I—do—not—know.

And then a boat pulled into the harbor. A big steamship pulled into the harbor and this steamship was going to America. Stopping over for a day or two at this small island in the British West Indies. As my grandmother says in those days it was all in the direction of America. Two brothers got off and they met my grandmother's Syrian father on the bay front because that's where they were at the bay front one brother stayed and the other went to America the next day with the large steamship. And the brother that stayed was given a suitcase full of goods and sent into the countryside to sell the things in his suitcases. This foreigner who arrived without a penny in his pocket was given a suitcase by my grandmother's father and sent into the countryside to sell goods to the "locals."

And soon after my great-grandfather pappy went into my grand-mother's room it was dark late at night in that room she shared with her sisters you see because it's not like up here where there is such a thing as having your own room maybe nowadays for rich people but then everyone slept in the same room

as I was saying my great-grandfather pappy went into my grand-mother's room and it was dark and she was fifteen and he pulled her out of the bed and made her kneel down and then he pulled up on her hair at the top of her head hard until it hurt she saw he had a razor blade in his hand because he put it to her throat close to her throat and held it there then she was married to the foreigner with the suitcase who had come off the boat. He spoke

Arabic. It was the beginning of her life with that man who spoke a language she didn't know the language her pappy and mammy knew

I knew my great-grandmother mammy was what they called her and after my great-grandfather died she was old and feeble and never spoke and you had to go right up to her and speak to her because she didn't like to talk loud she had grown used to the silence. She had grown comfortable with the rightness of silence. Awhyu. All you. All of you. All of us

pappy wasn't the nicest of people my grandmother says and mammy never told of how her two sons died and how the daughters. How the daughters had been treated. Like my grand-mother who was good in school. I never heard her say any of the things she knew mammy. She died in the hospital when I was ten. I know because I watched. I had to go I told my parents. She groaned as she died roared silently almost inaudibly I know I heard it her breath rumbling out of the silence like a train in the distance waiting to rush past no matter how much you know it's coming it surprises you sends a shiver through your body of the silences that don't come to anything except the sound of a train that simply lingers for seconds or if by chance memory gets passed on for generations

I felt it. Like some exchange of grief and sadness. It's all in the reading I thought standing there. I am sure she wanted to say something important I told them. Things she might have always wanted to say. Things no one ever wanted to hear. Stupidness. What kind of stupidness you chatting again girl. Hush. Keep yourself quiet. Mammy is dead they said. Mammy has died they cried

and the queen is coming the queen is coming get ready stand straight we were all pressed together black brown and white grateful colonial subjects in our school uniforms to make the perfect line to make the perfect wave with the perfect nose turned up just like the British people. My sister and I had it down noses in the pillow pressed upwards and out nightly to avoid hooked nose Arab. I made it a point never to wave. Pushed up sourfaced British people who smiled into nowhere I told my mother. Did the queen and her husband know the people who corrected my exams. Good very good excellent. I wanted to meet them those people in England my father said made the Balfour Declaration they were the reason for all the trouble over there I heard

time passed and my grandfather threw my grandmother down the stairs and he put a gun to her head again and he threw her down the stairs and he put a gun to her head. And the girl in the back room she was a "vegetable" you know they said keep quiet they said shame the girl in the back room who cried and screamed all night was my father's sister. And my grandmother tended her day and night and then she died and the back room remained empty as it still does today. And my grandfather ranted at the top of his lungs for someone to bring him his food his socks his his his and my grandmother for fear for fear of for fear of being slapped at the back of the head brought him his food and his housecoat and his socks

and when I was born my grandfather said a girl throw her in the river that's what girls are good for. In the old country we throw them in the river. And my antie Joyce told my mother we were like animals because we ran wild and made a lot of noise up and down the place. You call everyone antie down there. Except the white people said auntie. That's how I knew I was different from them too. And when I was old enough they said remember it's only those kind of whisper British and American women that behave like that you know not us. Antie antie antie. It was a mark like a cross or a tatoo or a scar. Antie. Civilized or uncivilized. How come we are the only kinda white looking people saying antie. Slap the teacher said in proper English. A—u—n—t—i—e. Repeat after me

they said people laughing shallow painted smiles looking straight through one another gesturing. Feigning interest. As if they had something to say. As if they wanted to hear. Be quiet. And so the party kept on. Year after year. The stillness

in the people's motions like death as I was stripped bare.
And silent the laughing gesturing skin hair. Chest of a man.
Exposing itself in slow motion. Because you know when you are
dead that's what happens. Everything happens in slow motion.
That's what I thought everytime. Now. In my dreams memories.
And those people laughing and smiling their fancy dressed up
smiling smiles. Like clowns looking for the right parade. Or
maybe for redemption I heard about that in church. Except they
didn't know. Selected oblivion to their confessions. To the hairy
chest moving around in front of me. Obscuring my sight line. My
vision way out. Some men have it. Hair. I had seen it before shh

before I was born when my father couldn't go to the beach
only the British people who spoke like this could go and
those people who spoke like this owned the beach so it was
easy because it was private property. If you own private
property you can say this and that and this and that about this
property because it is private I was told. Because. That's why I
was told. It's simple they said just be quiet. And then you can
say which kind of people can come and go. And you can talk to
who you want just so and so. Like my father who owns
property. Now. And then the tourists came. It ain jok ah mekin
wid yu. You tink it is joke I mek. Do you think I am joking with
you. Do you think I am joking around.

All this time my grandmother had to work hard everyday all day
in the store to give her children more than everything and my
grandfather soon returned to the old country for reasons I
wouldn't understand they told me I wasn't old enough but I can
see I said I can see the scars of war on the swelled joints and
faces of the "locals" resistance accusation accomplices perpetrators
you deserve to be sentenced without redemption shut shut up shut
your mouth what do you know that's not us it's the british you
don't know anything child said my drunk west indian first arab
second colonialist father whose vision is now obscured by two
white growths expanding at the edge of his pupils and not
long after we came to Canada. I was a teenager.

Marhaba what's happening hi hi hi my arab canadian cousins
seemed to say over and over again and when I first arrived they
told me about black licorice most disgusting thing I have ever
tasted I thought on the way to the countryside in Quebec where

all the trees looked the same and everyone said oh how beautiful how beautiful it is as if I had never seen beauty as if I had never seen beauty where I came from it makes me angry now. I didn't then understand the pine trees that all looked the same that didn't blow in the the wind so I tried to be grateful for all those straight looking trees and cement landscapes I tried hard to be grateful to those grinning canadian arab faces and those stretched out hiiiis faces widening interminably until the hiiii was complete what was I to do with the licorice anyway. Throw it away ungrateful for all the things that they had in this country because what would I know coming from some small uncivilized island where no black licorice grows

soon I learned about bleaches to blond hair on the forearms and upper lip and I got a blowdryer like the four other arab girls in my school who straightened their hair. Creme rinse much more than was necessary for the taking out of knots just enough to flatten the hair on the head a roll brush a blowdryer and some careful pulling from the roots down to the end of each strand. Small pieces worked best. You could be sure then not to leave out a single patch lest it expose itself accidentally to the force's wave and give you away. I often wondered whether the application of the heat twice a week for one or two hours each time would damage my brain since rumor had it on the island I was from that my friend's mother had died of cancer from hair dye chemicals seeping into her head and poisioning her. But what would they know down there anyway

now my grandfather is old and wears a three-piece suit and every-one thinks he is a dignified gentle man and he is he is a gentle man who almost died a few years ago now he tells people how much he loves them and my grandmother is old too and she still works everyday. And she came to Canada to have an operation on her hips and she walked by a bookstore because my grandmother spends most of her time alone reading watching CNN and Sunday morning church programs and she has never danced or swam or in her life anyway she told me she found a book and she bought the book and she asked me if I knew about this book and I asked her what the title was she told

me the book talked about her life what her life was like she was
surprised at what had been written

maybe that is what is wrong with my hips she said the times I
was pushed down the stairs did I know about this she asked this
book she asked that told the story of her life. There was no
emotion. No pain. Only shock to discover at eighty years of age
that this was something other women experienced did I believe
this happened she asked and she looked at me I wanted to cry
about this woman's life this Caribbean Arab woman this grand-
mother of mine pausing and talking pausing and talking without
flinching insisting in her pain that I should not show emotion
that I did not need to cry for her that I should not sentimentalize
a carcass. After all she was eighty and had died a long time ago.
At fifteen.

3.

Now I speak English. I learned it in the Caribbean. I didn't learn
Arabic and not long ago my mother told me how for years
growing up in Montreal her and her sisters walked the long way
to school and back every day. If they took the direct route home
or to school the other children in the neighborhood would throw
things and call them names. Names reserved for Arabs. Small bits
of anger slipped through the cracks between her words. How
did that feel I asked her. I don't know she said my mother
whose silence betrayed her I forgave for a moment now

a woman used to these trees now sometimes I even forget for a
moment and see they are different from one another. Most other
times I drive past them and they look the same like they did that
first time ugly and uneventful no large leaves and no small ones
no drooping branches and large imposing trunks no vine bushes
crawling over fences without indecision no flowers hanging over
prickle and kosha bush with pride

african jamaican canadian girlfriend jewish canadian friend. The
books and other things you have given me in this journey which
should have begun so long ago but this thing this thing in my
life had blocked my vision and stopped choked and strangled
throat gut tightened mouth hold chin up high out for fear

so I continued on after the black licorice through circuitous paths and winding roads to find comfortable places to rest to stop and stay awhile and then move on to the next rest stop never knowing what I was running from who which Caribbean Arab Canadian neither neither nor all in this splitting of communities falling apart at the seams existing within the crevices cracks hole identity constructed contrived reconstituted pockets of resistance on the battleground of visions closing in caribbean arab lesbian brown white privileged colonized healing thinking resting loving running party stopped. Remembered evidence. And the growth on the edge of my eye retreats reminds of threatened vision common affliction contagious inseparable unaware that I was planning my own rescue that change must be multifarious that I am more than the parts of who I am that things were the way they seemed as I searched the circumference of the still heavy surface. Now as I watch the oppressor(s) afflicted ailing with rotting of the soul.

One Room

LORENE ZAROU-ZOUZOUNIS

Grandfather Salem built a stone house,
one room for Grandmother Hilweh,
one room for seven of us,
one for a newlywed uncle,
Siham and her son in another,
a family upstairs.

Mother cooked near apricot and plum trees,
kitchen behind a curtain
in a corner near a jug reservoir.
Mother found her wedding ring there
many years after its plunge.
Siham and her son left.
We had a new kitchen,
complete with covered bucket to squat over.
No more frosty outhouse at midnight in December.

Mother feared baking bread in a taboon—
an outdoor igloo-oven for women
circled to gossip, flaming rocks toasting their toes.
Grandmother's round, hollow-center bread
was broken each night,
accompanied by well water only
Grandfather dared fetch. He scolded Mother for sneaking
our life-source for her hungry daffodils and tulips.

Tateh Hilweh and I roamed valleys filled
with narcissi, poppies, dandelions, cacti.
Stuffed baskets with wild greens.
A brew of camomile and anise calmed the tension;
four boys and a girl ran circles around dizzy Mother,
wringing cotton.

Round contented bellies over burning coals
protecting us from an open window
where home-made cheese sat on a sill,
chilled, fresh and firm for tomorrow.
Cardomon-flavored Turkish coffee
and farina sweets filled an evening's aroma,
fueling Grandfather's tales of Palestine past,
his hands flinging about, Father teasing him,
our eyes unblinking, our imaginations fed,
cuddled on the floor like newborn kittens.

We prepared our beds lined up against one wall,
looking like an orphanage on a meager budget.
Ready for another dream, blankets heavy.
Sleep-walking Sameer slipped into his pants,
crept out into the night,
until a scorpion's bite woke him.

Grandfather had a house
until the quarry rooms were flattened
by an over-worked bulldozer
in Ramallah,
burying our one room but not our memories.

Chalked Out

MARJORIE GELLHORN SA'ADAH

This is the way a generation ends. By writing the recipe down like this: "Take some good flour and add water slowly. Be careful not to add too much water too quickly, but do add enough until the mixture is just right." Mix it with your hands in the rhythm of a woman who has kneaded for a long time—years—and who kneads in such a way that the people—relatives—who finally come together in the living room or around the dining room table, have no idea how long it takes except by the perky remarks of some woman— who married in with no idea that any one was different from any other—saying, "Oh, Rose, you must have spent *hours.*"

Rosiegram we called her. I had thought we had been taught by our parents to attach a suffix of "gram" to our grandmothers' first names and call our grandfathers by their first names. When I was grown, I read something—probably while snooping—that my grandfather had written about his grandparents. He called them Grandmother and Grandfather. Any other word would have shown disrespect. I was horrified, terrified—I suddenly realized that I had been rude to my grandparents for my entire life. *I should have known better.* I asked my father, whose eyes would flash deep and angry if we ever, even in jest, called him by his first name, why we called our grandparents by their names. I can't remember exactly what he said, but he made it clear that he never called his parents or grandparents by their first names; still in his fifties speaking of Mommy, Daddy, and Grandmother. You start to think that this rudeness, this inappropriate behavior, this incorrect unknowing comes from an inherent place inside of you. *I should have known better.*

I should have known I couldn't help it so I could have changed something, done something, or at least been quieter. I should have known they would leave us out there having to figure it out alone.

---

*   This is an excerpt from *Chalked Out: Race, Culture, and Identity.*

"Say you took two cups of flour which is not too high in gluten content. Mix some salt and pepper into it and add water—maybe half a cup to begin with. Knead and if you need more water, add to it sparingly. The dough must not be liquidy and sticky. Knead well until it is smooth and firm—but not too firm." This is what happens. The recipe takes all day; if you cooked it the balls of your feet would ache from standing on the kitchen floor. You would get terse and frustrated when the walnut-sized balls of dough stuck to the rolling pin—too wet. And when you couldn't seal the triangles filled with American cheese *(I tell you, it is only the recipes that melted into the American pot),* green onion, and parsley—because the dough was too dry—you might give up and quickly think of something else to serve. When you had to fry them four at a time (and four wouldn't last even a child but a moment) you might realize that your damp towel covering the tasty morsels of your history was too damp, or too dry, but by then the oil is hot, though you hope not smoking. "Don't prick the dough while you are frying and see to it that the oil is never too hot or cold—they become soggy in cold oil and burn rapidly in too hot an oil. You need luck and practice. If you don't succeed, call me up, if I am still in this world."

It's not an image for anything, it's just what I have. A cookbook of recipes to be made from in exact amounts of ingredients converted to equivalents found in an American grocery store. A gold bracelet made from a child's necklace—my grandmother's—that I don't wear for fear of losing the connection. A fifty-page book of stories told out loud in earshot of my uncle, who knew enough to record and transcribe them. Makes up for the fact that you won't hear the stories unless you ask the right way.

But there you are nibbling in the living room, which sometime late in your life you realize is unlike any other living room you have ever been in, partly on account of all of the rugs that you probably call "oriental," and we just call rugs, and partly on account of the overall feeling that you always call "sparse," and we just call home. I've been in plenty of living rooms; I've been invited into plenty of your homes.

In 1968 nothing was burning, just integrating, on our block of Fourteenth Street NW. Wendy and I played on the brown wall-to-wall carpeting in her house. Etch-a-Sketch. Make-believe. She had black dolls. Even the one she made for me as a moving-away present had a black kneesock body and black yarn hair.

The 1970s: Renée's mom had this flair that surfaced vicariously in her hair color (a homemade—we watched—custom-mixed bottle of black, bottle of red) and in her interior decorating. White super-long shag rugs were anchored down at the corners by life-size ceramic pumas and green-eyed leopards. There didn't seem to be much other choice for self-expression in Army family housing (*Villagio Della Pace*/Village of Peace).

Bicentennial: wait for Juanita to sweep the carpets in Saxon Homes 1159-C so she didn't get in trouble when her momma came home. Actually, I didn't get invited to many white homes when we lived in South Carolina, except for Carroll Turleville's birthday party. I used to think "what a funny last name," because when she pronounced it "Tur-lee-ville" in her Southern accent, it sounded like some spinning saucer ride at the amusement park. Then I saw on the map that there was a whole town named Turleville a few miles away. It wasn't a coincidence. (And I don't think her name is all that much easier to say than mine, but obviously if hundreds (thousands?) of people have your last name as their address, they have to know how to say it right.)

By the 1980s I really feel like a transient, especially when we move to the Northwest where all these people act like their couple-of-generations of settling here is some sort of ancient scriptural thing. As if 100 years is a long time. Actually, here people have "Oriental" rugs, since the lumber, paper, and real estate industries (and their accompanying lawyers, financial planners, and governors) have made them wealthy. But in their houses, the colors all match, and rugs are chosen to bring out the deep red of a painting, or the burnt sienna of its frame.

College, even though I'm 3,000 miles away, is more of the same; wealthy refinished wood floors or wealthy worn rugs, with infusions of mud floors ("learning experiences") during the summers.

1988: I move away and move back. Fourteenth Street NW is still burned out, though the Mayor's new office is revitalizing from uptown and gentrification is moving from downtown.

Now when old friends walk into my home, no matter where I live, because now it's California, they always say, "This is just like your parents.'" And I never know whether that's a compliment or not.

It's not just the rugs that make our houses different. It's the art on the walls, the fragments of tapestries and the inscriptions on the huge hand-tooled trays that serve as tables. (These trays are never made for just one person—you, me, all of us could sit around one and eat and laugh and it could still hold it all.) But nothing is familiar enough to me that I don't have to ask what it is. Some people like it when you ask, because you're showing such an interest in their possessions. But these aren't possessions, and having to ask about each and every one of them makes me, in my Guatemalan dress and Kenyan jewelry, crazy. I find a magazine picture taped to the wall next to my Grandfather's reading chair—a boy throwing a rock— and my Grandfather tells me it is a symbol of resistance for him. And I think, "Now that is something I would do, tape a picture from a revolutionary struggle to a place where I would remember it." But then I think about how I would probably pick a different struggle, maybe in Central America or South Africa, or even meat-packers in the midwest, on account of how I know so much more about them. Or is that it?

I've just been looking for the scrap of paper—actually the part of a restaurant bill that you tear off and keep to prove you ate a certain amount's worth—that records my conversation with my father. Everywhere I have these backs of receipts and index cards and single sentences on old pages of legal pads. That's how I try to make up for lost memories. They pile up. When I browse through them, I think, "That's interesting, I should make some sort of conclusion from this," or "Hmm, well, that's certainly a point I should think about sometime again," or even, "Yes, I knew this was so, and here is the proof." But I am compulsively organized, so I file them away neatly, determining some sort of system that puts them out of sight.

But this one is unfiled, having been hidden in my jacket pocket for the week. I had borrowed the waitress' pen and wrote it down right in the restaurant. "You know, you could just check out the book from the library and read it yourself," my father had said. But that wasn't the point. The point wasn't so much that the quote was in the book (though that is another point) as it was that he had told me about it.

A year ago I first asked him what it was like to go to boarding school in New England. Wasn't it hard to go to that school with all those white boys? Did you have an accent?

"What are you talking about?"

I try again. Well, didn't you feel different from the other boys? Did they make you feel different? Weren't you different?

"I have no idea what you are talking about."

This time said quickly enough to make you realize you were going in that direction again. Or rather, all those other directions. By the end of the conversation, I am closing my eyes on tears, much to my dismay, and he really is sorry that I am crying but he's still not answering my questions. And I spend a year trying to figure out if he doesn't answer because he really doesn't understand what I am talking about or because he really doesn't want me to understand it.

And now, we're together again, in the same city as the last conversation. (Make a note—same place, that's not it.) And suddenly, over dinner (Make a note—same setting, that's not it either) I hear that he is answering my question of a year ago. (But already I have lost memory of what exactly we were talking about that prompted him to tell me. Pathetic, pathetic; I wrack my brain. It's no use, I can't remember the cue.)

"There were only two references to Arabs in my entire history book in ninth grade—Morison and Commager's 1950 edition." (He noticed that as a ninth-grade boy?) "We were studying the demographics of New York, the teacher was reading aloud to the class, and he read that New York was tarnished by 'the dirty stain of the Arab tribe.'" He could tell me the title, author, and edition of the textbook. The first, last, and nicknames of the teacher, his alma mater (Harvard, Harvard), and social class (upper). He remembered everything about the incident, right down to the chapter, section, and quotation mark.

But it is left to me to feel the heat of the words being read aloud. There is nowhere to go, because you have already fled there, and that place is here. So the heat just settles around our cheeks and ears; what is golden gets burnished.

Some day I will tell you how our ancestors for centuries stood at the gates of the Arabian Desert maintaining their Christianity and culture against the onslaught of the savage desert and the seductions of Byzantine decadence, absorbing their strengths but rejecting their dominance, subjected to the struggle for existence and for survival.

Some day also your Rosiegram will tell you how her folk and ancestors stood before the hammer and the anvil of the millennia, and in spite of all the martyrdoms and the near-genocide (including her own father), they maintained their identity and integrity. Only the dross was burned. The gold survived.

Some day, sit beside your other grandpa, your mother's father, and let him tell you of the great traditions of his noble family. Theirs is a story of the emergent United States, the real United States, the United States that we wish to purify and augment.

Be mindful of us occasionally, because as the sunset approaches, we do turn our eyes towards the dawn and ask, "What of the coming day?" He signs it, *Grandpa,* followed by his first name.

He doesn't know how much I know about my mother's father. About how even strangers at parties, in admissions offices, in libraries can tell me about him. He doesn't realize that even when I don't go to the parties or the schools, I can find it in a book, or in a catalogued archive. He must not know that even if I did none of these things, I could still find the instructions for how to ask my other grandparents myself. If he knew, he wouldn't be 500, 3,000, 7,000 miles away; he would talk louder, gossip longer, laugh more deeply so I would be sure to know what's so funny.

You can hear a generation end.

Unpicked Fruits

BARBARA NIMRI AZIZ

Muna, her son Mazin, and I are moving toward that beautiful occupied land, South Lebanon. We follow a potholed and dirty coastal road south in flight from our crowded West Beirut apartment.

A November day. Olive-harvest time in the hills. The sky is clear. Other young families pour out of the noisy city. Some drive northward, speeding along the coast. Then, as if slipping to a secret rendevous, their cars dart into an unmarked road and disappear into the hills—to their family homes. There they will pick olives and stroll with their cousins along the quiet lanes of their childhood.

I wait to hear my companion's comments about the recent Lebanese election, the first in such a long time; or will she discuss the Israeli shelling in the south? Nearby, less than an hour's drive away, fighting has erupted. Everyone knows; it arrives like a change in the weather—predictable and unwelcome. It destroys, then subsides. Its return is inevitable. All along that line that divides "free Lebanon" from the Israeli-occupied south, ambushes and airstrikes explode houses and skulls.

No comments are volunteered about the battles. It is pointless to discuss them. Why let them disrupt our weekend flow into family retreats where the old, silvery olive trees are heavy with their fruit?

To the hills. Beirut apartment dwellers are desperate for some respite in their countryside. They are not like other city people who moved from declining villages to become urbanites. All Lebanese remain part rural; their childhood homes are not places left behind; they keep them and make them modern and call them home. They risk venturing into these battle zones, especially at olive-harvest time. Besides, today's air-strikes are mild compared to the civil war years ago and the horrifying invasion in the burning summer of 1982. These shellings are inevitable, just as local resistance operations against the occupation forces are part of the pattern of life in the South.

Half of South Lebanon, like the Golan and the West Bank and Gaza, is under occupation. This, Muna's homeland, is known in the West simply as "Israel's security zone." There, Israeli troops arrive in a town and round up men and boys; uncles and grandsons are taken away at random "for a security check." Often they don't come back. Weeks pass before news arrives that they are in prison. Or that they have been expelled.

Resistance operations are also random. A strike on a United Nations convoy, the ambush of an Israeli patrol, a bombing of a South Lebanese Army post. Israeli air attacks follow. More round-ups. More torture. More funerals. Orphans.

We move deeper into the hills, and people point to a hilltop and say "There, look there—the Israeli army post." No alarm, no voiced objection, and no appeal for justice.

Because these people, absorbed in their work, said little about the attacks, I first thought they accepted occupation. I was wrong.

"Not for a moment! We never forget they are on our land." The resistance operations against the invaders enjoy widespread support. No one here feels a need to explain why they are fighting, and waiting. Meanwhile, old and young, watch the world. For that game, they have opinions. "Only a political solution will end this," ventures Muna. She follows the peace talks in Washington. She speculates on the outcome of the 1992 U.S. presidential election rather than who is hitting whom in the hills nearby. "We are waiting for the peace process to bring results. If there is to be peace, we too will have to have our land back."

Muna's no different from her friends. They share a deep conviction. It is deceptively, determinedly deep.

In the United States, in Syria and among Palestinians, from conversations about justice and about exchanges of land for peace, I had the impression that South Lebanon was dispensable. Surely, it would be given up for the Golan and for the West Bank and Gaza. But no. "Our land is "the bottom line' as Americans say." The Lebanese position is unshakable.

Our journey southwards is a series of dashes through the terrain, past a deepening blue Mediterranean. Every few kilometers, we slow to a stop—a military checkpoint lies ahead. In the middle of the highway is a battered sentry box buttressed with sandbags. Muna's arm is out the window, to gesture a greeting to the soldier standing outside his post. His rifle rests innocently on his forearm; he appears bored and apparently sees no reason to respond to Muna's cute smile. His hand rises for an instant and falls back on the rifle barrel. We are disappointed by his discourtesy.

"Are these guards Syrian or Lebanese?" I ask Muna when we are waved through the next checkpoint by an equally ungracious soldier. "Of course, Lebanese," she replies with a proud grin. "Can't you tell?" Actually I can not. Their churlishness I associated with Syrians. They do not wear the light blue fatigues I associated with Beirut policemen, the men with pistols on their hips. What a toughened lot they are. But they smile. Syrian soldiers and Lebanese army regulars carry rifles and seem equally unsmiling.

Muna recognizes her Lebanese men easily. "Besides, down here, no Syrians. Syrians you can see in Bekka. Here, all are Lebanese now." When the Lebanese deployed their army in the south last year, Muna and other southerners became optimistic.

What difference I could detect between the two armies was in the drape of their uniform. Chic and trim, the Lebanese soldier. Standing behind a sandbag or mounting his tank, his body says, "I am not really a soldier; I'm a civilized man with a grand history; in my closet at home are designer slacks." Self-conscious, he bathes in the pleasure of eyes following him as he strides across a gambling room or a cafe. We know these cultural markers—a Lebanese, the cut of his suit; an Iraqi, his haircut and high shoulders; a Syrian, his sad eyes and correct grammar.

Muna drives on, south out of Sidon city's neon lights, and onto the dark roadway. We'll soon turn away from the sea and enter the mountains, towards those villages of grandparents. "Have you ever seen an olive press?" My companion catches me by surprise. Her question marks a crossing, the border of a new language zone. "Tomorrow we'll go to the place where my mother takes the olives to make oil. You brought your camera, didn't you?"

From this introduction up to the moment we arrive in Dier Kyfa village, it is all about olives. Muna is speaking about home, about the orchards she ran through in little frocks, about sitting with her sisters and aunts on the veranda, sorting olives—the black from the green, the large from the small—about the gangs of cousins keeping secrets from the grownups, about noisy family weddings, about a time of peace when these towns were not simply for old folks, before Muna and her sisters moved to Beirut, before eldest brother left for Bahrain, and youngest brother for Ghana.

Most of the year Muna's parents are here, alone. "Father has too many trees to manage by himself. He can't strip the branches himself now. We hire local boys and girls to help, mainly girls. Young men cannot stay here. When I come down, I like to go into the fields, but I cannot work like those girls."

The car nudges its way deeper into the hills. We pass through a UN checkpost. The well-dressed Ghanaian soldier smiles back at Muna. Mazin shouts "hello" back out the window as we move forward.

We are near home. I cannot see the orchards on either side of the road, but Muna can. "We'll preserve them right away. Some we put in water for two days, then salt. By Tuesday we can eat those. Black ones are the best. Mother will have some ready, I am certain."

For another ten minutes we climb though hills. We slip quietly over narrow lanes, around hidden stone houses with their orchards reaching above their walled courtyards. No need to ask directions. We cross a motionless village square. A mosque without a minaret stands at the corner and we pass it on the right and slide down a lane and through trees. It's an orchard, the orchard of Muna's parents. We turn the motor off in front of the quiet bungalow. Inside, lights go on; young Mazin jumps from his sleepy trance and runs into the house to find his cousins.

Muna's mother slowly walks to the front of the open veranda and waits for her daughter. No loud shouts. Their embrace is casual. The welcome is eternal. Mother turns her eyes to a corner of the house. "Look there," she says with an uncomplaining voice. "I sat down to work at sunrise and I just got up." Clearly pleased with her day, she sits with us and takes a cigarette.

A young day worker, a girl of no more than sixteen, is seated on a mat on the floor. She continues to labor over the unsorted fruit. Behind her, three separate heaps of black and green olives flow onto the cool stone floor of the veranda. Against the wall rest sacks of olives she and Um Muna separated from the better quality olives. Those we will take to the oil press in the morning.

A tub nearby is full of the ripe, black variety. They are special. We go inside and Um Muna urges us to taste the black olives she has already preserved in oil. We each take one. "Still bitter," notes the daughter, pulling away the pit and reaching for another. "But I like them like this, don't you? Here." She insists I try another. "These we'll take back to Beirut with us, shall we?" Like every other weekend visitor, Muna will load her car trunk with a sack of ripe olives (ready to salt) and a bottle (or three) of freshly pressed oil. My host looks at me sadly: how can I take a sack back to New York next week? She pities me and will put her mind to the problem.

We see little of Muna's dad. He's in the fields all day. When his family was young, he supported all of them from these orchards: the olives, the figs, the grapes, the pomegranates, some pears as well. I will see heavy dark fig trees in the yard next morning when he escorts me through the fields behind the house to show off his arbors of grapes, the pear trees, the arching pomegranate branches. In the past every one of them was cultivated, their fruit sold in Tyre or shipped to Beirut.

War disrupted that. The young went to the cities when the war began; some died fighting or just standing in the path of a bullet or too close to a wired car that blew them apart. Others left Lebanon, temporarily, they thought.

Today the old man is able to keep his ancient olive plants in good health and to find a way to preserve what he harvests and to sell some of the crop. But he abandoned those figs and pomegranates and grapes five years ago.

I walk up the lane and reach into the dark-leafed branches for a ripe, rust-colored fig. At my feet is a blanket of the fallen fruit, dry and crushed among weeds. Others hang withered on their stems, half eaten by birds. The pomegranates are newly ripe—bright red, showing shiny seeds through their bursting skin. They will not be picked and neither will the huge clumps of grapes, now dried brown, hanging dense and dark under the arbor.

At the bottom of the hill is Litani River valley. Across the wide ravine I see another hillside once rich with lovingly cultivated grapes and figs but I detect no sign of life. Muna points to the Israeli military building on the ridge, the same place where, the night before, she distinguished the enemy line of bright lights on the horizon. Later we will spot helicopters crossing the far hills over the rows of red-roofed cottages of the same design as houses I saw all across the West Bank and penetrating Gaza; the houses of Jewish settlers.

Up to now, no one has mentioned the Israeli camps. But they are not forgotten. Never.

I do not ask the people of this house if they belong to a particular organization, or party—Amal, Hizbullah, Communist—or what they conclude about Palestinians, or Syria, or the shelling near the coast. I understand how, as time passes and peace recedes, farmers like Abu Muna, who grew up planting seedlings, will join the parties, Islamic or other, to ensure the resistance against occupation continues. Anyone who loves olives will do the same.

At the same time, every one of them awaits a peace treaty.

II

Bread

A Basic Desire : Going Home

Bread

Round, flat Arabic bread is served with most meals and is often used to pick up other foods. This common form of sustenance provides the backdrop for the section in which women describe their experiences of returning to the Arab world. The desire to connect with our homeland, in whatever ways we can, is as basic to us as the need to eat bread.

Khoobz Marouk–Basic Bread Dough

3 c. warm water
1 t. salt
1 T sugar (optional)
2 T dry yeast
3/4 c. wheat germ (alternate to using3 c. whole wheat flour)
unbleached white flour)
8 c. flour (3 c. whole wheat and 5 c. unbleached white)

Dissolve yeast in lukewarm water in a large bowl. Add salt, sugar, and wheatgerm; gradually mix in three cups of flour, breaking up lumps with your hands. Continue adding flour, kneading as you go. Add more water as needed, using your hands to blend in flour from the sides of the bowl. When the dough is thoroughly mixed and has a smooth, moist consistency that does not stick to your hands, divide into 5-6 parts and form into orange-sized balls. To make smaller loaves, roll into balls that are egg-sized. If you wish to freeze dough. Roll balls in flour and place on cloth-covered flat surface allowing space to rise. Cover with a damp cloth or plastic wrap and let rise for 1 hour or until doubled in size. Preheat oven to 475°.

Roll out as thick as you like on a floured surface, 1/8" for khoobz marouk (paper thin), or 1/4" for kmege (pocket bread). For khoobz marouk, gently stretch the dough over your hands, getting it as thin as possible. Here's where twirling and tossing in the air comes in. Watch pizza bakers for tricks unless you've seen your mom do it. Stretch the rolled, round dough onto a baking tray or slide it directly onto the floor of a hot gas or electric oven. Bake until air bubbles form or dough puffs up, about 5 minutes. Remove from oven and place in broiler for 1 minute or less until bread puffs up and lightly browns. In an electric oven: move tray to top rack briefly to brown. Stack loaves in damp towels to cool and soften, or eat hot and crispy. Yum!

To freeze dough: Roll the balls of dough in flour, wrap tightly in plastic wrap, and freeze in airtight bags. Remove from bag and leave at room temperature for a few hours or in the fridge overnight to thaw and rise. Proceed to roll out and bake as above in hot oven.

◔ Source: Linda Dalal Sawaya and Alice Ganamey Sawaya from The Ganamey: Sawaya Family Cookbook, Alice's Lebanese Restaurant

Boundaries: Arab/American

LISA SUHAIR MAJAJ

So much goes along with us
on the border of vision,
"street arabs"
orphans when we have no names
to bring them before our eyes.

—David Williams, *Traveling Mercies*

Beyond this world there are twenty other worlds.

—Naomi Shihab Nye, *Texas Poets in Concert*

One evening a number of years ago, at a workshop on racism, I became aware—in one of those moments of realization that is not a definitive falling into place, but instead a slow groundswell of understanding—of the ways in which I experience my identity as not merely complex, but rather an uninterpretable excess.

Workshop participants were asked to group ourselves in the center of the room. As the facilitator called out a series of categories, we crossed to one side of the room or the other, according to our self-identification: white or person of color, heterosexual or lesbian/bisexual, middle/upper-class or working-class, born in the United States or in another country, at least one college-educated parent or parents with no higher education, English as a native language or a second language. Although I am used to thinking of myself in terms of marginality and difference, I found myself, time after time, on the mainstream side of the room. White (as I called myself for lack of a more appropriate category), heterosexual, middle-class, born in the United States to a college-educated parent, a native speaker of English, I seemed to be part of America's presumed majority.

I learned a great deal that night about how much I take for granted those aspects of my life which locate me in a privileged sphere. It is a lesson of which I remain acutely conscious, and for which I am grateful. But looking across the room at the cluster of women representing what American society understands as "other," I was disconcerted by the lack of fit between the definitions offered that evening and my personal reality. Born in the United States, I have nonetheless lived much of my life outside it, in Jordan and Lebanon. My father was college-educated and middle-class, but Palestinian—hardly an identity suggestive of inclusion in mainstream American society. I considered myself white: my olive-tinged skin, while an asset in terms of acquiring a ready tan, did not seem a dramatic marker of difference. But I have received enough comments on my skin tone to make me aware that this is not entirely a neutral issue—and as I have learned the history of colonialism in the Arab world, I have come to understand the ways in which even light-skinned Arabs are people of color. Native speaker of English, I grew up alienated from the linguistic medium—Arabic—that swirled around me, living a life in some ways as marginal as that of a non-English speaker in the United States. Although I do not think of myself as having an accent, I have more than once been assumed to be foreign; I speak with an intonation acquired from the British-inflected Jordanian English that delineated my childhood, or from years of the careful enunciation one adopts when addressing non-native speakers. I have been the target of various forms of harassment specifically linked to my Arab identity, from hostile comments to threatening phone calls, racist mail, and destruction of property. I have feared physical assault when wearing something that identifies me as an Arab. And so, standing on the majority side of the room that evening, observing the discrepancy between the facts of my life and the available categories of inclusion and exclusion, I could not help but wonder whether these categories are insufficient, or insufficiently nuanced.

I recognize in this response my reluctance, here in this country which is so large, and which often seems—however inaccurately—so homogenous, to relinquish a sense of my own difference. When I arrived in the United States for graduate school in 1982, I felt oddly invisible. Walking down the crowded streets of Ann Arbor, Michigan I became aware, with a mixture of relief and unease, that no one was looking at me, trying to talk to me, or making comments under their breath. Years of living in Jordan and Lebanon, where my physical appearance, my style of dressing, my manner of walking had all coded me as foreign, had accustomed me to being the object of attention, curiosity, and sometimes harassment. Although in Amman and Beirut I had tried to make myself as inconspicuous as possible—walking close to walls, never meeting anyone's eyes—I always knew that people noted, assessed, commented on my presence. Even as I disliked and resented this attention, I grew to expect it. As a girl and woman with little self-confidence, the external gaze, intrusive as it was, perhaps offered the solace of definition: I am seen, therefore I exist. Without that gaze would I still know who I was?

The idea of such dependence upon external definition disturbs me now. I would like to say that I longed not to be defined by the gaze of the other, but to look out upon the world through eyes rooted in the boundaries of my own identity. But it is true that for much of my life I thought if I looked long enough I would find someone to tell me who I am. Turning to the world for some reflection of myself, however, I found only distortion. Perhaps it was asking too much of that younger self of mine, overwhelmed by a sense of my identity's invalidity no matter which culture I entered, to learn the necessary art of self-definition.

And if I had achieved that skill, would I have merely learned more quickly the cost of difference? Being American in the Arab world set me apart in ways I found profoundly disturbing. But I discovered soon enough that being Arab in the United States—worse, being Palestinian—offers little in the way of reassurance. My hopeful belief that moving to the United States would be a homecoming was quickly shaken. Once I claimed a past, spoke my history, told my name, the walls of incomprehension and hostility rose, brick by brick: un-funny "ethnic" jokes, jibes about terrorists and kalashnikovs, about veiled women and camels; or worse, the awkward silences, the hasty shifts to other subjects. Searching for images of my Arab self in American culture I found only unrecognizable stereotypes. In the face of such incomprehension I could say nothing.

But I have grown weary of my silence and paranoia; my fear that if I wear a Palestinian emblem, a *kaffiyeh*, use my few words of Arabic, say my name and where I am from, I will open myself to suspicion or hatred. I am tired of being afraid to speak who I am:

American and Palestinian, not merely half of one thing and half of another, but both at once—and in that inexplicable melding that occurs when two cultures come together, not quite either, so that neither American nor Arab find themselves fully reflected in me, nor I in them.

Perhaps it should not have surprised me to cross and recross that room of divisions and find myself nowhere.

I was born in 1960, in the small farming community of Hawarden, on Iowa's western border. My mother, Jean Caroline Stoltenberg, in whose hometown I was born, was American, of German descent. From her I take my facial structure and features, the color of my hair, and more: an awkward shyness, a certain naiveté, but also a capacity for survival and adaptation that exceeds my own expectations. I learned from her to value both pragmatism and a sense of humor. She liked to say that she was of farming stock, plain but sturdy. Twenty-three years in Jordan did not greatly alter her midwestern style; she met the unfamiliar with the same resolution and forthrightness with which she turned to her daily tasks. Despite her willing adjustment to Middle Eastern life, she never quite relinquished her longing for the seasonal landscapes of her Iowa childhood—summer's lush greenness, the white drifts of winter. Although I experienced her primarily against a Jordanian backdrop, my memories of her evoke midwestern images and echoes: fragrant platters of beef and potatoes, golden cornfields beneath wide, sultry skies, the strident music of crickets chanting at dusk.

My father, Isa Joudeh Majaj, a Palestinian of the generation that had reached young adulthood by the time of Israel's creation from the land of Palestine, was born in Bir Zeit, in what is now the occupied West Bank. From him I take the olive tinge to my skin, the shape of my hands and nose, the texture of my hair, and a tendency toward inarticulate and contradictory emotion. From him, too, I take a certain stubbornness, and what he used to call "Palestinian determination." Named Isa, Arabic for Jesus, by his widowed mother in fulfillment of a vow, my father grew from childhood to adolescence in Jerusalem, that city where so many histories intersect. Although distanced from each other by geographical origin, culture, and more, my parents held in common their respect for the earth and for the people who till it. My father, never quite reconciled to his urban life, spoke longingly of the groves of orange and olive trees, the tomato plants and squash vines, by which Palestinian farmers live. He could identify the crop of a distant field by its merest wisp of green, had learned the secrets of grafting, knew when to plant and when to harvest. His strong attachment to the earth—an emotion I have come to recognize among Palestinians—made me understand his dispossession as a particular form of violence. I associate his life with loss and bitterness, but also with a life-bearing rootedness reminiscent of those olive trees in Jerusalem that date back to the time of Christ, or of jasmine flowering from vines twisted thick as tree trunks.

After a youth punctuated by the devastating events leading up to Israel's creation in 1948, during which he fought against the British and saw relatives lose both homes and lives, my father worked his way to the United States for a college education. In Sioux City, Iowa he attended Morningside College, shovelling mounds of hamburger in the stockyards during school breaks. At a YMCA dance he met my mother, a quiet young woman working as a secretary in a legal firm. A year later the two were married.

I do not know what drew my parents together. My father may have seen and valued in my mother both the shy pliancy cultivated by girls of her generation and the resilience learned in a farming family. Though he seemed to take her strength for granted, he assumed she would mold herself to his delineation. My mother, who by her own account had grown up imbued with visions of true romance, may have seen in my father an exemplar of the tall dark stranger. At their wedding she vowed both to love and to obey. My parents' marriage, complex from its outset, promised the richness of cultural interaction, but bore as well the fruit of much cultural contradiction. It is the complexity and contradictions of their relationship that I have inherited, and that mediate my interactions in the societies, Arab and American, that I claim as birthright, but experience all too often as alienation.

When I was born my mother claimed me in a gesture that in later years I understood to have been quite remarkable. The birth of my older sister three years previously had disappointed my father in his desire for a son and the title "*Abu-Tarek*," father of Tarek. Forced by his work to be absent before my own birth, he refused to choose a girl's name before he left—hoping, no doubt, that this second child would be a boy, as the first one had not been. I was born, and my mother called me Lisa Ann. But my father asserted his will over my identity from many thousands of miles away. Upon learning of my birth, he sent a telegram congratulating my mother on the arrival of Suhair Suzanne—*Suhair*, a name meaning "little star in the night"; *Suzanne*, an Americanization of the Arabic *Sausan*—in what he may have thought would be a cultural compromise. By the time she received the telegram my mother must have had me home, Lisa Ann firmly inscribed in the hospital records. But this did not deter my father, always a stubborn man. On his return I was baptized Suhair Suzanne. In the one picture I possess of the event, I am cradled plumply in the arms of my aunt, indifferent to the saga of fractured identity about to ensue.

My mother, however, must have been stronger-willed than anyone expected. She acquiesced to the baptism, but her dutiful letters to the relatives in Jordan relate news of baby Lisa Suhair, with "Lisa" crossed out by her own pen. This marvelously subversive gesture allowed her to appear to abide by my father's wishes while still wedging her own claims in. And somehow her persistence won out. My earliest memories are of myself as Lisa: birthday cards and baby books all confirm it. Even my father only called me Suhair to tease me. But if my mother claimed victory in the colloquial, his was the legal victory. Both passport and birth certificate identified me as Suhair Suzanne, presaging a schism of worlds which would widen steadily as I grew.

When my sister and I were still very young, my parents moved first to Lebanon, then to Jordan. My father had had much difficulty finding work in the midwestern United States: people were suspicious of foreigners, and frequently anti-Semitic, and he was often assumed to be a Jew. Moving to the west coast did not greatly improve his opportunities. Finally, however, he was hired by a moving and packing firm that sent him to Beirut. From there we moved to Amman, where his mother and brother then lived. By my fourth birthday we were settled in the small stone house, in what is now thought of as "old" Amman, where we were to live for the next twenty years.

Despite the semblance of rootedness this move to Jordan offered, my childhood was permeated with the ambience of exile.

If to my mother "home" was thousands of miles away, beyond the Atlantic, to my father it was tantalizingly close, yet maddeningly unattainable—just across the Jordan River. My early years were marked by a constant sense of displacement, the unsettling quality of which determined much of my personal ambivalence and sense of confusion, as well as a certain flexibility I have come to value. I learned at an early age that there is always more than one way of doing things, but that this increased awareness of cultural relativity often meant a more complicated, and painful, existence. I learned to live as if in a transitional state, waiting always for the time that we would go to Palestine, to the United States, to a place where I would belong. But trips to Iowa and to Jerusalem taught me that once I got there, "home" slipped away inexplicably, materializing again just beyond reach. If a sense of rootedness was what gave life meaning, as my parents' individual efforts to ward off alienation implied, this meaning seemed able to assume full import only in the imagination.

The world of my growing-up years consisted of intersecting cultural spheres that often harmonized, but more frequently, particularly as my sister and I grew older, clashed. Home provided, naturally enough, the site of both the greatest cultural intermingling and the most intense contradiction. My mother worked, despite my father's objections, at the American Community School in Amman from the time I entered kindergarten until several years before her death in 1986. Though in later years she began to articulate the independence she had muted for years, for most of her married life she acquiesced to a hierarchical structuring of family codes. Although the prime agent of my sister's and my own socialization, my mother transmitted to us largely those lessons of my father's choosing. But my father's failure to fully explain his assumptions often resulted in a gap in the cultural translation from Arab to American. Thus, only *after* I had been away at college for some time did I explicitly learn that I should never go out except in large groups—a rule at the heart of which was a ban upon interactions with men. But such expectations hardly needed to be spelled out. My restricted upbringing and my own desire to maintain familial harmony had resulted in such an effective internalization of my father's expectations, most of which had to do with the maintenance of honor, that I lived them out almost unconsciously.

Looking back on our family life from the perspective of a painfully won feminism, the gender dynamics pervading our household seem unambiguously problematic. In addressing them, however, I find myself becoming defensive, wanting to preserve my deep-rooted family loyalties, however conflicted. I had learned to understand my relationship to others through the medium of Arab cultural norms filtered through an uneven Americanization. My childhood was permeated by the lesson, incessantly reinforced, that family is not just vital to self, but is so inherent that family and self are in a sense one and the same. I am more familiar than I would choose to be with the constrictions implicit in such celebration of family ties. But the mesh of familial expectations stressed in Arab culture provided a sense of security not readily apparent in my experience of American relationships, with their emphasis on individualism. However restrictively articulated, the stable definitions of self available in my childhood context held a certain appeal for me, caught as I was in a confusion of cultures.

I have come to understand the pressures that governed my life not as an innate characteristic of Arab culture, but as a particular, and gendered, product of cross-cultural interactions. In my experience, male children of mixed marriages are often able to claim both the rights of Arab men and an indefinable freedom usually attributed to western identity. Although the cultural mix imposes its burdens, a boy's situatedness between Arab and American identities is not debilitating. But for girls, relegated to the mother's sphere, the implications of a western identity in an Arab context can be so problematic that claustrophobic familial restrictions are often the result. Although modesty is required of all girls, those with American blood are at particular risk and must be doubly protected, so that there is neither opportunity nor basis for gossip.

As a child, however, I was aware only that being Arab, even in part, mandated a profound rejection of any self-definition that contradicted the claims of familial bonds. When I wished, as an adult, to marry a non-Arab man against my father's wishes, and engaged in a bitter, painful attempt to do so without irrevocably severing family ties, some friends seemed unable to understand why I would not rebel simply and cleanly, claiming my life and my feminist principles on my own terms. But to do so would have meant the abrogation not just of emotional connections, but of my very identity. Such absolute definitions make it extremely difficult for those of us caught between cultures to challenge restrictive cultural codes: without the security of being able to first lay full claim to the identity one rejects, rebellion becomes precarious and difficult.

Although I lived in an Arabic-speaking country, in my private world English was the main language of communication. My Arab relatives (who had all, except for my grandmother, learned English at school) wished to make my mother welcome by speaking her language, and wished as well to practice their skills in English—the use of which, in a residue of colonialism, still constitutes a mark of status in Jordan. Though I learned "kitchen Arabic" quite early, and could speak with my grandmother on an elementary level, I never became proficient in the language that should have been mine from childhood. This lack resulted in my isolation from the culture in which I lived. I was unable to follow conversations in family gatherings when people did not speak English. I could not understand Arabic television shows or news broadcasts, was unable to speak to storekeepers or passersby, or to develop friendships with Arab children. As a result I remained trapped in a cultural insularity—articulated through the American school, American church, and American friends constituting my world—which now mortifies me. My father's habit of speaking only English at home played a large part in this deficiency; it seems never to have occurred to him that my sister and I would *not* pick up Arabic. Perhaps he thought that language skills ran in the blood. Indeed, during my college years he once sent me an article in Arabic, and was surprised and dismayed at my inability to read it: he had expected me to be literate in his language.

These linguistic deficiencies, though partly self-willed, have come to haunt me. I mourned with particular potency when my grandmother died shortly after I started studying Arabic for the specific purpose of communicating with her more meaningfully. As a child I had received occasional Arabic lessons from a relative at home and during special lunch-hour classes at school. During my teens and early twenties, embarrassed by the limitations of monolingualism, I took various courses in spoken and written Arabic. Despite my efforts, however, I retained little of what I learned, and my father, perhaps taking my knowledge for granted, offered little reinforcement. During bursts of enthusiasm or guilt I would ask him to speak Arabic to me on a daily basis. But such resolutions rarely lasted. He was too busy and too impatient for my faltering efforts, and I must have harbored more internal resistance to learning Arabic than I then realized.

Similarly, my father seemed to believe that knowledge of Palestinian history was a blood inheritance. I therefore had only my personal experience of events such as the Six Day War, or Black September, and a basic awareness of key dates—1948, 1967, 1970, 1973—to guide me through this history that so defined my father's life, and my own.* Only when challenged by my college peers in Lebanon did I begin to educate myself about my Palestinian background, a task that assumed more urgency when I moved to the United States. Indeed, in a pattern that continues to repeat itself, I have come to understand myself primarily in oppositional contexts: in Jordan I learned the ways in which I am American, while in the United States I discovered the ways in which I am Arab.

Though my father's cultural codes regulated everything from the length of my hair to the friends I was permitted to visit, the surface texture of my life was indisputably American. I grew up reading Mother Goose, singing "Home on the Range," reciting "The Ride of Paul Revere," and drawing pictures of Pilgrims and Indians, Christmas trees and Santa Clauses, Valentines and Easter bunnies. At school I learned the standard colonialist narrative of white Pilgrims settling an empty new land, struggling bravely against savage Indians. Yet into this world came many Arab elements. My relatives would fill the house with their Palestinian dialect, the men arguing in loud voices, slamming the *tric trac* stones on the board, while the women chatted on the veranda or in the kitchen. Although my mother took advantage of my father's frequent business trips to serve meatloaf and potatoes, the plain American food she craved, much of the food we ate was Arabic: I grew up on *yakhni* and

---

* The state of Israel was established in 1948, dispossessing 750,000 Palestinians, more than 80 percent of the Arab inhabitants of the land that became Israel. The Six Day War of 1967 resulted in Israel's seizure of land from Jordan, Egypt, and Syria. During Black September of 1970 the Jordanian army killed thousands of Palestinians; militants who were not killed or captured fled to Lebanon. In 1973 war again broke out, this time between Israel, Egypt, Syria, and Iraq.

mahshi, wara'dawali and *ma'aloubi.* My father had taught my mother to cook these dishes when they lived in the United States: hungry for the food of his childhood, he was willing to enter the kitchen to teach her the art of rolling grapeleaves or hollowing squash. In Jordan my grandmother took over her culinary education, the two of them communicating through hand gestures and my mother's broken Arabic.

But even food was a marker of both integration and conflict. To my father's dismay, I learned from my mother to hate yoghurt, a staple of Middle Eastern diets. He took this as a form of betrayal. Holidays became arenas for suppressed cultural battles, as my father insisted that my mother prepare time-consuming pots of rolled grapeleaves and stuffed squash in addition to the turkey and mashed potatoes, sweet potatoes and cranberry sauce; or that she dispense with the bread stuffing and substitute an Arabic filling of rice, lamb meat, and pine nuts. For periods of my childhood, having two cultural backgrounds seemed merely to mean more variety from which to choose, like the holiday dinners with two complete menus on the table. I learned to like both cuisines, and to this day crave the potent garlic, the distinctive cinnamon and allspice of the Arabic dishes I rarely, for lack of time, make. But early on I learned that cultures, like flavors, often clash. And my sister and I, occupying through our very existence the point of tension where my mother's and father's worlds met, often provided the ground for this conflict.

Moving through childhood between the insular worlds of school and home, I remained constantly aware of the ways in which I was different. My relatively light skin and hair, while failing to grant me entrance to the blond, blue-eyed company of "real" Americans, set me apart from my Arab neighbors. There must have been some difference about me more elusive than that, however, for despite the fact that I knew Arabs with skin or hair lighter than my own, when I walked down the street I would hear the murmurs: *ajnabi,* foreigner. Even my body language marked me. When I was in my teens an Arab man once told me he would recognize my walk from blocks away. "You don't walk like an Arab girl," he said. "You take long steps; there's a bounce to your stride."

Instead of taking offense at what was in fact a criticism of my lack of "femininity," I hopefully interpreted this description to mean that perhaps I was, after all, American. I still clung to some shred of that old longing to be as confidently unambiguous as the diplomat kids who rode the Embassy bus, their lunchboxes filled with commissary treats—Oreos, Hershey bars—that we "locals" could never obtain. I wanted an American life like the ones I read about in the books I helped my mother unpack for the school library each year, the odor of glue and paper filling me with longing. I wanted an American father who would come home for dinner at 6 p.m., allow me to sleep over at friends' houses, speak unaccented English and never misuse a colloquialism; who would be other than what he indisputably was—a Palestinian. As a child I convinced myself that we lived in Jordan by mistake, and that soon we would return to the United States, where I would become my true self: American, whole. I wanted to believe that my confusion and fragmentation were merely temporary.

Meanwhile, I searched for someone to explain me to myself. I knew that Arabs—my relatives as much as neighbors and shop-keepers and strangers—thought me foreign, while "real" Americans thought me foreign as well. I knew, too, the subtle hierarchies implicit in these assessments. At school the social order was clear: Embassy Americans, then non-Embassy Americans, and finally those of us with mixed blood, whose claim to the insular world of overseas Americans was at best partial. At the interdenominational church we attended, my mother and sister and I fielded the solicitude of missionaries who never quite believed that my father was not Muslim. When, after exhausting the resources of the American school, I transferred to a Jordanian high school offering courses in English, I learned that there too I was an outsider. My father's name didn't change the fact that I couldn't speak Arabic, lacked the cultural subtleties into which an Arab girl would have been socialized, and as an American female had automatically suspect morals.

I see now how orientalist representations of the Arab world find echoes in occidentalist perceptions of the west. When I walked down the streets of Amman I was categorized as foreign, female; a target of curiosity and harassment. My appearance alone in public and my foreignness seemed to suggest sexual availability; whispers of *charmoota*, prostitute, echoed in my burning ears. The insidious touch of young men's hands on my body pursued me, their eyes taunting me in mock innocence when I whirled to confront them.

Once, when a young man crowded me against a wall, brushing my hips with his hand as he passed, I cried out wildly and swung my bag at him. But he advanced threateningly toward me, shouting angrily at my effrontery. If I had spoken Arabic to him he might have retreated in shame. Because I did not he must have seen me simply as a foreign woman, flaunting a sexuality unmediated by the protection of men, the uncles and brothers and cousins whom an Arab woman would be assumed to have.

Despite such experiences, early in my teens I claimed walking as a mark of my individuality. Determined to assert my difference since I could not eradicate it, I walked everywhere, consciously lengthening my stride and walking with a freedom of motion I longed to extend to the rest of my life. Walking offered a means both of setting myself off from and of confronting the Arab culture that I felt threatened to overwhelm me. I wanted to insist that I was "other" than these people whose language I barely spoke, even though they were my relatives; that I was American—as was, for that matter, my father. Lacking an understanding of his history, I remained oblivious to his awareness of his American citizenship as a bitter acquiescence to the realities of international politics and the denial of Palestinian identity. Instead, I clung to markers of our mutual Americanness. Didn't we cross the bridge to the West Bank with the foreigners, in air-conditioned comfort, instead of on the suffocatingly hot "Arab" side, where Palestinians returning to the Occupied Territories had to strip naked and send their shoes and suitcases to be x-rayed? Didn't we go to the Fourth of July picnics and Christmas bazaars? Weren't we as good as other Americans?

While my father shared my anger at being marginalized in the American community, he did not appreciate my attempts to reject his heritage. Despite his esteem for certain aspects of American culture—his fondness of small midwestern towns, his fascination with technological gadgetry, his admiration of the American work ethic—as I grew older he grew ever more disapproving of my efforts to identify as an American. Although he had left much of my sister's and my own upbringing to my mother, he had assumed that we would arrived at adolescence as model Arab girls: when we did not he was puzzled and annoyed. As walking became a measure of my independence, it became as well a measure of our conflict of wills. He did not like my "wandering in the streets"; it was not "becoming," and it threatened his own honor. I stole away for walks, therefore, during the drowsy hours after the heavy midday meal when most people, my father included, were either at work or at siesta. Walking in the early afternoon, especially during the summer months, accentuated my difference from the Jordanian culture I had determined to resist. A young woman walking quickly and alone through still, hot streets, past drowsy guards and bored shopkeepers, presented an anomaly: Arab girls, I had been told both subtly and explicitly, did not do such things—a fact that pleased me.

As my sister and I entered the "dangerous age," when our reputations were increasingly at stake and a wrong move would brand us as "loose," my father grew more and more rigid in his efforts to regulate our self-definitions. Our options in life were spelled out in terms of whom we would be permitted to marry. A Palestinian Christian, I knew, was the preferred choice. But even a Palestinian Muslim, my father said—though I did not quite believe him, conscious of the crucial significance of religious distinctions in the Middle East—would be better than a Jordanian. (I think of Black September, the days spent below window level, the nights of guns and mortars, my grandmother's house burned after soldiers learned of my cousins' political affiliations, the horror of Palestinian families massacred in their homes by the Jordanian army, and I begin to understand.) To marry an American, or Britisher, or Canadian was out of the question. Westerners, I heard repeatedly, had no morals, no respect for family, no sense of honor—an opinion that seemed to derive in part from observations of real cultural differences between Arabs and westerners, in part from the weekly episodes of Peyton Place and other English-language programs aired on Jordan television. (I have been asked by Arabs whether Americans really get divorced six or seven times, abandon their elderly parents, and are all wealthy. And I have been asked by Americans whether Arabs really ride camels to work, live in tents, and have never seen planes or hospitals.) Though I now appreciate the difficult balance my father sought to maintain in his identity as a Christian Palestinian in Muslim Jordan, between the American characteristics he had embraced after years in the United States and the cultural requirements of Jordanian society, at the time I experienced his expectations as unreasonable and contradictory. Most difficult to accept was the implicit portrayal of my mother's American identity as a misfortune for which we all, she included, had to compensate. On constant trial to prove my virtue and held to a far stricter standard of behavior than my Arab cousins, I both resented and felt compelled to undertake the ongoing task of proving that I wasn't, in fact, American.

In my experience cultural marginality has been among the most painful of alienations. My childhood desire, often desperate, was not so much to be a particular nationality, to be American or Arab, but to be wholly one thing or another: to be *something* that I and the rest of the world could understand, categorize, label, predict. Although I spent years struggling to define my personal politics of location, I remained situated somewhere between Arab and American cultures—never quite rooted in either, always constrained by both. My sense of liminality grew as I became more aware of the rigid nature of definitions: Arab culture simultaneously claimed and excluded me, while the American identity I longed for retreated inexorably from my grasp.

My experiences in the United States in many ways reinforced this sense of exclusion. Upon arriving in Michigan for graduate school, after four years at the American University of Beirut during which both my American and Palestinian identities had been inevitably politicized, I yearned, yet again, for the simplicity of belonging. Consciously drawing as little attention as possible to my name, my family, my background, I avoided Middle Eastern organizations, and made no Arab friends at all. A few days after my arrival in the United States, when a man asked me provocatively why I wore a "map of Israel" around my neck, I answered briefly that it was a map of historic Palestine and then retreated from his attempts to draw me into debate, shrinking deep into a cocoon of silence.

"Passing demands a desire to become invisible," writes Michelle Cliff. "A ghost-life. An ignorance of connections."* While the incidents that first made me afraid to reveal myself in the United States were minor—pointed questions, sidelong glances, awkward silences—they were enough to thrust me firmly back into a desire for invisibility. I sought anonymity, as if trying to erode the

* Michelle Cliff, *Claiming an Identity They Taught Me to Despise* (Watertown, MA: Persephone Press, 1980), 5.

connections that had brought me, juncture by juncture, to where and who I was, the product of histories I could no more undo than I could undo my bone structure.

But passing, as I was to learn, wreaks implicit violence upon the lived reality of our experiences. "Passing demands quiet," Cliff warns. "And from that quiet—silence." I have learned to understand silence as something insidious. As a child, lost between the contradictory demands of the worlds I moved between, I claimed silence as a tool of survival; I honed it still further in my American context. What I did not then realize was that silence, with time, atrophies the voice—a loss with such grave consequences that it is a form of dispossession. Silence made it possible for me to blend into my surroundings, chameleon-like; it enabled me to absorb without self-revelation what I needed to know. But its implications were disastrous. Silence wrapped itself around my limbs like cotton wool, wound itself into my ears and eyes, filled my mouth and muffled my throat. I do not know at what point I began to choke. Perhaps there was never a single incident, just a slow deposition of sediment over time. Until one day, retching, I spat out some unnameable substance. And I attempted to speak.

By this time I was beginning to claim the tools of feminism. In Beirut I had pored over a copy of *The Feminine Mystique*, startled by the wave of recognition it evoked. Later, graduate school exposed me to the analytical training and the affirmation of voice that I had been lacking. Although I eventually discovered its cultural insensibilities, American feminism enabled me to begin interrogating the entanglement of gender and culture in a search for my own definitions. While much in my experience had tempted me to reject Arab culture as misogynist, my growing awareness of the ways in which my experiences represented not Arab culture *per se*, but a conflicted interaction between Arab and American, led me to explore my Palestinian background for positive symbols, not just nationalistic but gendered, on which to draw for identification and strength.

This exploration reinforced my acute awareness of the representation and misrepresentation of Arab culture in the United States. There are ways in which Palestinian women escape the typical stereotypes of Arab women—exotic, sensualized, victimized—only to be laden with the more male-coded, or perhaps merely generic, images of irrational terrorists and pathetic refugees. But none of these images reflect the Arab women I know: my widowed Palestinian grandmother, who raised three boys and buried two girls, raising two grandchildren as well after their mother was killed by a Zionist group's bomb, whose strength and independence people still speak of with awe; or my Lebanese aunt, a skilled nurse who ran a Jerusalem hospital ward for years, raised four children, gracefully met the social requirements of her husband's busy political and medical careers, and now directs a center for disabled children. My increasing anger at the portrayal of the Middle East as a chaotic realm outside the boundaries of rational Western comprehension, and a slowly developing confidence in my own political and cultural knowledge, came together with my burgeoning feminism to make possible an articulation that, although tentative, was more empowering than anything I had experienced.

At some point I began to feel anger. At the jokes about *kalashnikovs* in my backpack, grenades in my purse. At the sheer amazement of a woman who asked my mother, "But why did you marry a terrorist?" At an acquaintance's incredulous look when I spoke of Arab feminism. At the comments that it must be dangerous to live in Jordan "because of all the terrorism." At the college professor who did not believe that Arabs could be Christians. At the knowledge that when I posted announcements of Arab cultural events on campus they would be torn down moments later. At the look of shock and dismay, quickly masked, on the face of a new acquaintance just learning of my Palestinian background. At the startled response of someone who, having assumed my Arab name to be my spouse's, learned that I chose to keep an *Arab* name. At the conversations in which I am forced to explain that Palestinians do indeed exist; that they claim a long history in Palestine.

And with the anger has come fear. Of the unknown person in my apartment building who intercepted packages I had ordered from an Arab-American organization, strewing their contents, defaced with obscenities, at my door. Of the hostility of airport security personnel once they know my destination or origin point: the overly thorough searches, the insistent questions. Of the anonymous person who dialed my home after I was interviewed by my local paper, shouting "Death to Palestinians!" Of the unsigned, racist mail. Of the mysterious hit-and-run driver who smashed my car as it was parked on a quiet residential street, a Palestine emblem clearly visible through the window of the car door.

Such actions inscribe their subjects within a singular, predetermined identity, and often elicit responses validating precisely this identity. However, such exclusionary identification remains, finally, untenable. During the Gulf War a radio commentator proclaimed, "In war there are no hyphenated Americans, just Americans and non-Americans." It is a familiar, and chilling, sentiment: Japanese-Americans in particular can speak to its implications. But what is to become of those of us in-between, those of us who are neither "just" Americans, nor "just" non-Americans? I could say that I opposed the Gulf War as a human being first, as an American second, and only third as a Palestinian. But in fact my identities cannot be so neatly divided. I am never *just* an American, any more than I am *just* a Palestinian. Yet I am not therefore any *less* of an American, or *less* of a Palestinian. As I was rarely given the choice in the Middle East to claim or not claim my American identity, so I am not often given the choice in my American context to be or not to be Palestinian. At best I can attempt to pass, suppressing my identity and resorting to silence. And when this strategy fails—*or when I reject it*—then I am forced to take responsibility for *both* American and Palestinian histories in their contradictory entireties—histories articulated through idealism, but resorting too often to violence. And in so doing I come to a fuller understanding of the contradictions, the excesses, which spill over the neat boundaries within which I am often expected to, and sometimes long to, reside.

It has taken personal loss to bring me to a fuller understanding of the connections and contradictions forming the warp and weft of my experience. The devastation I experienced at my parents' deaths, at the foreclosing of their attempts to negotiate difference in their lives together, compels me to claim and validate their legacy—the textured fabric of my own life. I look in the mirror and recognize their mingled features in my own; I lift my hair and note the curl, the color bequeathed by their mixed genes. My skin, lighter now since my years away from the strong sun of Jordan and Lebanon, retains the faint tinge of olive that set me apart from my white-skinned playmates even in babyhood. Tata Olga, my Palestinian grandmother, used to lament my propensity to stay in the sun. "You'll never find a husband, dark like this," she would scold, speaking the words of internalized racism and sexism. But I search now for color in my life. On the shelf above my desk I keep a card depicting a small Maldivian girl whose richly hued skin, deep brown eyes, and dark, unkempt hair compel me with their beauty. The Lebanese-American poet who gave me this card recently adopted a vibrant Guatemalan child; the girl in the picture reminds me of his daughter. She reminds me as well of a group of Maldivian students from American University of Beirut whose embracing presence and steady endurance during our exodus from Lebanon in 1982 sustained and comforted me. And she brings to mind all the small girls growing up in a world where women are less valued than men, dark skin less valued than light skin, poor people less valued than wealthy people, non-western cultures less valued than western cultures.

She reminds me, too, that it is through a willing encounter with difference that we come to a fuller realization of ourselves. I possess no representative photograph of a Palestinian-American, no non-personal touchstone of my mixed heritage. And despite my longing for such tokens, perhaps they are unnecessary. Although I remain acutely aware of the importance of communal symbols in affirming individual and group consciousness, I find glimmers of myself in people I do not recognize, in faces that share with mine only questions. No closed circle of family or tribe or culture reflects from the Maldivian girl's eyes. She looks slightly away from the camera, her gaze directed wistfully at something just over my left shoulder, something I cannot see and that she may not be able to claim. The card identifies her as Laila, from a Maldive fishing family, noting that Maldivians are a mix of Arab, Singhalese, and Malaysian: there are, after all, some connections between us. But I cannot intercept her gaze. Laila looks steadily beyond me, light planing her pensive face. Whatever she sees remains unspoken. I look at her often, remembering how much I do not know.

Like my parents, I am grounded in both history and alienation. But if it is true that we are ideologically determined, it is also true that our choices allow us a measure of resistance against the larger patterns that map us, a measure of self-creation. Constructed and reconstructed, always historically situated, identities embody the demarcation of possibilities at particular junctures. I claim the identity "Arab-American" not as a heritage passed from generation to generation, but rather as an on-going negotiation of difference. My parents articulated their relationship oppositionally, assumptions colliding as they confronted each other's cultural boundaries. Child of their contradictions, I seek to transform that conflict into a constant motion testing the lines that encircle and embrace me, protect and imprison me. I am caught within a web: lines fade and reappear, forming intricate patterns, a maze. I live at borders that are always overdetermined, constantly shifting. Gripped by the logic of translation, I still long to find my reflection on either side of the cultural divide. But the infinitely more complex web of music beckons, speaking beyond translation. Who can say how this will end?

Claims

I am not soft, hennaed hands,
a seduction of coral lips;
not the enticement of jasmine musk
through a tent flap at night;
not a swirl of sequined hips,
a glint of eyes unveiled.
I am neither harem's promise
nor desire's fulfillment

I am not a shapeless peasant
trailing children like flies;
not a second wife, concubine,
kitchen drudge, house slave;
not foul smelling, moth-eaten, primitive,
tent-dweller, grass-eater, rag-wearer.
I am neither a victim
nor an anachronism.

I am not a camel jockey, sand nigger, terrorist,
oil-rich, bloodthirsty, fiendish;
not a pawn of politicians,
nor a fanatic seeking violent heaven.
I am neither the mirror of your hatred and fear,
nor the reflection of your pity and scorn.
I have learned the world's histories,
and mine are among them.
My hands are open and empty:
the weapon you place in them is your own.

I am the woman remembering jasmine,
bougainvillea against chipped white stone.
I am the laboring farmwife
whose cracked hands claim this soil.
I am the writer whose blacked-out words
are birds' wings, razored and shorn.
I am the lost one who flees,
and the lost one returning;
I am the dream, and the stillness,
and the keen of mourning.

I am the wheat stalk, and I am
the olive. I am plowed fields young
with the music of crickets,
I am ancient earth struggling
to bear history's fruit.
I am the shift of soil
where green thrusts through,
and I am the furrow
embracing the seed again.

I am many rivulets watering
a tree, and I am the tree.
I am opposite banks of a river,
and I am the bridge.
I am light shimmering
off water at night,
and I am the dark sheen
which swallows the moon whole.

I am neither the end of the world
nor the beginning.

Wherever I Am

MARY SALOME

"You speak Hebrew, and you're not Jewish?"

The surprise in the man's voice alarmed me, despite the fact that most people respond that way upon learning that yes, I speak Hebrew and no, I am not Jewish. In this case, my last name made it obvious that not only am I not Jewish, I am Arab-American.

"Yes," I responded. "I learned in high school. It was taught just like any other foreign language."

"But isn't this a bit...unusual?"

"I suppose so." My insides tightened. This was no ordinary conversation, it was prefaced by three hours of questioning and searching that occured before I could board my El Al flight to Israel. What little I knew of life in Israel didn't prepare me for my first visit. I felt shocked, and angry. I expected my knowledge of Hebrew would be an asset, a sign that I had opened myself to Israeli culture in a gesture of understanding and good will. O.K., I was ignorant, and wrong.

It was the fall of 1989 and I spent four months travelling in Egypt, Jordan, Cyprus, Greece, Turkey, and Jerusalem. Part of the reason for my trip was a search for myself and my identity; for communities where I might feel at home. Identity is a complicated subject, and it is always hard for me to say who I am in a few words. I identify myself as a living being, a human being, a woman, a lesbian, a Syrian/Irish-American, and a feminist. My feeling that there is rarely room for me to claim all of who I am increased on this trip. The most noticeable parts of my identity were those which made me different from the people around me, and people usually viewed these differences as negative. For example, in mainstream Israel our common humanity felt less important than the fact that I am an Arab, an American, a lesbian, and a feminist. Among Arabs, my Arab identity came into question because I am part Irish, and an American; my feminism and lesbianism also seemed to set me apart. I don't believe it is my identity that creates these divisions, but rather anti-Arab, anti-woman, and homophobic sentiments that create feelings of fragmentation and disconnection.

In my mind, home is a place where I can be whole and bring all of myself. Even in the United States, I often feel that in order to connect, I must leave some part of myself behind. This feeling was exacerbated during my travels. When I felt powerless, I forgot I had a choice regarding what parts of myself I could express. However, sometimes I intentionally left parts of myself behind. I did this when I felt that acknowledging all of myself would endanger me; when I didn't care enough about my companions to share all of myself with them; when I couldn't spend enough time with someone to give meaning to my identity. But maybe I wouldn't have felt so disjointed and "homeless" if I had made room inside myself for all I am, instead of waiting for the outside world to accept me first. That's not a simple task under any circumstances, especially when the world tells you, "You don't belong, you do not fit, you are not welcome, you don't exist."

In West Jerusalem, an Israeli teenager, without provocation, "accused" my cousin (who is not Arab) and me of being Arabs, then threatened to hit me when I told him to leave. In East Jerusalem, a police van stopped in the street and a badly beaten Palestinian man was pushed out the back doors. He collapsed on the sidewalk in front of us, and other Palestinians carried him away as the police van sped off. Apparently this is a common occurrence; no one seemed surprised and it happened in the middle of the day. On buses, young Israeli boys pretended to shoot Palestinians on the street. An Israeli woman confronted me on a bus for reading an anthology of writing by Asian American women. She thought "Asian" referred to Arabs, and demanded to know why no Israeli writers appeared in the anthology.

A woman in the passport office complained to another woman that she only had three babies, and needed to have more. The numbers of women having babies for the state and their god astounded me. There are many examples of misogyny in Israel (as everywhere): some women cover their hair, elbows, and knees, and hide themselves when they menstruate; some men thank God every morning that they were not born women; porn theatres in Tel Aviv display posters of women, legs splayed, under titles that read "I Want to be Teased" and "Start Something I Can't Stop."

When I was visiting Israel, Palestinians in Israel could be arrested for no reason, without charges, and held in prison for up to a year without charges or a trial. People's license plate colors correlate with their ethnicity and place of residence; thus police know who to stop and question at roadblocks. Young Palestinians are stopped for no reason and routinely interrogated by police; sometimes they are strip-searched on the street. "Troublemakers" have their houses blown up.

Visiting Arab countries also presented problems. A young Palestinian tour guide made an offer to my father. Was it 100 camels he offered for me? I can't remember. When I got angry, the response was "Can't you take a joke?" with a hint of "You should be flattered." In Jordan, my father told me about a Jordanian woman political candidate who called for an end to wife and child beating. In response, she was threatened with violence, fundamentalists took her to court and, needless to say, she was not elected.

In Egypt, dozens of people pointed at, stared at, and reached out to touch my "light" cousin. In my journal I wrote, "Dark hair and skin are not valued here, and Emily earns a higher price than I do. My pride wells up and I feel hurt and jealous for an instant; then I realize the sexism and racism built into these values and I feel disgusted."

My cousin is of Polish and Irish descent, and while our features are similar in some ways, our height and coloring are different. People noticed this. Our tour guide said, "You are so dark and she is so light. You are like night and day." One thing that made this dynamic so difficult is that it reminded me of similar situations with my sister.

As I grew up, there was a definite, if subtle, message from the world that dark is ugly and light is beautiful. I call it subtle only because I can't remember hearing it explicitly stated. My sister looks like the Arab side of the family and I look more like the Irish. When compared with my sister, I was usually designated the "light/Western/pretty" one, while she was usually designated "dark/foreign/ugly." My brother also looks more Arab than I do, but I believe the dynamic is different among girls and women. As girls we are taught, again often by unspoken means, that one of the few ways we can become powerful is if we happen to fit the narrow mold of what is considered beautiful. As adults, my sister, brother, and I are aware and critical of these messages.

So as not to support the stereotype that Arabs and Mediterranean people are more sexist than Westerners, and to present a truer picture of the trip, let me report that sexism is alive and well among tourists and Westerners in the area. In Jordan I heard a white American tourist advise his friend to slap his girlfriend for "getting smart." We also met a white Canadian woman living and working in Saudi Arabia. She laughed as she told us about postcards she had bought in Egypt—a topless Arab woman standing next to Santa Claus, who held her bathing suit top. In Cyprus, we saw similar postcards. One showed the smoking barrel of a gun and a woman in a bikini on the beach; the caption read, "Hunting in Cyprus."

Of course anti-Jewish sentiment also abounds. When leaving Cyprus and again when leaving Greece, airport officials asked me why I was going to Israel, in ways either subtly or blatantly anti-Jewish. For example, a man who checked my passport in Athens as I left for Tel Aviv asked if I lived in Israel, and whether I had dual citizenship with the United States and Israel. When I told him no on both counts, he said, "Good, because I only like Christians," and made the sign of a cross on himself. Another Greek man told me he hates Jewish tourists. I realized how hard it is to engage in honest criticism of Israeli policies without feeding this kind of hatred.

Let's Go: Israel and Egypt informed me that the Middle East doesn't open its arms to gays and lesbians. Nevertheless, I packed my copy of *Gaia's Guide* and set out in search of other queer people almost as soon as I arrived in Israel. My copy of the *Guide* is old, and the section for Israel is small, so I was hopeful but not optimistic. First I called a gay and lesbian switch board; no one answered after several tries. I then decided to look for actual addresses. From Jerusalem I took a bus to Tel Aviv, armed with a tourist map and a few phone tokens. I found the street I wanted, but an automechanic's shop stood where the bookstore was supposed to be. I called a few more phone numbers with no success, then gave up for the time being.

There are reasons for being underground in hostile environments. I know a gay and lesbian community exists in Israel; I just couldn't find it. The forced closeting of the community and my own cultural ignorance made it hard to uncover. By cultural ignorance I mean the fact that signs that could be read to imply that a woman is a lesbian in the United States—very short hair, assertive personality and manner, androgynous clothing, direct eye contact—might mean nothing more in Israel than that a woman had been trained in the military.

For me, part of being a lesbian is uncovering empowering aspects of women's culture and history. On this trip, I found several of these—carvings of women scribes in Egypt, Artemis' temples in Jordan and Turkey, women's collectives in Palestine, and Israel's Women in Black. I also managed a day trip to the Isle of Lesbos.

I told Emily why I wanted to go there—that it had been the home of Sappho, who wrote love poems about women, and the term "lesbian," used in the United States, stems from this woman. Emily went with me, and we managed to get from Turkey to Chios, from Chios to Lesbos, and then from Lesbos back to Turkey again, as if we had planned it months in advance. We only had a day in Lesbos, but it meant a lot to me. In my journal I wrote, "I'm not sure if Lesbos was a disappointment or not. I had sense enough, even when I was still in Israel, to realize that the image of attractive "lesbians" lounging in front of cafés was a fantasy, that it probably wouldn't be like that, just as Israel turned out to be much different from what I'd imagined. But I still have hope, because we didn't have time to go to western Lesbos, Sappho's birthplace, where you can find 'havens for carefree lifestyles,' as the brochure put it. Oh well, next time."

It struck me later that I had travelled a very long way to find "lesbians"—women who love women—when I know we are everywhere. While I enjoyed Lesbos for its historical significance and the ritualized sense of importance I had given to journeying there, it saddened me that I could not find a sense of "lesbian" history or existence anywhere else I went. Besides the reference to "carefree lifestyles" in the brochure, there was no sign that "lesbians" (as we use the term in the United States) live or ever lived on Lesbos. I had only learned about this aspect of our history in Women's Studies classes.

My trip to the Middle East both confused me and broadened my perspective. As a traveller there, I did my best to maintain respect for the different cultures and to remember the importance of cultural autonomy. However, as an Arab/Irish-American woman, a lesbian, a feminist, and someone who opposes oppression in any form, I felt affronted on many levels in every country I visited. And, just as I speak up about this in the United States, I must speak my mind about what I felt in the Middle East.

First, I did not resolve anything on this trip. I did not figure out who I am. That's something that's always changing, I suppose. Community is still a complicated thing. I don't know exactly what it means. I find connection where I can, and I have noticed that the places where I expect to "fit" are often the places where I feel I don't. But fitting has become less important to me, too.

Second, when I came back from the Middle East, every uniformed U.P.S. man looked for a second like an Israeli soldier. Every newspaper stood out for what it didn't say about the Middle East, particularly Israel.

Third, I returned to the United States with new, not necessarily productive anger. I no longer believe that because our languages are similar and our faces so familiar, Arabs, Jews, and other people of Middle Eastern heritage should be able to simply overcome the wars that divide us. This feels like delusion in the face of the hatred and violence there and oversimplification of complicated situations.

Finally, the trip put me in touch with issues around my ethnicity in the United States. Most people in the United States can't tell my ethnicity by looking at me ("You must be Italian/Greek/Jewish/'Hispanic'"). I have decided, though, that my own definition of myself is more important than anyone else's definition of me. I know that because I have a "small nose," blue eyes and light olive skin I will be perceived as "white" by many people in the United States, and there are privileges that go along with that. On the other hand, I feel a sense of loss and invisibility when my ethnicity goes unrecognized. In this country, though, claiming my ethnicity is in many ways a choice I can make that many people of color can not. In Israel and other places in the Middle East and Mediterranean, as I have noted, my perceived ethnicity takes on different meanings.

Like being out as a lesbian, my claiming of my ethnicity is a political choice as well as a personal one, wherever I am.

ℋomecoming

MAY MANSOOR MUNN

Going home is what some of us try to do throughout our lives—although many of us are already home, a chosen place where we live and relate to family and friends. Yet always, that other, almost mythical home wraps us in memory, hints at who or what we are—and sometimes points the way. It's that *other* home that we must occasionally return to and, despite our former rebellions, learn to embrace. Only then will the splinters of our many selves merge into a single strand.

I went back to that other home in 1989, not a former home in Dalton or Richmond or even Onalaska, Texas, but to my old home where my mother and sister still live, where my brother-in-law teaches school, where a sixth-grade classmate is now a minister's wife, and where Aunt Selma, at eighty, still bakes her thick round wheat bread in the old *taboun,* and cooks for a ninety-five-year-old brother. That is the place I left at age fifteen for college in the United States, returning at nineteen—to teach, to marry, and to leave again.

In that other home, early morning mist drenches valleys, moves stealthily across boundaries, sometimes hides the sun. That long-ago home where my mother, in August, leaves for her early treasure hunt in the vineyard, returning with grapes and figs she sets before us: an offering. Once, in this place of memory, shops opened mornings *and* afternoons, stone walls and buildings were free of politics, and instead of gunfire, the honking of cars disrupted equilibrium in the streets.

My mother's house has new aluminum screens now and is white-washed, its high ceiling no longer peeling. Roses and zinnias grow in her garden, basil just below the waterpump, mint under the clothes line, and the sweet-scented Louisa plant at the edge of our veranda.

But in the front yard of our Quaker Meeting House, no flowers bloom. Instead, a broken-off post now lies on its side amid tin cans, bottles, bits of paper, and leftover falafils from the stand next door. The sight of rubbish on Meeting House grounds arouses guilt, and propels me to make amends. I dress in an old shirt and jeans and wind my way to the Meeting House built in Ramallah, Palestine, in 1910, with chiseled-stone flooring, where once my mother's father, Elias Audi, sat in silence in our unprogrammed meeting until he felt inspired to speak, and where my mother still teaches First Day School. And in this once-lovely town, boarding students from Friends' schools made their orderly Sunday trek here and occupied benches to the right and left of the center where adults sat and worshipped.

No one then talked of closing the Meeting House, or selling the property, as they do now. For in this summer of my return, a mere handful of local Quaker adults warm the benches, their small number occasionally bolstered by a trickle of visitors from abroad.

When I get to Meeting House grounds, I discover children playing: a girl, eight, and her brother, six, have carved out their place in the midst of bottles, cans, and mounds of paper and debris, and marked it with stones.

"Would you help me clean?" I ask, fearful of intruding, of usurping their time. As a visitor in this wounded land, I barely glance up as soldiers stand guard on rooftops, looking down at papers and plastic bags swirling in the streets. Looking down at us.

The children do not seem to mind: this curly-headed girl who clutches a notebook possessively to her chest or her brother with his large green eyes. This may be a game for them and I, in my old jeans, am a curiosity—newly arrived from Mars. They help me carry box after box to the wheeled trash can on the side street. My mother lives up the road a bit, I explain, and try to establish authenticity in this place that still has its hold on my life. We establish a routine, the children and I, filling up boxes, moving gingerly with our small loads, returning to fill again.

The children live on the second floor above the shops, across from the Meeting House, and see everything that happens in the street. Much has been happening in the streets while I've been away these past two years. An intifada has been going on here.

We sit on the veranda in my mother's house overlooking flowers and vineyard and fig trees and sip lemonade as my young friend holds her notebook discreetly.

"Is this your homework?" I, once-teacher, ask, curious of homework in Intifada Country.

Children's heads shake, eyes grow wider still. "No. Not *school* homework. This is our *Martyrs'* notebook."

I hold my breath, then ask again to clarify matters. As awkward as a visitor from Mars or even Texas, I ponder children's voices giving cryptic answers. "But how does a *Martyrs'* notebook look from the *inside?*"

The notebook is opened, pages begin to turn. Naturally, a *Martyrs'* notebook has obituaries of those killed in the Intifada. Not the 500 or 600 killed...but only those names my little friend has managed to cut out of newspapers before they were thrown away.

She points out the latest one—killed four days before my homecoming: Yasser Abu Gosh, 17 years. *Martyr.* "I saw it happen," she says softly. "Afterwards, the soldiers threw his body in the jeep and drove him around the street, his head dangling, almost touching the dirt."

Her eyes do not blink in her tiny grown-up face. Her brother's green eyes remain intent on hers. All this comes from asking questions. Curiosity killed the...What you don't know doesn't—or does...?

Welcome Home!

Banned Poem

NAOMI SHIHAB NYE

(East Jerusalem, 1992)

The Palestinian journalists have gathered in a small, modestly elegant theater that could have dropped out of any neighborhood in Paris or New York. We are shivering, having just whirled through a gust of bone-chilling wind on the street outside. Our friend tells us it is always cold and windy on this one street.

Mulling together with their notebooks, the journalists—mostly men in dark jackets, a few using kaffiyehs for scarves—speak quietly. Some sit at tables, smoking over small cups of coffee and plates of sweets.

I feel overcome by a speaker's worst horror—nothing to say. Too much, and nothing. What could I possibly say that these people might want to hear? Why would a group of beleaguered journalists wish to listen to a Palestinian-American poet who lives in Texas?

We shake hands, greet, get introduced. The niceties of human encounter weigh heavily upon the room. Moments later, as if detecting my sudden reluctance, they speak of cancelling today's meeting, of gathering tomorrow instead, once they have better spread the word. Apparently not enough people have arrived to make them feel the crowd is a respectable size. I tell them the smaller, the better. I would be happiest to speak to a mouse just now.

Because it is not hard to have some idea of their situation, and because their faces house such strong dignity nonetheless, I keep asking questions. How do you stand this life here? How do you sustain hope?

And the answers come slowly, cloaked in the mystery which says, "We keep on going. See? We wake up and we keep on going."

Amidst daily curfews, closures, and beatings, my friend the bookseller arranges her lovely series of British Ladybird books for children. "I never know, on any given day, if I will be able to come to work, since I live in the next town."

At a famous east Jerusalem restaurant, Walid stuffs succulent carrots and baby eggplants, stirring a pot of lentil soup for my five-year-old son. I think of Walid's gracious greeting to everyone who enters. "You may sit wherever you feel best." We've chosen the table next to the heater every time.

My new friend the English professor teaches contemporary American and British literatures behind a university door riddled with at least fifty ungrammatical bullet holes. Israeli soldiers approached the campus recently while the students held a small party, a rare occurrence in Intifada times, to celebrate the end of semester. "The party had nothing to do with politics," he tells me. "You know that relief which comes after exams, before break, that sense of lightened load and sweeter days? A very momentary sense, I can assure you, particularly here in the Occupied Territories. My students were eating cake when the soldiers started shouting outside. The students called down to them, 'This is a private gathering,' and they started shooting. Believe me, there was no more provocation than that. We are leaving the door with the bullet holes to remind us of the terrible times we live in."

The times. They are hard to forget. And the journalists carry notebooks and pens, though every paragraph they write must first be submitted to the Israeli censors. In my mind a censor is a huge hulking man at a wide desk with a cigar and a massive inkpad for stamping NO NO NO. The journalists file into their seats. I say how often journalism has frustrated me, and maybe that is why the world needs poetry, too.

After the start of the Intifada, our local newspaper in Texas ticked off the Palestinian dead in tiny token back-page notes: seventy-sixth Palestinian dead, 425th Palestinian dead—as if keeping score in a sporting event. Only when the number fattened to a ripe round 500 did the victim receive a story. Ibtisam Bozieh, age thirteen. She'd dreamed of becoming a doctor, but was shot in the face by an Israeli soldier when she peered curiously through the window of her village home, perhaps to see what was going on out there.

After reading that slim story, I could not stop thinking about Ibtisam Bozieh. She followed me, in waking, in troubled sleep. A small poem was born, written to her, which includes the lines,

"When do we become doctors for one another, Arab, Jew, instead of guarding tumors of pain as if they hold us upright?"

The journalists ask for a copy of the poem. I read a few others. I try to tell them, in a way they may believe, how many Americans I know, both writers and otherwise, who have their interests at heart. But quite obviously we do not run the government. They grow energetic. They tell me we will meet tomorrow too, same theater, same hour. Tomorrow my father, the retired Palestinian-American journalist, will speak, and I will sit in the audience. This sounds better to me.

Next day a small hubbub greets us in the theater, brimming with excitement. The journalists arrange a microphone for my father. Today a few women with strong, careful faces filter in with the men. The way they look at me, I can tell what they think of the United States. Tear gas canisters scattered in the fields by Israeli soldiers say, "Made in Pennsylvania." My grandmother's village home was gassed yesterday as we sat in it, for no reason, as if to give us a small taste of what people experience here on a daily basis. My female cousins stayed shockingly calm. "Don't worry," they said to me, unscrewing the cap on a little bottle of perfume. "It goes away in twenty minutes."

My friend Lena arrived late for a meeting this morning because her shaken neighbor told her this story: Yesterday soldiers dragged off the neighbor's husband while he took care of his little boys, ages four and two. The soldiers left the boys locked in the house by themselves, after smashing the toilet and bathtub and sink. "This is a new tactic," says Lena. "Israeli soldiers like to smash Palestinian bathrooms. Don't ask me why." Water poured into the rest of the house; the little boys stood on chairs, screaming, until their mother came home from work and found them.

I keep thinking of those signs in the United States at construction sites: YOUR TAX DOLLARS AT WORK HERE. I keep feeling dizzy, as if these stories create an altitude unsuitable for living. Yet journalists and date-cake vendors and taxi drivers and schoolgirls in blue pleated skirts keep on living, if they are lucky. A boy in a stationery store arranges a display of vivid children's stickers shaped like chipmunks and ducks and bears, as he would at a happy sales counter anywhere. What happens to people to make them worse than chipmunks and ducks and bears?

Yesterday after our meeting the journalists translated my poem about Ibtisam into Arabic on the spot. I can picture them—smoking, arguing over words. They submitted it to the censors with the rest of their stories last night. It came back today slashed with red X's, stamped at the bottom of the page, REJECTED ENTIRELY, in Arabic and Hebrew. The journalists have encircled it with barbed wire and placed it on red velvet under a frame, presenting it to me at the microphone in front of the crowd, a gift to take home. So I may remember them and the shape of their days. "Now you are one of us," they say. It's a strangely honorable linkage, to be rejected by their own censors.

Think of it: two peoples, so closely related it's hard to tell them apart in the streets sometimes, claiming the same land. The end of the twentieth century.

I keep shuddering. I keep feeling gripped, as if someone has placed an icy hand on my shoulder. None of this does any good for Ibtisam, of course. She's probably buried in her high-up village between the craggy, endlessly patient olive trees. It seems wrong to me that soldiers wear olive-colored fatigues.

Peace Is Tossed to the Wind

LEILA DIAB

The reality of a situation affects you the most when you are placed dead center in the heart of a conflict.

In the course of my yearly trips to Occupied Palestine, I seldom witness any relaxation of discrimination, racism, harassment, and subhuman treatment of Palestinians living under Israeli occupation. And the many Palestinians with whom I speak fear justice and peace are an elusive dream. "The Israeli government can violate Universal Human Rights laws or a series of articles under the fourth Geneva Convention of International Law, and still manages to receive billions of dollars in United States aid. So tell me, how can there be a decisive peace with justice for the Palestinians?" asked a Palestinian refugee from Gaza. Peace is tossed to the wind.

I want to describe what happened when I, a Palestinian-American, visited my relatives in Occupied Palestine in fall, 1991. At the end of my trip, at Tel Aviv Airport, I went through a security check. If you happen to be an Arab, regardless of where you were born, the odds are never in your favor. You are automatically singled out.

As I approached the ticket counter to obtain a boarding pass for my Chicago flight, an Israeli airport security guard said, "You must first pass our security check." Fine, I thought, everybody must go through this. But then I realized this racist treatment is not for everyone. It is reserved for us. There should be a sign, "For Arabs Only." But there is none.

As an Israeli Security Officer searched through my personal belongings, she wanted to know why I had two cameras. I told her I am a photographer and always carry an extra camera. She continued to drill me on why I need two cameras and what type of pictures I take. I told her I took pictures of my relatives, friends, and nature. "I want to know the names and places you visited," she responded. I explained that I grew up in Occupied Palestine and it is only natural for me to return to the land and capture its beauty on film.

Irritated by my comments, she then proceeded to take my two cameras to a back room to remove the batteries. After an hour, she returned with both cameras, and insisted I place them in my luggage. I told her they would be crushed if I did as she requested. However, she forced me to do so. (When I arrived back in Chicago both cameras were crushed.)

Tired and bewildered, I approached the KLM ticket counter to receive my boarding pass. The KLM ticket agent told me she could not give me one until everybody else boarded the plane. She told me if I had purchased my ticket in Israel, this would not be a problem, and made me stand to the side while other passengers were given boarding passes. I insisted upon speaking to the manager, but he simply forced me to wait.

There were two additional security checks for Arabs before we were allowed to board. During the five hours I spent at Tel Aviv Airport, my luggage was searched and x-rayed three times. The final security check for Arabs, before boarding, is a body search behind a closed curtain. In a pleasant voice Israeli security agents say, "You know it's for security reasons that we are obligated to do this."

Knowing only Arabs are subjected to this type of treatment caused me a considerable amount of distress and discontentment. It really doesn't matter if a person of Arab descent has an U.S. passport. I have to wonder if peace is possible for Palestinians in refugee camps, for Palestinians who need identity cards and special license plates, for Palestinians detained and imprisoned without charges or trial, for Palestinians whose land is confiscated so that more Israeli settlements can be built to house the Russian and Ethiopian Jews arriving by the thousands each week.

And at my uncle's home in Beitunia (West Bank), where I spent three formative years, I was told my cousins, twenty and twenty-six years old, are imprisoned for defying the Israeli occupation. Four days before I arrived, Israeli soldiers stormed the village in the middle of the night and forced males between the ages of sixteen and sixty to stand outside in the chill of the night for three hours. The soldiers searched their homes for a young Palestinian wanted for throwing stones.

I desperately hope the Israeli/Palestinian peace agreement, signed on September 13, 1993, marks a new beginning in this vicious cycle of injustice and human suffering. The seeds of peace must be given a chance to germinate and blossom.

Moroccan Steam

LINDA SIMON

"We are going to the hammam today," Janat said, "Bring a big towel."

I shared lodgings with Janat in Morocco. I had been looking forward to my first visit to the hammam, or steam bath, and hurried to pack. We drove to Aisha's near the old walled city, and found her loading a straw basket. We hugged and smiled and kissed each other repeatedly on both cheeks. "I can't wait to see the hammam," I enthused.

Aisha, the teacher, smiled at me and explained, "It's not a health club—and it's not a class thing," she added, anticipating one of my usual questions, "Everyone goes to the hammam."

We brought much more than towels. In fact, the preparations reminded me of going to the beach. Each of us carried a bright plastic pail filled with soaps, creams, homemade potions, pumice stones, and combs.

From the outside, the one-story building looked ordinary, just another arch off a narrow alley in the oldest part of town. We entered through two sets of swinging doors and found ourselves in a large dressing room where women were changing or, swathed in towels, sat cooling on benches that lined the walls. We paid the sixty-cent fee to a middle-aged woman staffing the counter, then removed all our clothes and left them folded on a bench with our shoes tucked underneath. This is it, I thought, and we skittled through a heavy wooden door.

The picture that greeted my eyes remains vivid. In a gray stone room with high, opaque windows, 100 nude women and children doused their bodies with bowls of water, washing hair and scrubbing skin. Vapor rose from stone walls and floors. Voices and clattering sounds echoed all around. Every size and shape of body, hue from cream to chocolate, swayed in the mist like reflections on a pool.

The hammam was a series of three progressively hotter rooms, the innermost of which held the flowing hot water supply. With our paraphernalia we staked out a sitting area in the middle room, and walked gingerly to the stone tub brimming with steaming water. Wooden buckets were piled against a wall. We filled three and returned to our spot where we sat, backs to the wall, on the hard, warm floor. Sweat began to break out on our foreheads. Soon I was suffocating, and moved to the outer room to cool off a bit.

Languidly, I watched the bath rites. The women in their nakedness were reposed and beautiful, with uniformly thick, long, black hair. It took hours to clean and condition those luxurious manes, and I watched, fascinated, as women combed first one homemade unguent, then another, through their tresses.

We rubbed our bodies with a natural brown soap called rassoul. It lathered little, but I felt the fine grit doing its work. A *guellassa* who worked in the hammam asked if we wanted to hire her to scrub us. Aisha's eyes twinkled at me. "Do it," she recommended.

Both of us sitting cross-legged, the guellassa donned a mitt of slightly rough material and began a slow deliberate scrub of my limbs. She raised my arms to get at their neglected undersides, pushed away hair to expose the crevice behind my ears, and attended to my roughened knees. I let her arrange me face down, anticipating a backrub, and fell under her spell as the long, even strokes glided from shoulders to buttocks. The tension in my neck gave way. I felt comforted and also amused: this thorough worker was stroking almost as much of my body as a lover would. As sensual as a massage, the scrub ended much too soon.

Tingly and glowing, I rose for a rinse. Bucket after bucket the guellassa poured over my head. I closed my eyes and tilted my face into the stream, delighting in the warm cascade. I had never felt cleaner, nor more relaxed, and my skin had never been smoother— a shower has seemed inadequate ever since.

I thanked and tipped the guellassa, and settled next to my friends. Through half-closed eyes I beheld the variety of womanhood before me. A plump young woman with the largest buttocks I had ever seen was washing her two-year-old daughter, a vivacious child who already showed promise of her mother's extravagant behind. In the next room three generations of a family were combing each other's hair. Many women did not shave, and the hair of their legs and underarms remained soft and downy. There was no ego here: the firm of body and the sagging seemed to accept each other without a thought.

I recrossed my ankles and my feet brushed Janat's. Her toes danced against mine, and we giggled dreamily. I felt an enormous rush of affection for Janat and Aisha, for all the bathers, for women everywhere. Why is western women's modesty motivated by shame? Why do we hide from each other under layers of clothes, turn backs on each other and furtively cover up? In the hammam, the nonchalant acceptance of nakedness was enlightening, even liberating. I felt myself leap to a new plateau of consciousness, more in touch with my own body and the community of women than ever before.

Nakedness is a great equalizer. I found that every Moroccan woman, from farmer to intellectual, cherished her time in the hammam. It was more than a few hours break from the demands of home and husband. For an American used to rushing, the lesson was clear: slow down and take care of each other's body and spirit. Sisterhood is everywhere. Reach out for it.

She Makes Me Tea In Cairo

LEILA MARSHY

There is a woman who makes our tea at work and
coffee when we tire and
pours water over ice
to keep us cool in the heat
that falls in from the walls and window

She is
sitting straight, her cotton dress
splattered with water and soap
stained with the floor and walls
and toilet
her eyes close
tenderly, hesitantly   and there she sits
a breathing refugee from the tomb of the dead *

A cry from the hall:
her name is called
she bolts upright
in the trance of response
she looks afraid
she looks at me
          most times I look away

But (I am no different)

* One of the densley populated areas in the city of Cairo is "the tomb of the
dead"—a very old cemetery where receiving rooms were constructed to
temporarily house mourners. Thousands of families now crowd into these
sparse cement rooms, built over the graves.

If she were a baby on my doorstep
I'd pick her up
live with her till she grew old

If a twisted shrapnel skewered her body
and Uzi guns deafened us both
I'd hug her throbbing shoulders
running together
for the cover of bandages and worried kisses

If she carried a piece of paper
that had been ratified by this or that
convention
that had been validated and publicized by this or that
politician
I'd sign the petition
and whispering hotly
lower my eyes in homage
to her flight

But
she just makes tea
barely older than I
whose four children have died
who comes to work
on the yellow and crowded and slow slow train
who nods asleep by noon
who runs to the kettle when it shrieks
runs to the door when it knocks
runs for my coffee when I am tired
runs to the toilet
when she is tired

And that
is the story of our lives

III

Thyme

Growing Against the Odds:

Surviving the Gulf War

Thyme

Thyme is used in many dishes, and grows wild in many parts of the Arab world; often it grows out of rocks. This herb is a survivor, and for that reason it expresses the spirit of this section which discusses the Gulf War. Thyme is an apt symbol for Arab-Americans and Arab-Canadians who experienced Gulf War trauma and came out of it with a renewed commitment to celebrate our culture and resist assimilation.

๛ Za'tar ๛

dough
5 pounds flour
1 package fresh or dry yeast
1 t. sugar
1 1/2 t. salt
water
3/4 c. oil

Put flour in large bowl. Make an indentation in the flour. Soften yeast in lukewarm water. Add sugar and mix to dissolve yeast. Place mixture of salt and oil in indentation. Add enough warm water to make a dough of firm yet pliable consistency. Knead until dough does not stick to side of bowl. Let rise. Punch down. Let rise again.

Za'tar topping; Mix thyme, sumac, and sesame seeds to taste (or buy za'tar pre-mixed at an Arab grocery store). Mix the za'tar with olive oil to make a syrup-like consistency. Spread the dough on the pan, then spread the topping across the dough. Bake in 500° oven. Brown lightly.

A shortcut here is to put the za'tar topping on already-made pita bread, then warm in oven until ready.

๛ Source : Carol Haddad

Amara

LAMEA ABBAS AMARA

O my memories of Amara,
I hear the rockets destroying my memories.
Amara, where many rivers branch out from the Tigris.
There my life began.
In summer the sound of a single mournful flute wafts
   over the sleepless rooftops.
My beloved Amara,
The home of my grandfather,
The alley of my school,
My daily walks on the banks of al-Kahla,
My song...
Even the songs have been silenced, not spared from the killing.
What hurts more is that I must pay the price of every bomb
   which fell on my people.

---

* Translated from the original Arabic by Marcia Hermansen and Lamea Abbas Amara.

A Woman's Place is in the Struggle:

A Personal Viewpoint on Feminism, Pacifism, and the Gulf War

NADA ELIA

I am Lebanese, or so I tell people I think I will not be seeing again. Friends get the longer version. My parents are Palestinian. My birth occurred in Iraq. We moved to Beirut when I was still a baby. I grew up in Lebanon. I also make it a point to specify that although my family is Christian, I grew up in West Beirut; that is, that part of the city the media refers to as "mostly Muslim." Why should my narrative be simple? Can any narrative be simple if one of its themes is related to the Palestine question? I also identify with Muslim culture, because it is my experience that, whether you are a believer or not, you carry values of the predominant religion. Thus, in the United States, you need not be Christian to identify with certain Christian values, or to punctuate your calendar with Christian dates. Similarly, I believe Islam to be part of Arab culture, my culture. I am sure the Lebanese Christians will choke on this one...

In 1991, I "fought" Desert Storm as a member of a peace coalition. We tried very hard, during the all-too-brief "Desert Shield" period, to educate the community about the issues at stake. We organized two teach-ins at which I was the only local Arab speaker. My Arab friends supported our initiative but preferred not to join me. Did they, too, feel this was an anti-Arab war? The issue is complex, for I am convinced that racism disguised as patriotism (so what else is new) lay at the bottom of the pro-war movement. But did the Arabs in my community in Lafayette, Indiana really believe the best way to retaliate against racism was to keep silent?

I joined all the marches and political protests I could. Until then, my complex background allowed me not to feel personally involved because I could always claim to be someone else:

Palestinian when the Lebanese were being criticized, a resident of West Beirut when the East Beirutis were described as bloodthirsty savages, Christian when the Muslims were called ruthless murderers. But I avoided all of that during the Gulf War. I was appalled at the arrogance of the United States appointing itself World Cop and couching everything in the hypocritical. "We're doing this for democracy." Centuries earlier, colonial England had said it was acting in the name of Christian charity by spreading "civilization across the world...

I had prepared a number of responses to the argument I expected from the American supporters of "Desert Storm" who believed this was not an anti-Arab war but a war to preserve "democracy." Sadly enough, I never had to use them. This alone proved to me that the United States is overwhelmingly anti-Arab, so much so that the average citizen does not need to pretend otherwise. Anti-Arab oppression carried over to intimidation on U.S. streets. The day I was harassed for wearing my Arab scarf, I rejoiced at the opportunity of telling those jerks who had mud-splashed my newly-cleaned coat, their car decorated with "Support the Troops" stickers, that they should not be opposed to me on the basis of my Arab identity. I wanted to explain their troops were fighting alongside those dark-skinned people with flowing robes and multiple wives. I never had the chance: they were driving a mean, fast car, not seeking an enlightened discussion.

Although the war is over, these issues and questions are as relevant as ever. In March 1992, organizers of a symposium on feminism and multiculturalism asked me to participate in a panel titled "International Feminism and the Gulf War." I accepted and did not anticipate any problems. After all, I am a peace activist, a "politically aware" feminist woman from the Arab World. I research narratives of resistance from the Middle East, I am able to address audiences—both friendly and hostile—and have experience as a journalist. I planned to write a paper on the Orientalism that still underlines American discourse on the Middle East.* It would be easy to construct an argument: the Iraqi leadership has been depicted as irrational, emotional, tribal, and lacking in strategic foresight. President Bush, on the other hand, was seen as a model of restraint, a wise and mature leader of the "civilized" world.

Every night for two weeks I tried to come up with something, anything, to say at the symposium. The sterility of my attempts amazed me. As a journalist, I had to fill ten pages a week, every week. As a graduate student, I have produced papers on incredibly uninspiring topics. I once managed a twenty-page paper on the origin of the *fabliaux* ** in twelfth-century French literature. So why couldn't I say anything on feminism and the Gulf War? The day of the symposium arrived, and I ended up reading from my various unfinished attempts.

I explained that women have always been resourceful enough to secure new rights under any circumstances. I listed achievements by Arab women that were directly related to struggle. In Algeria, as a result of the War of Independence, women successfully fought for literacy and won the right to vote in 1962. More recently, in the Palestinian context, women such as Hanan Ashrawi and Zahira Kamal have achieved international political recognition.

I then explained that I did not feel like I belonged on the panel. In my mind, we women have measured our achievements in terms of masculine history for too long. To examine international feminism in terms of the Gulf War would, once again, validate the patriarchal, militaristic discourse feminism seeks to undermine. I am at a point in my development where I am much more woman-centered. I know I fought Desert Storm as a peace activist who is also a feminist. Unfortunately, I am also convinced that, for the time being, we must still distinguish between feminism and pacifism.

---

* I borrow the term "Orientalism" from Edward Said, who uses it to refer to the Western definition of the Orient as "its contrasting image, idea, personality, experience," but also as "a Western style for dominating, restructuring, and having authority over the Orient" (*Orientalism* [New York: Pantheon, 1978], p2-3).

** short, satirical poems

It is sad but understandable that so many working-class women of color join the army as an alternative to welfare or minimum-pay, no-benefit jobs. However I do not see the entry of women into the war machine as a feminist achievement. Nor do I think that feminists should refrain from fighting in cases of self-defense or against the oppression of the underdog. But I believe American women enrolling in an arrogant, sexist army in the name of "feminism" is a gross mistake.

I often ponder what brought me to political consciousness. I could say I came to political consciousness, or was thrust into it, at age thirteen, when I was briefly arrested by the Beirut police for joining a demonstration in support of the South. Of course, I had no notion of what I was "demonstrating" for or against when I joined a bunch of older students marching in the streets. I think I did it because school was dismissed, and I didn't want to go home yet. Being arrested by the brutal "Squad 16" police force, when I had done nothing wrong, shocked me.

And then again, perhaps I came into political consciousness at age sixteen, while talking to a young man who noticed the band-aid on my arm. I explained I had donated blood the previous day. "Red Cross, or a personal acquaintance?" he asked. "Red Crescent," I replied. The man was awed by my "noble generosity," donating my blood to those who need it most, even though they were the enemy. This confused me, since blood is precious, and should be put to the best possible use. Even less did I understand how one could think of Muslims as "the enemy."

The terms this man used to refer to Muslims were so derogatory they reminded me of an earlier childhood incident. During Ramadan, my mother asked our maid, Shahnaz, if she was fasting and if she was Shiite. I was angered by that question, because I liked Shahnaz and had been taught that Shiite was a dirty four-letter word. I went to a relatively large Catholic school with no more than a handful of Muslim students—I realize only now how alienated they must have been—and in our young minds, shaped by French nuns, Islam was so closely associated with all things ugly that Shiite became synonymous with "disgusting." I grew up believing "Shiite" was an insult, not a religion.

I could go on like this, enumerating moments of conscious-
ness, trying to locate the one external crisis that made me the peace
activist I am today—if indeed I was transformed by any one event.
However, I know my feminism is a consequence of more personal
circumstances.

My father died when I was six. Hard as I try, I can only recall
him as an "absence," for he was always gone on seemingly
never-ending business trips to Africa or Europe. Yet when he died,
everybody around me said our family was as good as dead, for he
had left "only women" behind him. My mother, my three sisters,
and I now made up the Elia household. I grew up surrounded by
people who believed that, because none of us had a penis, we were
worthless. In vain I tried to comprehend this. And I came to strongly
resent the suggestion that it was my father, this occasional visitor,
who had given meaning to my existence. Didn't my mother
matter—who had always been there, feeding me, changing my
diapers, washing me, staying up by my bedside when I was sick,
rising before dawn to prepare our lunch-boxes? Later, as an
adolescent, I frequently overheard discussions between my mother
and some "wiser" family member—female more often than not—
urging her to get my sisters and me out of school because a
high-school degree would do us no good. Invariably, my mother
refused. She had been denied an education and did not want her
daughters helpless and dependent on husbands, as she had been.

I left Lebanon at age twenty-seven because of the fighting.
Having earned my "bachelor's" (sic) and "master's" (sic again)
degrees in Beirut, I entered a doctoral program in comparative
literature in the United States. (This is no longer offered in Beirut
because of academic difficulties resulting from the civil war.) I have
my mother to thank for it. Decades after her education was
interrupted by the creation of the state of Israel, this "helpless
female" put herself through vocational school in order to support
us. She wanted to make sure we went to school and obtain the
degrees we were ambitious enough to seek.

Across the cultures and ages, women have achieved tremen-
dous feats, all the more heroic because they lacked the encourage-
ment, the "you can do it" showered on men. But we still have a

long, long way to go before this is common knowledge. And whether it be at home, at school, in the office or on the battlefront, a woman's place is still in the struggle.

꙰꙰꙰꙰꙰ᕉ꙰꙰ᕉ꙰꙰꙰꙰

"Offensive" Art by Palestinian Children:

Anti-Arab Racism and the Gulf War Fallout on Campus

MONA MARSHY

In the first weeks of 1991, during the U.S. massacre of Iraqis commonly known as the Gulf War, members of the Pro-Palestine Students Association (a mixed Arab and non-Arab group of men and women) at Carleton University waged a public and private battle of our own. I was acting president of the association at the time, and remember the beginnings of this local battle coinciding with the first midnight images of silver bombs falling out of the sky. The experiences of our group on campus coincided also with the silencing of the voices of Arab-Canadians during the war, a silencing that was part of the effort to keep the victims of the bombs voiceless if not nonexistent in our minds.

The war effort was fed by the media, by the Prime Minister's call for Canadians (read non-Arabs) to be vigilant, and by the Canadian Secret Intelligence Services (C.S.I.S.), in what the Canadian Arab Federation calls the most encompassing security sweep in the country's history. Up to 1,000 Arab-Canadians were questioned after being tracked and photographed, their phones bugged, their employers questioned, and bank accounts monitored. Non Arab-Canadians could speak out against the war, but Arabs and non-Arab Muslims who opposed it were seen as potential saboteurs.*

Our club was a loosely-organized group of students mostly wired on school deadlines, bad dreams, and a kind of psychological shellshock. We identified with the unnamed, faceless targets of raining bombs. We were emotionally drained from mental calisthenics

* Zuhair Kashmeri, *The Gulf War Within: Canadian Arabs, Racism and the Gulf War* (Toronto: James Lorimer & Co., 1991), 105.

in front of lit-up TV screens. But floating, glazed images registered only as pin-pricks at the base of my skull, pin-sized doses of reality seeping in, violating each neuron with a psychic disease as my Iraqi friend threw up in the toilet. I knew something was being written into a history, a history I did not want to live in.

On campus our club held several events during the 1990-1991 school year. These included information tables in the university's unicentre, individual speakers, panel discussions, and video showings—to let people know about the day-to-day living conditions of Palestinians in the Occupied Territories and about the urgency of the Palestinian national struggle. As a club on campus, we had a display window situated across from the library entrance in the tunnel system under the university. In the display we pinned up a Red Crescent (a division of the Red Cross) poster consisting of four crayon drawings by Palestinian children (See pp. 142-145). The poster in question depicts scenes of stick-people, representing Palestinian girls and boys, waving flags, throwing rocks, wearing kafiyyas, facing Israeli soldiers. The inscription on the poster reads, "As a Palestinian child I learned that there is occupation, deportation, tear gas, and peace." The final drawing depicts a dove with an olive branch.

Then came the reactions. What happened, as events unfolded and wrapped around us, made us realize the extent of anti-Palestinian sentiment and how it can be manifested. We found out how much objection there is to images of Palestinian voices, frozen lives suspended in so many shades of crayon drawings by children. During the first days of the onslaught of violence in Iraq, we were told that complaints about the poster's "offensiveness" had been made to the Carleton University Students Association (C.U.S.A.). C.U.S.A. representatives assured us we did not have to remove the poster, and they would take responsibility for complaints as they had previously approved it. A few days later, someone attempted to burn the poster and managed to blacken the plastic window. One week later, someone took a blowtorch to the display case, melting the window and burning most of the poster as well as other documentation. Then the display case was broken into, the remaining contents removed and replaced with newspaper clippings of an Israeli soldier killed in South Lebanon.

During the same time period, someone or some group broke into two of our club members' lockers. We felt increasingly vulnerable, followed and targeted as a group and as individuals. Meanwhile, a "well-meaning" C.U.S.A. representative began to arrange for a meeting between our group and individuals who had complained about the poster. We did not know their identity and were asked to attend a closed session whereby we would hear complaints about the destroyed poster, and answer "their" questions about "us." Supposedly, the poster was not the issue. Rather, "they" wanted to inquire about the issue of blame for the torching of our display case and the burning of the poster. Also, we were told through C.U.S.A., "they" wanted to know our "intentions" as a group. Deciding if and why we should attend this meeting and account for our activities took a lot of time and energy. Club activities were side-tracked, planned events postponed. Stress, perplexity, and anger dug into me. We discussed whether or not we should attend the "closed" session, and noted how ludicrous it was that now we were being put on trial. I know that if we were an anti-Apartheid group on campus being the target and victims of violence, we would not have been pressured to calm fears about our "intentions." But as a Palestinian club during the war, with "ordinary" Canadians called to be vigilant, we were caught in a trap of justifying ourselves.

We voted to attend the meeting. I had a restless night after a long discussion with a Jewish friend who insisted that "Nothing will change until Palestinians convince them that we are human." Associated with our right to put up the Palestinian children's drawings—to display life in the Occupied Territories—was the notion that Palestinians need not only to justify our cause, but also soothe fears and convince people that Palestinians are in fact (and in deed) human.

During the scheduled meeting, a professor and C.U.S.A. representative acted as "mediators." They met with a group of Jewish students earlier in the morning, then with us. The professor and C.U.S.A. representative expressed the students' concerns: What events did we have planned for the rest of term? Did we blame the Jewish Students Union or any particular students for the torching of the poster? Did we plan to invite a member of the PLO to campus?

We explained the public education aims of our club and answered their questions in good faith, noting we weren't trying to solve the crime as that was not our responsibility. We expressed our concern about the increased anti-Arab racism. In response, the professor and C.U.S.A. representative asked if we were similarly concerned about the possibility of increased anti-Semitism (a misnomer as Arabs are Semites) as a result of the poster burnings. The assumption that somehow we could be held responsible for such a backlash amounts to blaming the victims. In the end, we were "checked out," investigated.

In an odd way, the work of the C.S.I.S. was carried out by average Canadians, by Carleton University students, by the Carleton University student government, and by the mediating professor. It took a year to record these events, to dig out the anger at the systematic shrinking of our entitled social and political space on campus. During that year I have come to question the tendency to embrace the growing "mediation" ethos which can, in an already skewed context, be a more sophisticated means of controlling political space and expression. Our options as a club were constricted. I think we can hold onto some pride that we participated in the "mediated" session. But I still have questions. Why was the professor "impressed" with our reason and integrity? When will we no longer have to bare our souls and personal anguish and hopes to gain legitimacy? Should we have so dutifully bared our humanness? What can we do with the knowledge that we are often left with very little ground, with the knowledge that we are standing in a space very near the edges of any benefit of doubt?

I now have some ironic distance. The irony is that there are so many countless ways the war machinery is dutifully internalized, transmitting the bigger wars into sharp personal anguish, torment, and confusion—and a deeper, clearer sense of injustice. The irony, I tell myself, must not serve to distance us from organizing, from staying together as a group to voice and keep voicing the words, images, drawings, and demands of Palestinian and other struggles.

The "poster incidents" occurred as our psyches were assaulted by the knowledge of bombs raining on Iraqi children, women, and men. They occurred as many Arab-Canadians were "checked out" by C.S.I.S. and as many more felt the increased stereotyping in the media—which embedded more deeply the racist images and notions constructed through hundreds of years of western Orientalism.

The commotion surrounding the poster began with complaints made to C.U.S.A. and ended with three incidents of burnings and blowtorching. I cannot say I know how or if these events were connected. What I do know is we felt alienated. We were targeted and yet made to explain ourselves—as if we were somehow responsible for the violence, or had somehow provoked these problems. What I find most repulsive is that, once again, we had to convince others of our humanness, stripped from us by anti-Arab racism.

And an image lingers of my then-roommate poring over the poster drawings as she expressed her suspicion that the children's crayon drawings might really be the work of a propaganda artist who made them look like children's art. Palestinian children live, eat, breathe, think, and dream occupation, deportation, and tear gas. I have yet to remind the roommate of her remark and find out where just such a notion might still reside in her mind. Or maybe I do know, and do not want to be reminded.

Military Presences and Absences

Arab Women and the Persian Gulf War*

THERESE SALIBA

In the postmodern era, news media, with their subservience to corporate advertisers and government interests, have come to emulate the disinformation of fashion magazines, popular films, and talk shows, suggesting that the discourses of fashion and politics are not so disparate. U.S. political discourse on the Persian Gulf War created an illusion of consensus to a fashionable war with "picture perfect" bombing assaults that were supposedly "saving" Iraqi lives.** The marketing of the Gulf War to U.S. audiences was consistent with popular culture's marketing of the Arab world to the West through the circulation of stereotyped images of Arabs which alluded to the benevolence of the United States or Western influence in their lives. The specifically *gendered* representations of demonized Arab men and captive or absent Arab women fed a revival of colonialist attitudes, and heralded George Bush's new world order to reassert U.S. dominance in the Middle East.

The absent Arab woman has been deployed within the U.S. media both as a resonant and as an efficient signifier of so-called Western cultural superiority over the Arab world. By the *absent Arab*

* This essay was originally presented at the Modern Language Association conference in San Francisco, December 1991. A longer version was published in *Seeing Through the Media: The Persian Gulf War,* ed. Susan Jeffords and Lauren Rabinovitz, (New Brunswick, NJ: Rutgers University Press, 1994). My special thanks to Laura Brenner, Susan Jeffords, and Tom Wright for their challenging suggestions and comments on various versions of this piece.

** The *Newsweek* cover for February 18, 1991 read "The New Science of War/High Tech Hardware: How Many Lives Can It Save?" Cited in "Gulf War Coverage: The Worst Censorship Was at Home," *EXTRA!,* May 1991, 7.

woman I mean two notable forms of absence: the first, a literal absence, when the Arab woman is not present or is entirely missing from the scene; the second, a symbolic absence, when she is present but only for the purpose of representing her invisibility or silence in order to serve as a subordinate to the Western subject of the scene. She is also granted moments of presence when her actions and speech are manipulated and exploited to serve the interests of her Western interpreters. In all these instances, the *absent* Arab woman is objectified and contrasted to the "liberated" Western woman, who often serves as a representative for Arab women. The white woman is granted agency to speak for Arab women, usually on behalf of their liberation.

In *Women and Gender in Islam,* Leila Ahmed defines "colonial feminism" as "feminism used against other cultures in the service of colonialism" (p.151), a "feminism" that is racist in its assumptions and exploitative of both "native" and Western women in its appropriation of feminist language to serve imperialist/patriarchal interests. In the case of the Persian Gulf War, the neocolonialist rhetoric of Western intervention to save Arab women from Arab men mirrored "colonial feminist" strategies in its attempt to discredit Arab culture as universally oppressive to women. The relentless absenting of Arab women, from its most banal forms in popular culture to U.S. news reports on the Persian Gulf Crisis and War, I argue, supports the neocolonialist interests of the new world order and the U.S. media's repressions of the war's destruction. The U.S. media's predictions of Saudi women's liberation exemplified in "Images of 'GI Jane' fuel Saudi Women's advance on tradition" (*Chicago Tribune*, September 19, 1990) juxtaposed U.S. military women in camouflage to Saudi women in their *abayahs,* to depict Arab women as the agents of Western influence. However, in contrast to its anticipated liberatory effect, U.S. military presence in the region did nothing but reinforce the invisibility of Arab women.

The veil plays an important symbolic role in the absenting of Arab women. In a Western context, the veil has traditionally been viewed as a signifier of inaccessibility. It is associated with the hidden, forbidden woman shrouded in mystery, masked in a cloak of purity, underneath which lies unbridled sensuality. In the Arab world, the veil takes many forms and may signify piety, class differences, or even a radical fashion statement against Western influence, particularly in those countries where women have the choice of veiling.* • French and British colonialists of the nineteenth century saw the veil as a major obstacle to the modernization [read *Westernization*] of the Arab world and sought to abolish the practice of veiling. With the rise of colonialism, the discourse on women and the veil came to the forefront of nationalist debates both in the West and in the Middle East, where the veil allowed women a private space within public spheres, but did not necessarily negate their presence. But the U.S. media interprets cultural practices such as veiling as captivity and powerlessness. Furthermore, war propaganda and colonialist discourse constructs the Arab woman as captive to Arab patriarchy rather than as captive to imperialist forces, or to both. The dominant discourse's emphasis on the Arab woman's body and her position within an alleged despotic family structure allows external forces of racism and imperialism to continue unquestioned.

Much of the U.S. media "foreplay" to the Persian Gulf War relied on gender issues and "women's liberation" in order to mask the war's racist intentions and to prove the moral superiority of the United States. These media distortions included repeated images of absent Arab women, "liberated" American women, and demonized Arab men. For example, the film *Not Without My Daughter*, released one week prior to President George Bush's January 15th deadline, reinforced U.S. notions of the brutality and "primitivism" of Muslim men who

* The debate among Arab scholars and feminists regarding the history and socio-religious significances of veiling is complex. For more information on the practice of veiling, refer to Leila Ahmed, *Women and Gender in Islam* (New Haven: Yale University Press, 1992); Fatima Mernissi, *Beyond the Veil* (Bloomington: Indiana University Press, 1987) and *The Veil and the Male Elite: A Feminist Interpretation of Women's Rights in Islam*, trans. Mary Jo Lakeland (New York: Addison-Wesley Publishing, 1991); and Malek Alloula, *The Colonial Harem*, trans. Myrna Godzich and Wlad Godzich (Minneapolis: University of Minnesota Press, 1986).

confine and oppress women and children in the name of their religion.* Although the film takes place in post-revolution Iran, media propaganda succeeded in creating a monolith of Islam and associating it with the war effort. (Over a year after the war, I was listening to a radio talk show in Los Angeles in which a woman called in and made reference to the film. The deejay then said, "Oh yes, I saw that movie. Didn't it take place in Iraq or Saudi Arabia?" "Yes, that's right," the woman said, as if both could be correct. The specific geographical and historical context of the film becomes irrelevant, making its racist propaganda more effective).

Another example of this fixation on the "sexism" of Arab-Islamic culture occurred in a post-invasion episode of The Donahue Show,** which examined the "volatile" relationship between Arab men and their U.S. wives. The underlying assumption: If the American public could understand the marital relationships and problems between a U.S. wife and an Arab husband, then we might decipher the Persian Gulf Crisis. The guest panel consisted of one Palestinian-American man, Dr. Hassan El-Yacoubi; his U.S. wife Dr. Amar El-Yacoubi (who was consistently identified as a doctor, while Donahue refused to recognize her husband's equal title); Laurie Kofahi, who "Loves being a Jordanian Wife"; Kristine Uhlman, who lost her children when she divorced her Saudi husband; and "Shelly," who divorced her Kuwaiti husband and cannot see her children. While the panelists discussed their varying attitudes toward Arab men, there was only one Arab man present as their representative; and while the predominantly white female audience joined in bashing Arab men, Arab women were absent from the scene.

The title of the show, "American Wife/Saudi Husband: Culture Clash," subsumes gender relations under a Saudi model, which is the most conservative of all Arab countries in its treatment of women. In fact, there were no Saudi Arabians on the

* Anne Norton, "Sexuality and the Gulf War," *Middle East Report: Gender and Politics,* November-December 1991, 27.

** Unfortunately, I was unable to view this show, which was brought to my attention by a friend who described much of its visual contents to me. All quotations are taken from *Donahue* transcript #3061, "American Wife/Saudi Husband: Culture Clash," Oct. 23, 1991.

panel; the only Arab man on the panel was Palestinian, and only one woman on the panel was married to a Saudi husband. The avowed purpose of the program, that of cultural understanding, was undercut by assumptions of a particular "Arab character," one represented exclusively by its men. When Dr. Hassan El-Yacoubi respond to Donahue's questions by repeating religious phrases, the women in the audience booed and hissed at El-Yacoubi's responses. As the only Arab male in a show about Arab sexism, Dr. El-Yacoubi was positioned as a spectacle, an oddity, the thing we must fight against on an individual or national level.

The notable absence of Arab women both on the panel and in the audience suggests one of the many ways that U.S. women serve as stand-ins for invisible Arab women. The veiling of these U.S. women enables them to "put on" an Arab identity, suggesting that the fashionability of "Arabia" might be merely a matter of dress. This manipulation of female agency accords Anglo-American women the right of representing, or speaking for, as well as "re-presenting," or acting as a fashionable semblance of, the Arab woman. Although the U.S. women panelists said much in defense of Arab culture, their words were often subsumed by the culture clash dramatized on stage.

A third media event, the driving demonstration by Saudi women, was highly dramatized in national news reports to exemplify the gender politics of Islamic fundamentalism and to stress the West's superior treatment of women. On November 6, 1990, forty-seven Saudi women dismissed their drivers and drove themselves through the *suq* (marketplace) in Riyadh, many with the support of their husbands and brothers, who watched. The women insisted that the protest was a practical matter; they feared the war would leave them without drivers and they wanted the right to drive, especially in the event of an emergency. Despite Saudi women's insistence to the contrary, U.S. reports emphasized the connection between U.S. military presence in the region and the Saudi women's struggle. The assumption that women's rights were a Western rather than an international value fed into the ideology of the new world order, which demanded respect for the Western values of liberation and democracy that the United States was purportedly in the region to defend. Reports of the demonstration were framed by displays of weaponry to suggest to U.S. audiences the vulnerability of the Persian Gulf and the chivalry of U.S. troops sent in to protect these feminized regions. Yet to cover over the contradiction of U.S. support of the repressive Saudi regime, the reports also fairly consistently ended with claims that the Saudi royal family and King Fahd supported women driving, and that "by all indications" were moving slowly towards more liberal policies concerning women's rights.* Another embarrassing fact to U.S. media predictors, however, was King Fahd's punishment of these women who had achieved a momentary presence in the U.S. media, his deference to the conservative religious leaders, and his use of the incident to reassert his control over his kingdom, which many Saudis felt had fallen under spreading Western influence. These facts were subsequently covered up by the media, and Saudi women slipped once more back into invisibility when they no longer served U.S. propaganda needs.

Whatever happened to Saudi women in the Gulf War, particularly those who participated in the driving demonstration? Although the mainstream media abandoned them for more picturesque bombing displays, reports have appeared in alternative presses (including *Middle East Report* and *Ms.*). The women, among them university professors, businesswomen, housewives, students, and teachers, were detained for twelve hours, interrogated, and released to their closest male relatives. They were denounced by fundamentalist leaders as "corrupters of society," and their "immoral behavior" was rebuked in a song recorded in a chorus of children's voices and broadcast on children's television.** According to an anonymous Saudi woman writing to *Ms.*, "The women's phones were

---

* *New York Times*, November 7, 1990, and Associated Press reports. It is also significant to note that the Saudi women who participated in the driving demonstration were from the upper echelons of Saudi society. Their struggle for driving privileges hardly compares to the sufferings of the women guest workers, from the Philippines, Sri Lanka, etc., who have been abused and raped by their masters, both in Saudi Arabia and in Kuwait. These details were conveniently omitted from the U.S. media until after the war had ended.

** See Eleanor Abdella Doumata, "Women and the Stability of Saudi Arabia," *Middle East Report*, July-August 1991, 36-37.

tapped; they were fired from their jobs, and stripped of travel papers. Their families were threatened. They have lived for a year in terror."*

After the driving demonstration, the National Organization for Women (NOW), which had been outspoken against the War since the early days of the crisis, joined in the battle to free Saudi women from the hands of Arab Islamic patriarchy. The media ignored NOW's anti-war agenda and highlighted their statements against the subjugation and oppression of women within Saudi Arabia, the assumption being that NOW as a women's group had the right to speak, and be heard, on women's issues alone. However, NOW capitalized on the media attention they received. On November 27, 1990, NOW issued a statement "denouncing Saudi Arabia for its attitude toward women—both its own citizens and female U.S. troops based there." According to a *USA Today* article entitled, "NOW Blasts Saudis for Treatment of Women," NOW president Molly Yard connected Saudi Arabia's oppression of women with South Africa's apartheid policies, saying, "We would be outraged if the administration sent American troops to defend South Africa from invasion, ordering black soldiers to 'respect the culture' by bowing their heads in the presence of white racists." Yard's analogy, conflating racial and gender apartheid, privileges gender oppression over racial oppression. In doing so, she fails to account for the complex and contradictory positionings of Arab women within the existing imperialist structure or for the ways in which Arab women have defined their struggle. Although NOW's concern for Saudi and Kuwaiti women is viable, within the existing racist structure, NOW's position was predictably treated by the press to reinforce anti-Arab racism in this country and the absenting of Arab women. Like the U.S. wives and converts to Islam on *Donahue*, NOW stands in for the seemingly absent Saudi woman. In taking this position, the organization denies Arab women subjectivity and reinforces notions of the West as their cultural savior. NOW further failed to see how gender issues were being invoked by the U.S. military/media to support not only a racist agenda, but, in fact, the massacre of

* "Saudi Arabia: Update on Women at the Wheel," *Ms.*, November-December 1991, 17.

thousands of Iraqis, including women and children. In formulating a feminist anti-war agenda, NOW might have more effectively attacked the U.S. military for posing as liberators of Arab women and for their treatment of U.S. military women, rather than targeting Saudi Arabia and Kuwait as the seats of patriarchal oppression.

In a war where reality was defined in terms of visibility, the invisibility of Arab women both in the U.S. media and within the Saudi kingdom served to reinforce existing power relations, both gendered and geopolitical, and to silence voices of dissent. The repeated imaging of the *absent Arab woman* in the U.S. media reinforced these notions of Western cultural superiority and effectively stripped Arab women of agency by disallowing their "illegitimate voices" to be heard, voices which might have disrupted the racist, gendered stereotypes of Arab women and men. Many of the U.S. women who operated as the "legitimate speakers" or stand-ins for Arab women played their roles too well, reinforcing racist assumptions and aiding in the further oppression of all women. The U.S. military's visible performance of liberation stands in stark contradiction to the invisible events censored from the U.S. media—bomber pilots watching porn movies, sexual assault of U.S military women, Saudi women under house arrest, and tens of thousands of Iraqi women and children killed by U.S. bombs and in the aftermath of the war's destruction. These contradictions remind us that war, while often justified in the rhetoric of liberation, is rarely intended to liberate anyone—least of all women.

Gulf War

D. H. MELHEM

When the sky is rent asunder; when the stars scatter and the
oceans roll together; when the graves are hurled about; each
soul shall know what it has done and what it
has failed to do.

—*Qur'an, 82:1*

Eighty thousand sorties nonstop express over Baghdad
a sound and light show takeout boxed into your livingroom
(you can only see the nightskytop on TV;
the bloody bottom of the picture mars the image).
Look at the stars! *look, look up at the skies!*
O look at all the fire-folk sitting in the air!
Smart bombs and cruise missiles, F-16 fighter jets,
Patriot antimissiles and rocket hardware.
Everyone wants them now.
(Was this a carnage
commercial?)

In the bomb shelter children are sleeping
in the arms of their mothers. Not hungry,
having supp'd full with horrors **
Are targeted. Deliberately hit.

* Gerard Manley Hopkins, "The Starlight Night."

** Shakespeare, *Macbeth*, v.13. The reference here is to an actual occurence,
in which the air force corrected the misconception that the bombing of an air
raid shelter was accidental.

Well, enemies are enemies.
May hide anywhere.

Your red-and-white kaffiyeh was edged with lace
crocheted by your mother in the family's pattern.
You wore a blue bead to ward off evil.
It didn't work.

Iraq is a dry place, mostly, dry as cobblestones,
and hot. "Iraq, with its Soviet-style strategy and
Soviet-made arms, was the kind of opponent the Army has
spent decades preparing to fight." * No figures, as yet,
on civilian deaths. Maybe a hundred thousand.
Plus a hundred thousand soldiers.
A thousand of theirs to one of ours.
We're still number one.

Try to make sense of it—
boys who will kill other boys who will kill
children asleep in the arms of their mothers
and their mothers asleep with them.
Arms and armaments twist into smoke.
Even the tanks writhe and scream.

Men and women kneel in the prayerful dust
of ancient cities, in the new museum
of bones and shell fragments.
Daily they kneel five times,
facing Mecca.

* *New York Times* editorial, March 30, 1991.

Between the Tigris and the Euphrates
Mesopotamia once flourished.
The Tigris and the Euphrates
carried great deposits of silt.
The Tigris and the Euphrates
carry dead bodies to be oiled
in the Persian Gulf.

Cheetah, hyena, wolf, jackal, desert hare,
and small mammals, the jerboa. The vulture,
the raven, the owl, the hawk. In the west
the country is nearly treeless. Places
devoid of vegetation except for
the bush of Christ's thorn.

"Although many think of it as a lifeless place, the desert
is actually a teeming, though fragile, ecosystem. Home to a
variety of spiders, snakes and scorpions as well as larger
creatures like camels, sheep and gazelles, it is literally
held together by microorganisms, which form a thin surface
crust. This crust catches the seeds of sparse shrubs and
prevents surface soil from blowing away. Once it is
disturbed—by the maneuvers of a million soldiers,
say—recovery can take decades. The Libyan desert still
shows tank tracks laid down in World War II."*

The Mesopotamian desert is strewn
with the ruins of ancient cities,
their royal tombs and hecatombs. In Sumer,
five dynasties ruled before the Flood.

* *Time*, March 18, 1991, 37. Information on Iraq is culled from various
reference works.

The first capital was founded at Kish by 4000 B.C.
Sippar lay on the edge of the glacial shore-line.
South of Sippar rose Akkad and its armies of Sargon.
Below Cuthah stood the great temples of Kish.
Fifteen miles westward lie the ruins of Babylon.

When the Euphrates changed course it deserted
its settled embankments. In the south,
lakes became marshland. Now
ancient cities are mounds, waterless, bare.
Kish, Akkad, Babylon, Nippur,
Nineveh, Borsippa, Uruk, Ur.
Levels of excavation
on caravan routes
from Baghdad.

Baghdad, the Abode of Peace, foremost city
of Mesopotamia, preserved the name it has held
for 4,000 years. It was once a fertile land of gardens,
the home of merchants and scholars, renowned for learning,
for silks and tiled buildings, enlightened caliphs,
tales of the Arabian Nights.

In 1258 Hulagu Khan, grandson of Genghiz, sacked the city.
The Mongols destroyed irrigation systems
and converted Mesopotamia into a desert.

"Already a U.N. report concludes that Iraq has been bombed
back to the 'pre-industrial age,' its infrastructure
destroyed, its people beset by famine and disease." *

---

* Tom Wicker, *New York Times*, April 3, 1991.

I prayed for the people and I prayed for
food, water, electricity, and I prayed
for the museums, that our history not be obliterated
into a footnote of rubble.

"It was a great sight—all those fireworks,
like Christmas," said a U.S. airman.

The tank was running out of gas and the planes kept coming
and everyone was running and I prayed to Allah that I not be
burned in the tank and we were just like everyone else,
scared and running like the people on the road,
running to Basra.

"It was a turkey shoot," said a U.S. airman.

"After the third day as I say, we knew that we had them. I
mean we had closed the back door. The bridges across the
Tigris and Euphrates were out. We had cut highway 8 that
ran up the Tigris and Euphrates valley on this side of the
river. There was no way out for them. I mean, they could
go through Basra. There were a few bridges going across Al
Fao to the Al Fao but there was nothing else and there was
literally about to become the Battle of Cannae, a battle of
annihilation." *

Schwartzkopf at Cannae, Schwartzkopf as Hannibal,
the Carthaginian general, who stunned the Romans
by a rapid march to the city.

---

* General H. Norman Schwartzkopf, excerpt from TV interview with David
Frost, published the following day in the *New York Times*, March 28, 1991.

Caritas. *Though I speak with the tongues of men and of angels, and have not charity, I am become as sounding brass, or a tinkling cymbal.*—1 Corinthians 13.1.

And Cato the Elder cried, "Delenda est Carthago."
Carthage must be destroyed.
Carthage destroyed Tyre and ruled the Mediterranean.
It warred with the Greeks and was defeated at Salamis.
It fought three Punic Wars with the Romans
and was destroyed. Delenda est Carthago.

Madam, Saddam Hussein is mad, bad, and
dangerous to know*. A Hitler.**
(Have I no friend will rid me of this living fear? ***
His soldiers? his generals? his people?
The Kurds? The Shi'ites? Rambo?)
Saddam Hussein must not remain
to retain his domain. He must eat
the Breakfast of Humiliations.
And yet, if his neighbors
come nibbling at his table
they may elect to dine well,
so let his helicopter blades
whip the dissidents
into a mix, a sort of blend,
not too crumbly, one that can

* Written of George Gordon, Lord Byron, by Lady Caroline Lamb in her *Journal* (1812).

** An opinion notably expressed by President George Bush.

*** Shakespeare, Richard II, V.iv.2.

hold together when pressed
in the fist.
This is called
stabilizing
the region.

"Increasingly, it becomes hard to distinguish victim from
victor in the gulf crisis."..."What we have now is worse
than what we had when Iraq was in Kuwait." *

They want the oil **
But they don't want the people.
They want the oil
But they don't want the people.

Everything ventured, chaos gained.
Everything ventured, chaos gained.

Feast on scorpions
on jackals
the petroleum-dipped
tongues of politicians
the excrement of bombers
dropping their loads
on the people.

Sorties of sound and light.
Fuel-bombs of flaming blood.

---

* Christine Moss Helms and Patrick E. Tyler, Middle East scholar, *New York Times*, March 30, 1991.

** Jayne Cortez, "Nigerian/American Relations," *Firespitter* (NY: Bola Press, 1982).

They took everything.
Who did?
Enemies. They shot my father
in front of us.
What did this teach you?
To hate them.
My children will hate them
and their children, also.

The oil burns and will burn.
The eye of the sky
will glare through a tear
in the ozone. (Oh-oh. The ozone.)

My child is a beggar.
My child is a running sore in the street.
She looks for food, for water.
I must find our lost family.
I can hear them laughing
under the rubble of our house.
The planes do not stop.
Why must they kill us all?

"The burning wells emit a daily load of 50,000 tons of
sulfur dioxide—a prime cause of acid rain—and 100,000 tons
of sooty smoke into the atmosphere....Saddam Hussein...
had plainly warned that he would do it, however; so the
United States, by its decision to launch the war anyway rather
than rely on non-combat pressures,
bears some responsibility....
the Kuwaiti well fires...'the most intense burning
source, probably, in the history of the world.'" * Meanwhile,

The Country Is in a Better (or Worse) Economic Mood.
Kurdish Refugee Plight Worsens. The "Star Wars" Program
Will Go On. The Third World Seeks Advanced Arms. Wars Will
Become More Destructive. The Baseball Season Begins.

"From the overcast skies drips a greasy black rain, while
sheets of gooey oil slap against a polluted shore.
Burned-out hulks of twisted metal litter a landscape
pockmarked by bomb craters, land mines and shallow graves
scraped in the sand....No one knows how long it will
take to undo the damage done by the war. Most of the oil in
the gulf will probably be left for nature to dispose of, a
process that could take decades given the sluggish movement
of the water. The job of disarming or exploding the land
mines is also likely to go on for years; fifty years after
World War II, people are still stumbling on mines in Egypt's
western desert." *

Pilgrim, behold Death Highway, afterwards. A road that
stumbles into next year, groans into the future. Mother of
Battles, pray for us now and in the hour of our
devastations.

****Tom Wicker, *New York Times*, April 3, 1991,
*   Joel S. Levine of NASA in *Time*, March 18, 1991, 36-37.

As a Palestinian child, I learned that there is

Occupation

Deportation

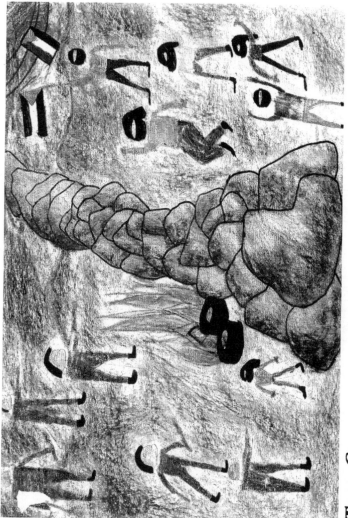

Tear Gas

and Peace

IV

Laban

Silent Victims and Belly Dancers: (Mis) Representations of Arab Women

Laban

Laban accompanies most meals and is known in the West as yogurt. While properly made laban carries several nutrients, the yogurt available in most places in the West has been usurped and appropriated; of all Arabic foods commonly available, laban has been the most altered, and not in any positive way. Here, sugar and fruit are routinely added to yogurt, and it is usually made from such a weak culture that important nutrients are gone. That made it a good choice for this section focussing on the ways Arabs are silenced, made invisible, and appropriated. Keep in mind that this recipe is the way our grandmothers made it.

↝ Laban ↜

1/2 gallon milk
1-2 T roube (yogurt culture for starter)

Simmer milk until it rises and becomes frothy, stirring frequently so it does not scorch. Bring it almost to a boil, but do not boil. Immediately remove from heat. Cool until you can put your baby finger in and count to 10. Add roube that you have smoothed out in a saucer. Stir in thoroughly; immediately pour into a crock with a lid. Sito, Mom, or Dad would always make the sign of the cross over the laban to bless it and insure that it comes out. Place crock in a warm spot wrapped in several blankets where it can remain warm and undisturbed for 6-12 hours while the bacterial action happens and the milk is converted into yogurt. Let it sit overnight if made in the evening, or, if made in the morning, leave it all day. It's as though a special magic happens transforming the milk into laban. Refrigerate and remember to save a little of this batch as roube for the next batch.

Hints:

~ Thickness can be controlled by how long milk is heated, whether you use whole or low fat milk, and how long you've let it set.

~ Sourness or tartness can be controlled by the temperature at the time the roube is added. The warmer the milk, the more sour. If roube has been refrigerated for one week or more, it will be tart. If roube is fresher, the laban will be sweeter.

~ If the yoghurt hasn't set, the milk may not have been kept warm enough during incubation. Another reason for not setting could be that the milk may not have been heated enough to kill certain bacteria which will inhibit the yoging. Conversely, if milk is too hot, it can kill the needed bacteria. Finally, culture may not be good. Some commercial yoghurts cannot be used for starter.

~ Source : Linda Dalal Sawaya and Alice Ganamey Sawaya from The Ganamey: Sawaya Family Cookbook, Alice's Lebanese Restaurant

say french

D. H. MELHEM

say french:
who knows what lebanese is? .
or syrian? (serbian? siberian?)
protectorate is close to
protector

of course there's your culture
a tradition of teachers and doctors
an elegant descent
from phoenicians

but
immigration officials
and neighbors
employers
perplexed by exotics
non-anglo-saxon
non-westeuropean-nontoxic
attest
the best are
types here
longer

the immigration official
said to me,
syrian?
what's

that?

(and sallow
with a menacing
guttural tongue)

your teacher accused
arabic spoken
at home:
"you have an accent"

though fearing strangers
and the foreign school
I went
showed myself
clean   educated
stopped her

still she detested
your rivalling
the girl on her lap
whose braids she caressed
before the class

people don't mean
to be mean
nevertheless
better say
french

Global Sisterhood:

Where Do We Fit In?

MICHELLE SHARIF

I am an Arab-American woman. For most of my life, however, I distanced myself from my ethnic identity. Growing up in the United States meant being constantly bombarded by negative images of Arabs. The popular stereotype portrayed Arab men as at best rich oil sheiks, and at worst sadistic terrorists with no regard for human life. U.S. society painted a more uniform picture of Arab women: passive and silent. Portrayals of Arab women outside their harem—I mean home—usually included images of scantily clad belly dancers performing for a roomful of horny men. Even at a young age, I understood that calling myself an Arab woman would entail ridicule and ostracism. I am light-skinned and can pass, so why make waves?

The identity I spent so much energy running away from finally caught up with me on December 8, 1987, the beginning of the Palestinian uprising. The nightly images of continued Palestinian resistance in the face of a brutal Israeli occupation made me reevaluate my life and the decisions I had made. When Palestinian and Arab groups began organizing on my college campus, I decided the time had arrived to "come out of the closet" as an Arab-American woman. The environment in which I publicly acknowledged my ethnic background turned out to be anything but hospitable. Most of my "feminist" female friends—women with whom I walked hand in hand during Take Back the Night marches, attended consciousness raising groups about gay and lesbian rights, and worked closely educating our campus about domestic violence and women's reproductive rights—tried to downplay that part of my identity. They could not understand why I would choose to identify myself with the negative traits they attributed to Arab women. Moreover, their stereotypes of Arab women meant they felt discomfort thinking of me as Arab-American. A few friends hoped I would use my knowledge as an American woman to help educate and rescue Arab and Muslim women from their horrible predicament.

Six years later, the reaction to my ethnic identity remains generally the same. Acceptance by the west, particularly western women, is going to be a long and arduous process. Still, I remain convinced that Arabs must struggle for equal recognition. For sisterhood to become truly global, both Arab and western women must invest time and energy in understanding one another. The myths western women hold about Arab and Muslim women belong to the colonial legacy that still influences feminist thought in the west. By examining the origins of these myths as well as analyzing their effects on current-day attitudes towards Arab and Muslim women, I hope to encourage dialogue between all women on the subject of racism and bigotry against Arab/Muslim societies and its effects on global sisterhood.

Historical Baggage

Current western perceptions about Arab and Muslim women can be traced back to early European writings about the Middle East and North Africa. The myths manufactured by Europeans hundreds of years ago still influence modern western notions of the east. It needs to be stated that, like gender roles, the categories "east" and "west" also are largely social constructs. As such, they are not "natural" categories neutrally and faithfully reflecting reality. Defining the term "western" poses a number of problems. In this chapter, the term is used in reference to Europe and peoples with historical connections to European culture (e.g., most Americans, Canadians, Israelis, and white South Africans).

In Europe, a special area of study developed which devoted itself to the examination of non-European or "Oriental" culture. Orientalists, who considered themselves unbiased, sought to systematically define "the Orient" by contrasting its people and customs with Europe, which represented the norm. Although religion has long been recognized in western societies as only one of many social institutions, European scholars perceived religion as the bedrock of Middle Eastern and North African societies. Many

Orientalists viewed these areas as unchanging and used seventh-century Islam to explain the workings of those societies.* These ideas still find acceptance among twentieth-century European scholars. One such scholar, Dominique Sourdel, viewed the last 500 years of Middle Eastern history, including western colonialism, as negligible.** Sourdel failed to give much weight to the effects of economics and recent history on Middle Eastern societies and cultures. He and his peers perceived the Middle East as static and showed no interest in revising the west's image of this region, regardless of how inaccurate.

Sourdel's point of view is far from unique. Indeed, for years Orientalists have held that Islam has been preserved since the seventh century and has remained relatively uninfluenced by contemporary history, politics, and economics. Further, they believe Arabs and Muslims can not analyze their own societies. For example, English Orientalist Sir Hamilton Gibb argues that only western scholars are in a position to study Islam and these societies because "in contrast to most western societies, [Muslims and Arabs] have generally devoted [their time] to building stable social organizations [over] constructing ideal systems of philosophical thought."***

Such notions permeate Orientalist writings. From the beginning of western speculation about the Orient, western scholars refused to give credibility to easterners' thoughts on subjects such as their own society and religion. Muslim and Arab analysis of Middle Eastern society and Islam became credible only after being examined by and made "scientifically acceptable" by European scholars.

Orientalists' writings about Islam included statements about the degrading conditions of Muslim women. Westerners have used such degradation as a theme from the time they began writing about Islam.**** Scholars discussed veiling and the harem to illustrate the

* Islam originated in the seventh century. The prophet Mohammad created the first Islamic community during this time.

** Dominique Sourdel, *Medieval Islam* (New York: Routledge & Kegan Paul, 1979), 187.

*** Sir Hamilton Gibb, *Mohammedanism: An Historical Survey* (New York: Oxford University Press, 1953), 83-84.

east's inferiority, while conveniently ignoring Muslim women's rights to own property and to inherit that had been in place since the eighth century—rights western women did not enjoy until hundreds of years later. Nineteenth-century Orientalist art and literature depicted the harem as both a place where women socialized with one another and as a system that permitted males sexual access to more than one female. Middle to late twentieth-century European literature represented harem women as occupied only with men's pleasure. The west came to define the harem as prison for women and their captors as violent Muslim males.* Islam thus became closely associated with violence against and subjugation of women.

The West created myths and ideas about the Middle East and North Africa from dubious data. Perceptions of the East formed largely during the colonial period live on today through unchallenged doctrines and theses.** Although many European and U.S. feminists have made some progress in rejecting their culture's sexist myths, they continue to believe those myths about Muslims, especially Muslim women.***

Western Perceptions of Middle Eastern Women

Many westerners use the veil to identify Muslim culture with women's exclusion and exploitation. The argument goes as follows: the greater the number of women who wear the veil, the more universal is the sexual segregation and control of women. In *Time* magazine's Fall 1990 special issue on women, the article on Muslim women is entitled "Life Behind the Veil." The article blames the growth of Islamic fundamentalism—epitomized by the veiling of

****Leila Ahmed, "Western Ethnocentrism and Perceptions of Harem, *Feminist Studies* Fall 1992.

* Anne Norton, "Gender, Sexuality and the Iraq of Our Imagination," *Middle East Report* Nov/Dec 1991.

** Edward Said, *Orientalism* (New York: Pantheon, 1978), 2.

*** Ahmed, 526.

women—for new legislation in the Middle East and North Africa that discriminated against women.*

This shallow analysis denies any cultural and historical significance to the veil or social problems. Rather than focusing on the right of women to choose whether to veil, the article views veiling itself to be a source of women's subjugation. Veiling is put in the same category as the new laws restricting women's legal rights.

During the Gulf War, the National Organization for Women (NOW), one of the largest women's organizations in the United States, issued the following list of demands to the United States government:

> Whereas, both Saudi Arabia and Kuwait subjugate and systematically oppress women, denying them basic human rights of self-determination, freedom of speech, association, transportation, and the right to vote; and Saudi Arabia further denies women by isolating them in purdah, denying them employment opportunities and education...
>
> Now therefore, be it Resolved, that NOW demands that...the U.S. insist on democratic and feminist reforms in Saudi Arabia rather than capitulating to that government's misogynist, totalitarian monarchy.**

Rather than working with indigenous women to find out their concerns and wishes, NOW made demands on their behalf without input from either Saudi or Kuwaiti women.*** The demands reflect western values and perceptions of Arab women. Instead of empowering Arab women in these countries to define their own struggle, NOW assumed these "passive" women must be "saved" by enlightened and liberated U.S. women. This type of reasoning assumes that there can be no change without reference to an external standard, which here is obviously western.

* Lisa Beyer, "Life Behind the Veil," *Time* Fall 1990.

** National Organization for Women, *Resolution on the Status of Women in Saudi Arabia and Kuwait* (Washington D.C.: NOW, November 18, 1990).

*** Personal interview with Marie-Jose Ragab, the International Program Director for the National Organization for Women, April 18, 1992.

Recently, popular culture has begun using the theme of rigid, backward, anti-female Islam. The best-known example of this recent trend is the film *Not Without My Daughter,* in which a U.S. woman marries an Iranian who takes her and their daughter to Iran. Shortly afterwards, her husband turns into an anti-woman Muslim extremist who refuses to allow her and the girl to return to the United States. In keeping with this theme, several talk shows have interviewed American female "victims" of Islam. Sally Jessy Raphael devoted a show to fathers who kidnapped their children and took them out of the country. Two of the three women on the show had been married to Muslim men. These women, with the prodding of Ms. Raphael, named Islamic teachings as the reason their ex-husbands kidnapped their children. The show portrayed the third woman's experience as a freak occurrence—incidentaly, her ex-husband is an American.

Even when the media decides to focus on a "good" Arab, the end result is problematic. When Arab and Muslim women, such as Hanan Ashrawi and Benazir Bhutto, attain international recognition, U.S. periodicals feel obligated to paint these women as enigmas in their societies. *Mirabella*'s article on Hanan Ashrawi, a Palestinian activist and advisor to the Jordanian-Palestinian delegation, illustrates this point. The article makes continual reference to the "typical" Arab woman who stays at home and out of politics, in contrast to Ashrawi's unique position as an Arab woman. In a region where many women still live behind the veil, her prominence is nothing less than astonishing.*

Talk shows and articles such as the ones mentioned above have a profound affect on U.S. ideas and attitudes about gender relations in the Middle East and North Africa. While earning my master's of arts degree in Arab Studies at Georgetown University, I often hesitated to discuss my area of study. Many times when I did, the response was "As a woman, don't you feel threatened going to the Middle East?" or "Those Arabs are such violent people—a nice girl like you should focus on something else." The latter group was often the most shocked when I revealed my identity.

---

* Ann Louise Bardach, "Send in a Woman," *Mirabella,* April 1992, 96.

I have learned to accept as part of life the ignorant and racist comments people make about Arabs and Islam. Still, there is the occasional unconscionable remark that, even after all these years, manages to amaze me. One such incident happened on my wedding day when my hairdresser started asking questions about my husband-to-be. When she found out he is Arab she asked, "So, does he beat you?" After overcoming my shock, I answered, "No, and if I were looking for that quality in a husband I could have just as well married an American."

Such comments help create more distance between Arab and U.S. women. Arab and Muslim women who hope to join in a dialogue with Western women instead spend most of their time defending our culture. In such a hostile atmosphere, a productive dialogue becomes next to impossible. Arab and Muslim women need to feel westerners respect their culture before talking frankly about the problems within their societies. Otherwise, Arab and Muslim women will continue to distrust the motivations behind western women's criticism.

Toward a Common Goal?

Despite differences in culture, religion, and class, many women have reached out to one another in an attempt to forge a universal women's movement. When the United Nations named the 1980s as the decade for women, many feminists hoped global sisterhood would finally become a reality. Women throughout the world greeted the declaration as an opportunity to meet with one another in an attempt to define common struggles and goals.

At the 1985 Nairobi Women's Conference, women from all corners of the world gathered to discuss experiences, concerns, and goals for the future. Many western women wanted to confine discussions to issues they perceived as common to all women independent of nationality, race, and class. Politicizing the conference, they believed, would be counterproductive. Most Third World women argued that gender oppression could not be separated from national, class, or racial oppression.[*]

[*] Nilufer Cagatay, Caren Grown, and Aida Santiago, "The Nairobi Women's Conference: Toward a Global Feminism?", *Feminist Studies* Summer 1986, 402-03.

For women around the world, forms of subjugation are intertwined. For example, the source of Arab and Muslim men's oppression overlap with the source of Arab and Muslim women's oppression. The problems facing Palestinian women illustrate this point. The poverty, overcrowding, prison terms, gas attacks, curfews, beatings, death squads, and torture affect the lives of both Palestinian men and women. Although Palestinian women embrace the concept of gender identity, they reject an ideology of change based solely on gender, since such a simplistic analysis does not address their life under Israeli occupation. For sisterhood to truly be global, feminism must be a comprehensive and inclusive ideology and movement that incorporates yet transcends gender-specificity. All sources of oppression to women, whether based on race, sex, class, or imperialism must be included in the definition of feminism. Otherwise, feminism loses its relevance and ceases to be an ideology of change.

Agreement on an issue's importance does not necessarily guarantee that eastern and western women can decide upon an approach. The debates surrounding female circumcision epitomize this problem. U.S. and European efforts to eliminate genital mutilation by lobbying international health and development agencies have met with mixed reactions from Arab and African feminists. Nawal el Saadawi, an Egyptian feminist and physician active in this struggle, accuses westerners of racism for failing to point out that clitoridectomy has occurred in many cultures including the West, and for presenting it as an "Islamic" practice, thus fueling anti-Muslim sentiment.*

At the 1980 Copenhagen Women's Conference, the issue of clitoridectomy was extremely contentious partly because a group of western women attempted both to define the problem and impose their own plan of action on the women directly affected by this practice.** A number of Middle Eastern and African feminists believed that this type of approach—outside interference—made

* Margot I. Duley, "Women in the Islamic Middle East and North Africa," *The Cross-Cultural Study of Women*, ed. Margot I. Duley and Mary I. Edwards (New York: The Feminist Press, 1986), 423-25.

** Cagatay et al., 407.

their task harder. They argued that because the practice arises in contexts of extreme poverty and lack of education, any solution must be connected with the demands of Third World nations for a new economic order.*

Conclusion

As long as Orientalist views of Middle Eastern and North African culture continue to influence western thought, the dream of global sisterhood will continue to elude all of us. To assist in building bridges of understanding between cultures, western women must explore their own racism. Doing so would help them gain the respect and ultimately the trust of Arab and Muslim women. Only after the defeat of Eurocentrism can we begin developing a universal feminist agenda. Some Israeli women's groups, such as Women's Organization for Political Prisoners, have made progress in this arena. Besides publicizing the conditions of Palestinian female prisoners, they have begun exploring Israeli attitudes toward Palestinian culture, particularly those stereotypes that justify the torture and rape of Palestinian women.

Arab-Americans belong to both cultures and therefore occupy a unique position. We can and must help this dialogue develop. Our struggle, like all women of color, includes overcoming racism as well as sexism. By joining women's groups in the United States, we can put issues such as anti-Arab racism on the agenda. Our time for recognition and respect in western feminist movements has come.

* Duley, 425.

Tear Off Your Western Veil!

AZIZAH AL-HIBRI

In Ireland, I attended the 1992 Global Forum of Women as a participant in the panel entitled "Reclaiming Religious Freedom." Yet again I heard feminists denounce the practice of clitoridectomy. While sharing a table during the Irish president's opening reception, the other participants and I had an opportunity to discuss our upcoming panel. Berhane Ras Work, a panelist and president of the Inter-African Committee on Traditional Practices, said that she would be discussing, among other things, the practice of clitoridectomy in certain African regions. The classical question came up: "But how could they *justify* it?" I listened attentively. Such a question is usually a prelude to subtle, sanctimonious denunciations of Islam. On this occasion, I was more curious than worried since Burhane was not an Orientalist, or someone who had obtained her information from Orientalist publications. She gave a straightforward answer. Burhane replied that the various tribes justify clitoridectomy on the basis of religion, whether Christian or Muslim. There was a gasp. "Christian, you say? How could they justify such a horrible practice on the basis of the *Christian* religion?!" I smiled and interjected, "The same way they justify it on the basis of the Muslim religion!"

For decades, western feminists have continued to latch onto the issue of clitoridectomy, not only as a symbol of the backwardness and hence inferiority of African and Asian Muslim societies, particularly Arab ones, but also as proof that Islam, as well as Muslim and Arab societies (which the west often conflates into one), are inherently patriarchal and oppressive. While these beliefs are not always openly articulated, they are always communicated. In holding these positions, western feminists do not attempt to educate themselves about Islam as a world religion, or about the points of view of Muslim or Arab women. Instead, western feminists hold an Orientalist view of Islam, and act on that view. This attitude has already resulted in western feminists silencing Muslim/Arab-American women, not through coercion, but rather by their astounding inability to hear us regardless of how loudly we protest. And that inability to hear is not the result of a cultural gap! Some of us were right here, in the forefront of the U.S. women's movement in the 1960s! Oh yes; you may not have noticed, but many of us *are* U.S. feminists. We are part of you. We live among you, and we have invisibly struggled by your side for decades.

It is not difficult for the U.S. women's movement to stray into patriarchal modes of thinking because it perceives itself as the vanguard of the international women's movement. After all, how could white, middle-class, U.S. doubt their leadership role when their own government has taken upon itself the leadership of the whole world? Only recently we sent our troops to Somalia to save its people from extinction. Earlier, we saved the whole world from the Iraqi "madman."

These days, we wring our hands over Bosnia. If only it met *our* criteria for salvation. But it does not, and those Bosnian Muslim women keep getting impregnated by Serbs, the latter-day champions of "ethnic cleansing" who have corralled these women in "stud farms." So we turn our heads sadly, and forge ahead as though none of this has happened. We fight against Muslim/Arab veils, and for Muslim/Arab clitorises. We push for a United Nations human rights declaration which says that no country may commit violence against its women, even if that country justifies its violence on the basis of religion, a statement which quietly implies that some religions (read Islam) condone violence against women.

In the meantime, the true story about all this multifaceted, international suffering is lost. The story about the culpability of our government and other white governments in Europe for arming undemocratic regimes in Africa and Asia beyond the means or true desire of their people remains untold. It is infinitely more satisfying to hear that these nations are hapless and in dire need of our charitable intervention than to hear that the arms flow into these countries is encouraged by us to shore up the U.S. economy, to foster destructive factionalism in some countries and to prop up dictators and protect them from the wrath of their people in others. To add insult to injury, we now criticize these very people for the absence of democracy in their countries, as if any people, throughout history, have ever preferred oppression to freedom.

I miss the 1960s. I miss the intuitive understanding that my friends had of all these matters. Not only did they understand acts of war, but they also understood acts of "peace," like the Nestle campaign to end the prevalent "uncivilized" practice of breast-feeding in Third World countries, and to instead promote, you guessed it, powdered milk. Where did that consciousness go? What thick veil is the U.S. women's movement wrapped in these days? Can we help you tear it off? Please tear off your western veil. It is blocking your insight.

Lest these complaints about racist and religious insensitivity are dismissed too quickly, let me provide a historical perspective by quoting from a speech I gave at the National Women's Studies Association (NWSA) in 1983. The sad thing is, nothing has changed since then.

> It is not easy for me today to speak about racism in the women's movement. For many years I have attended NWSA conferences and shared with you my thoughts, my fears, and last year—when my country of birth [Lebanon] was being bombed— my tears. You have always been to me a relatively safe enclave from the brutal reality of the outside. For this reason, I tolerated many a racist incident. But now, you ask me to speak to you not about my feelings of sisterhood towards you, but about the racism amongst us. I would be remiss in my duty if I do not grab the opportunity and bare to you the many scars I have acquired from the women's movement over the years.

> To be an Arab-American in the women's movement is to be an inferior "Other." This notion did not originate from within the movement, but it certainly does permeate the movement. It manifests itself in a variety of ways, not the least of which is the fact that the suffering of Arab women, somehow, does not seem worthy of your attention. "What do you mean?" you object. "The women's movement has dedicated a substantial amount of energy discussing issues like 'the veil' and 'clitoridectomy'." But that is precisely the point. The white middle-class women's movement has bestowed upon itself the right to tell us Arab and Arab-American

women what are the most serious issues for us— over our own objections.

In 1988, I delivered a speech in Amherst at a conference entitled, "The Muslims in America." My wounds had not then healed. I went back to the same issues of racism in the women's movement and provided the following additional history:

> In 1982, I was due to deliver a paper at NWSA's annual conference. Israel was bombing Beirut and I was not sure whether my elderly father was safe, or whether he was hungry, thirsty and bleeding in the rubble under the scorching summer sun of Beirut. But I went to the conference, delivered my paper and shared my anxiety with American feminists. I asked for a resolution, in line with other NWSA resolutions, calling for peace and denouncing the bombing of the civilian population in Beirut. The Third World Caucus unanimously recommended such a resolution to the delegates, who were overwhelmingly white, but the delegates rejected it.
>
> ...[W]e have been informed by some feminists that the topics we raised were sensitive ones which they did not want to touch. In the past, however, women have differed on many matters, and have discussed with vigor many a sensitive topic, including lesbianism and the overthrow of Patriarchy. However, they have not yet been willing to differ over those Muslim women dying in the East, perhaps because these women appear, through the reductionist and Orientalist perspective, as an irrational and inferior 'Other' not worth splitting ranks over. Thus, tactical considerations at home override the ideology of sisterhood; and to appease their conscience, American feminists, with even greater vigor, denounce U.S. policy in Nicaragua, hoping to drown with their loud voices the faint moaning of dying Muslim women...

So little has changed! When this book is finally in print, there will be new problems for people of color in this country and new trouble spots in the Third World: new famines, new rapes, new murders, new destruction. Perhaps these excerpts from my speeches will be just as relevant in another ten years. Or can I hope that by then a true foundation for dialogue in good faith will have sprouted among us like an unexpected burst of sunshine?

Arab-Americans:

Living With Pride And Prejudice

ELLEN MANSOOR COLLIER

After a whirlwind trip touring London and Paris a few years ago, my friends and I returned to Houston, exhausted. But as we filed through customs, an agent blocked my path. He pointed to me and my brother, saying, "Come with me." Our friends waited while two inspectors examined our luggage, demanding to know, "What was the purpose of your visit?" Was it mere coincidence that—with our Arabic looks and surnames—the agents singled us out? Not only was I angry, I felt humiliated that my friends and fiancé had to witness this degrading scene.

As an American of Palestinian background, I'm all too aware of anti-Arab discrimination. Since the 1973 oil embargo, Arabs have served as scapegoats for a number of world problems—everything from gas shortages to bomb threats. The recent Persian Gulf War incited a new round of Arab-bashing. In Houston, vandals often attack a local Islamic mosque, smashing cars and windows, throwing rocks and smoke bombs. Once they spray-painted "Death to Evil Arabs" in black on the walls. Such blatant acts of racism usually ignite a public outcry but in this case they did not. Why is it socially acceptable to defame Arabs?

Perhaps the media should shoulder much of the blame. As a writer and editor, I'm especially offended by derogatory images of Arabs in the media. In movies, Arabs appear as characters straight out of *Arabian Nights*. Notice the evil villains in "Aladdin" have stereotyped features and accents as thick as their moustaches. Handsome, heroic Aladdin looks and sounds more like a tanned Tom Cruise than an Arab.

Worse, the lyrics to the film's theme song "Arabian Nights" include: "Oh, I come from a land/From a faraway place/Where the caravan camels roam/Where they cut off your ear/If they don't like your face/It's barbaric, but hey, it's home." Pressure from the American-Arab Anti-Discrimination Committee (ADC) forced Disney to change some of the racist lines for the home video version, but others were left intact.

Some writers pass off ethnic slurs as "humor." In *Men: An Owner's Manual*, author Stephanie Brush writes:

> At a very early age, young Arab men practice having sex with laundry...If you say, "Praise be to Allah" after most sentences...he may buy Sweden for you or let you count his rings. If you are bad at sex...He may remove your nose or feed you drugged falafil and have you raped by goats.

Such blatant slander turns up in various forms. Not long ago, I wrote to Harper & Row, publishers of Robert Chapman's *American Slang*, protesting their listing of the word "scuzzy or scuz": "Dirty; filthy; repellent = Grungy: a bunch of scuzzy Moroccan A-rabs— [quoted from the] *Village Voice*." Even the Merriam-Webster *Thesaurus* defines "arab" as synonymous with "vagabond, drifter, bum, huckster, roadster, tramp, piker, vagrant, derelict, peddler, transient, hobo."

Three million Arab-Americans don't deserve to be labelled derelicts, tramps, and bums. Yet, in spite of the number of celebrated Arab-Americans—Marlo Thomas, the late Danny Thomas, Paula Abdul, Casey Kasem, Dr. Michael DeBakey, journalist Helen Thomas, actor F. Murray Abraham, Ralph Nader, poet Naomi Shihab Nye—we remain a much-maligned and misunderstood minority.

Throughout history, Arabs have made notable contributions to the Western world—in medicine, science, mathematics, and art—including our numerical system and the concept of algebra. Still, Arabs continue to be enigmas to most Americans largely because of ignorance.

When my mother first came to the United States after winning a scholarship to a Quaker college, classmates asked her, "Does your family live in a tent and ride camels?" She'd explain that her father was a physician—not an oil sheik—and her mother was a teacher;

they lived in a modern stone house in Ramallah, near Jerusalem, and owned a car, not a camel.

To protect us from discrimination, my mother insisted my brother Jeff and I become "Americanized." We didn't disappoint her. Unfortunately, in these efforts to assimilate and "fit in," I am afraid much has been sacrificed. I regret not speaking Arabic and sometimes feel out of place at Arab functions. Must we deny our ethnic identity to gain acceptance?

I'm proud of my Palestinian heritage and, whenever possible, I try to meld both cultures. Meanwhile, I look forward to the day when bigotry towards different ethnic groups will be replaced with understanding, acceptance, and peace. Perhaps then, certain reference books will find new descriptions for "Arab"——words that are more enlightening and far more accurate.

Exotic

PAULINE KALDAS

dark   your hair is the soil
    eyes lined with the dye of an olive
       and your walk is the wind that moves a palm tree

Here,   dark woman
    I will leave my golden beauty
           and take you
who are also permitted:

"Hey girl, how you doin'?"
      "Que pasa niña?"
  "Hey baby!"
"What are you—Lebanese, Armenian, Spanish,
                  Puerto Rican, Italian, Mexican
    c'mon what are you?"
"You're either Spanish or Italian."

The square edges me
    as it extends *White*
     includes People from North Africa and the Middle East

White?
    as fava beans stirred green with olive oil
    falafel fried with sesame seeds burned black
    baklava and basboosa the aroma browned crisp in the oven

White is not my breasts growing at nine
　　　not the gang of fifth grade boys hurling snowballs
　　　　　cornering me to the side of my house
　　　and not my last menstruation at sixty

I will draw four sides
contain my X in the box and write my name next to it.

　　　for food, pronounce guttural kha script
　　　twirl into ABC　　　　found in the exotic section
　　　for body, untwirl lengths of cloth
　　　　　　　　　　　mummy encased in glass

taste a color not confined
by the squares

The Arab Woman and I

MONA FAYAD

I am haunted by a constant companion called The Arab Woman. When I shut myself alone in my home, she steps out of the television screen to taunt me. In the movies, she stares down at me just as I am starting to relax. As I settle in a coffee shop to read the newspaper, she springs out at me and tries to choke me. In the classroom, when I tell my students that I grew up in Syria, she materializes suddenly as the inevitable question comes up: "Did you wear a veil?" That is when she appears in all her glory: the Faceless Veiled Woman, silent, passive, helpless, in need of rescue by the west. But there's also that other version of her, exotic and seductive, that follows me in the form of the Belly Dancer.

As a construct invented by the west, this two-in-one Arab Woman is completely intractable. Her voice drowns mine. It is no use pointing out that in Syria, Arab school girls wear khaki uniforms and are required for school credit to work on urban improvement projects, planting trees and painting walls. Or that Syrian television is constantly running ads for women to join the army. As I try to assert my experience of being an Arab woman, the Arab Woman tries to make me write about *her*. For a brief moment, I give in.

My one personal encounter in Syria with a fully veiled woman happens during my third year at the University of Damascus. I take a bus home. (Yes, we do have buses in the Middle East. We did away with camels as a means of transportation five years ago.) A veiled woman climbs aboard, the only one on the bus. I pay her no attention until she rushes up and embraces me enthusiastically. "Mona, how wonderful to see you!"

I know the voice, but somehow I can't place it. Realizing my predicament, she raises the veil for a minute. It's Mona, a friend of mine from university that I haven't seen recently. A bouncing, energetic person, she is very active socially. I have never seen her veiled. I ask if it's a recent decision.

"Not really. I come from a conservative neighborhood, so I prefer to wear the veil when I arrive there." She shrugs. "My family isn't very concerned, but I prefer to do it this way."

The old souk (market) in downtown Kuwait is one of my favorite places to go. The tradition of bargaining is still in practice. It's a sharp contrast to the cold, impersonal supermarkets that have now almost completely eradicated the social exchanges that have been a part of buying and selling in the Middle East for centuries. In this section of town, many women wear burqas or are completely veiled since they belong to an older generation. Here the real haggling happens, and the high-pitched shouting of women dins the lower and more cracked voices of the men. "What a cheat," the woman announces to whoever is willing to listen. "Can you believe how much he's asking for this worthless piece of cloth?"

In another corner, two women selling men's underwear laugh good-naturedly as they target a young man whose embarrassment is apparent. "How *big* did you say you were?"

These are some veiled Arab women. Neither silent nor passive, they have a place within their culture, like women all across the world. But once again, The Arab Woman has intruded, preventing me from talking about myself, pushing me to feed you what you want to hear.

Part of the reason I obey her is that it's easier to be exotic. To talk about an ordinary Arab woman, one who wears pants or a plain dress or a suit and walks around looking like everyone else is uninteresting, to say the least. I feel pressured to produce something *special*, something different. I try to shut out The Arab Woman who is controlling my thoughts. She is asking me for facts, figures, ways of classifying women so they can be clearly placed in boxes and the doors can be shut on them once and for all. She wants order, a rational explanation, something easy to understand.

After much thinking, it occurs to me that it is you who veil the Arab woman, it is you who make her into a passive victim, it is you who silence her. Arab women get on with our lives. I try to get on with my life, but it is difficult to constantly confront what I am not.

I am not The Arab Woman. And, further, I cannot represent Arab women. Each Arab woman must represent herself, with the range of identities that include Syrian or Saudi Arabian, Berber or Copt, bedouin or society woman from Beirut, Druze or Alawite, villager in the Upper Nile or Minister of Culture from Damascus. We're not an object that can be crushed together and concentrated for Western consumption in a box labelled: Organic Arab Woman.

There's no doubt within *me* that I'm an Arab woman. The problem is whether you will believe me.

The Arab Woman in U.S. Popular Culture:

Sex and Stereotype

MARSHA J. HAMILTON

Images of Middle Eastern women can be found in every form of popular culture in the U.S. including literature, art, music, fashion, cartoons, advertisements, television, and film. Textbooks, educational and documentary films, and news all of which are heavily influenced by popular culture, reinforce the same few images. The stereotype of Arabs as billionaires, belly dancers, and bombers has been documented by Jack Shaheen in *The TV Arab*.* The images of Middle Eastern peoples found in contemporary popular culture are not new. Most would be familiar to late Victorian audiences, some date back to colonial times, and a few have their origins in the economic, political, and religious conflict known as the Crusades.

A stereotype is an image, trait, or mode of behavior that is inappropriately applied to all individuals who share a common religion, sex, ethnic origin, geographic location, political party, socio-economic bracket, or other discernible factor that may set them apart from others. One hallmark of a stereotype is its persistence over time. An event or character can enter popular awareness, and through retelling and exaggeration, transform into an image that comes to represent millions of individuals for dozens or hundreds of years.

---

* Jack Shaheen, *The TV Arab* (Bowling Green: Bowling Green State University Popular Press, 1984).

Stereotypes have a specific effect on the way the holder processes incoming information. The holder of a stereotype will accept any information, no matter how improbable, which reinforces the image. Conversely, the holder will discard as irrelevant any data which does not confirm the stereotype.

A stereotype is a shortcut. It allows novelists, artists, cartoonists, news reporters, and politicians to raise an image and make a point without having to provide tedious background information."Right-wing Christian" or "left-wing Muslim" can define a complex coalition of people in an unknown part of the world in a short phrase. The viewer understands exactly how he or she is supposed to feel about each group. Announcers guide our reactions to an event such as a bombing by making the object either a "refugee camp" or a "guerrilla base." While one term may elicit an expression of concern or outrage, the other does not. Stereotypes allow the holder to easily identify one group as "us" and another as "them." This can produce a reassuring sense of self-identification. A stereotype gives the holder the ability to easily judge who is right and wrong in complex situations. It instills a feeling of cultural superiority over beings unlike oneself.

Stereotypes can be examined by identifying beliefs or assumptions held in common by a group. Several formal and informal surveys of U.S. schoolchildren, teachers, television audiences, college students, and others have been undertaken to see how people respond to words associated with the Middle East.* Most audiences, despite differences in age, education, and socio-economic background, tend to share the same narrow set of stereotypes about Arab women. This often includes association with the words harem, polygamy, belly dancer, sexy, uneducated, oppressed, and veiled. These images are a result of the frequent representation of Middle Eastern women in U.S. popular culture in terms of the character of the belly dancer and seductress, Cleopatra of the Nile, the harem

---

* Michael Suleiman, *American Images of Middle Eastern Peoples: Impact of the High School* (Brattleboro: Middle East Studies Association of North America, 1977); Suleiman, *The Arabs in the Mind of America* (NY: Amana Books, 1988); William J. Griswold, *The Image of the Middle East in Secondary School Textbooks* (NY: Middle East Studies Association of North America, 1975).

beauty, and the veiled woman with bewitching kohl-circled eyes. Another image is of the veiled, uneducated, oppressed, silent female. Once sensitized to their presence, these images can be seen weekly on television, in grocery store tabloids, and in a variety of unexpected sources.

The image of the harem beauty entered western popular thought following the translation of *The 1001 Arabian Nights* into French and English. Their publication created an eighteenth-century popular cultural phenomenon.* *The 1001 Arabian Nights* were originally a series of medieval bawdy stories recited to adult male audiences in the Middle East. European readers, unfamiliar with their original context or age, were fascinated by the tales of sex, wealth, power, and revenge. However, European scholars also mistakenly viewed the stories as accurate representations of contemporary Middle Eastern society, values, and behavior. These popular stories continue today, forming a staple of western children's literature and an integral part of U.S. popular culture.

Perhaps the most memorable woman portrayed in *The 1001 Arabian Nights* is Scheherazade, who by cunning and skill saves her own life from her cruel ruler and husband. Scheherazade is a perfect example of the harem beauty character in popular culture. The concept of the harem enthralled many eighteenth- and nineteenth-century western male writers who incorrectly considered it synonymous with the state of polygamy. It is true the Qur'an granted Muslim men the right to marry up to four wives but only on the condition that all be treated equally. Because of the expense, polygamy had been the exception, not the norm, for most Muslim men. In Europe, where laws forbade multiple mates and made divorce practically impossible, the idea of a society that allowed both was fascinating to men and women. Western men unfamiliar with the complex social and economic factors involved in divorce assumed Muslim men regularly put aside their wives for any offense, no matter how small, and thereby kept women in a constant state of fear and subjugation.

* Muhsin Jasim Musawi, *Scheherazade in England: A Study of Nineteenth Century English Criticism of the Arabian Nights* (Washington, DC: Three Continents Press, 1981).

In the Middle East, the harem is the women's quarters for living and working protected by male members of the family from outside intrusion. It is the sphere of women, in many ways comparable to the ideal Victorian household where the modest wife creates a protected environment for family, children, and the domestic necessities of the household. The Victorian home, upheld as an ideal in the west, has been represented in countless sentimental songs, paintings, and novels. However, the equivalent women's environment in the Middle East, the harem, came to symbolize the opposite to eighteenth- and nineteenth-century Europeans.

Many European men who discussed, wrote about, and painted scenes of the secrets of the harem had never been inside one. Some European women, such as Lady Hester Stanhope, did visit harems and women's baths and wrote detailed, realistic descriptions of women's lives.* This work stated both advantages and disadvantages to the role of women in the Middle East compared to European women at the time. Western men, for the most part denied access to Middle Eastern women's quarters, developed all manner of stories about the forbidden realm of women complete with tales of sexual orgies, lesbian affairs, violence, greed, lust, and unimaginable wealth.

The perception of the Arab woman as a harem girl continued throughout the nineteenth century. At the 1893 Chicago World's Fair, the representation of a street in Cairo was a popular attraction. The site, designed by Henry Ives Cobb, had minarets, camel and donkey rides, and a bazaar. The star who drew crowds to the attraction was "Little Egypt," a woman of uncertain identity and nationality who did a "hootchy-cootchy" dance. By the end of the Fair, over 27.5 million admissions had been counted. Little Egypt and her scandalous dance entered U.S. popular culture and became the basis of numerous songs, jokes, cartoons, and stories. One hundred years later, we are still familiar with that event and the catchy tune associated with her dance. It appears in children's cartoons on Saturday morning and is a staple in jokes about Middle Eastern women, yet few people realize where and how it entered

---

* Hester Lucy Stanhope, *Memoirs of the Lady Hester Stanhope*, 3 vols. (Salzburg: Universität Salzburg, 1985).

the popular memory. This seemingly unimportant event has affected generations of film producers, television script writers, songwriters, and novelists because the repeated representation continues to reinforce our image of women from the Middle East as belly dancers and harem girls.

The predominant Western image of the harem beauty is not a homemaker but a young, beautiful woman who must share a wealthy but cruel master or husband with dozens, perhaps hundreds of rivals. She must be sexually active and trained in alleged ancient Eastern sexual secrets, ruthless with her many rivals and fiercely protective of her position and her children. There is some historical reference for this stereotype. Ruling sultans did have large harems which were the site of intrigue and political infighting. Wealth and power were at stake. Then as now, sex was used as a weapon and a tool in the struggle for political power. As with most stereotypical images, an unusual or occasional situation expanded to define all situations. The harems of a small percentage of the ruling population at one point in history came to represent the norm by which all Middle Eastern women have since been indentified.

Popular images quickly become a part of new media or technologies. Stereotypes of Middle Eastern women appeared in silent films in the character of Theda Bara, the Vamp. The studio gave the name, an anagram of "Arab Death," to Theodosia Goodman, a bit player from Ohio. The vamp or vampire, a mysterious, sexually aggressive woman, lured men to their doom. Salome, Cleopatra, and other vampish women became popular characters in early films. Cecil B. DeMille and other producers noted that ticket sales increased for films including scenes with scantily clad actresses, and that historical and Biblical temptresses could be dressed in revealing costumes. Even after the Hayes Office implemented the Production Code of the Motion Picture Producers and Directors of America in the 1930s, the most revealing costumes and dances, such as the "Dance of the Seven Veils," often involved Middle Eastern women characters. Needless to say, these roles were not played by women of Middle Eastern background.

Middle Eastern women have seldom been presented in U.S. or Western art, literature, song, theatre, or film as loving daughters, sisters, wives, or mothers. They are not portrayed as bravely struggling for a better life for their families or for women's rights. They are never shown fighting beside men for national independence. We see no Arab women writers, artists, doctors, teachers, politicians, or businesswomen. Women have performed all these roles and more. We can see their photographs in Sarah Graham-Brown's *Images of Women: The Portrayal of Women in Photography of the Middle East, 1860-1950.* * We can read the journals of Huda Shaarawi,** we can learn about other women involved in the professions, public life, and politics in the Middle East. On the news, we can see Kuwaiti ambassadors and Palestinian delegates who are women. But these women, three-dimensional Middle Eastern women, are invisible in U.S. popular culture.

The Arab woman in western popular culture has been a sexual object, a projection of the suppressed sexual fantasies of eighteenth- and nineteenth-century Europeans constrained by societal and religious taboos. Until the early twentieth century, writers and artists unable to represent Western women in sexually explicit settings could substitute non-Western women. The character of the Middle Eastern woman could be represented in the harem, in the bath, in groups of African and Eastern women, as slaves, in any imaginable mode, unfettered by the need for accuracy. This can be seen in the work of the Orientalist school of painting, produced primarily by French and English male artists between 1830 and 1910. These genre scenes relied heavily on imagination and colorful props to create a fiction of women's lives. Some Orientalist painters, like Ingres in his famous bath scenes, used European models to substitute for inaccessible Middle Eastern women. A double standard also applied to display of harem scenes. Erotic scenes of Eastern and African women lounging in naked abandon in a Turkish bath guarded by black eunuchs, for example, could be displayed in a public gallery at a time when it would have been unacceptable had the painting represented French women. It is also interesting to note that while

* Sarah Graham-Brown, *Images of Women: The Portrayal of Women in Photography of the Middle East, 1860-1950* (New York: Columbia University Press, 1988).

** Huda Shaarawi, *Harem Years: The Memoirs of an Egyptian Feminist (1879-1924)* (New York: Feminist Press, 1987).

the majority of Orientalist painters were French, the largest markets for Orientalist art were in U.S. and England.*

The image of the Middle Eastern woman in the nineteenth century was that of an alien creature of a different nation and religion, sometimes dark-skinned, and by the late nineteenth century, the symbol of a defeated and occupied empire. The image of Middle Eastern women in art and literature as being sexually available to western men, and preferring western men to their Middle Eastern counterparts, is a part of the sinister side of political domination, sexual repression, and cultural violence inherent in the western colonialization of much of the Middle East and North Africa.

A new stereotype of Middle Eastern men and women emerged in the late 1960s and early 1970s—the terrorist. This image appeared after the emergence of groups like the Palestine Liberation Organization. Televised coverage of isolated terrorist activities created the association of Arab, Middle Eastern, and Palestinian with terrorism in the minds of many Americans. These hostile feelings were further reinforced by the stereotype of oil-wealthy sheikhs robbing Americans of their hard-earned money at the gas pumps during the oil embargo of the mid 1970s, and by the kidnapping of U.S. and European nationals during the Iranian Revolution and the Lebanese Civil War.

What do popular cultural images of Middle Eastern men, women, and children have to do with our own experiences as Arab-American women? To me, very little. My image of Arab women has been created by observing four generations of the women in my family and from interacting with Arab and Arab-American women at work, church, community activities, and in my research. I have never met the Arab woman portrayed in films or television. Conversely, the image of a perfect Middle Eastern woman is as two-dimensional as that of a harem girl. The only trait possessed by all the Middle Eastern women I have known is strength, a strength

* Lynne Thorton, *The Orientalists: Painter-Travellers, 1828-1908* (Paris: ACR Editions, 1983); Philip Hook and Mark Poltimore, *Popular 19th Century Painting: A Dictionary of European Genre Painters* (Woodbridge, Suffolk: Antique Collectors' Club, 1986); *The Orientalists: Delacroix to Matisse: The Allure of North Africa and the Near East,* ed. Mary Anne Stevens (London: Thames and Hudson/National Gallery of Art, 1984).

often born of adversity. Some have been stubborn to a fault, did not speak to each other for years over a minor falling out, and were very harsh in their judgement of others. Some were kind, gentle and soft-spoken. Most were fiercely proud of their families and lavished love on all children. Some were distant and kept to themselves. Most were generous to a fault and would go to any length to help a friend, relative, or neighbor in need. The same woman could be opinionated and aggravating one day and humble and supportive the next. They were all very human, exhibiting the strengths and weaknesses of people everywhere.

Stereotyping.
Arab American
East Asia

Orientalism in Science Fiction

HODA M. ZAKI

Science fiction is a form of popular culture that speculates about the human condition by creating imaginary societies located in the future. Enormously widespread, science fiction is found in a variety of forms, ranging from novels and short stories to films and cartoons. Science fiction's imaginary societies are linked to the author's and reader's imaginations through extrapolation, a process by which an author extends a pattern from the past or present society into the future. These patterns may be economic, social, technological, political, or religious. Grounded in the author's present, these imagined societies often carry over prejudicial assumptions without comment. This is true of even the most "alien" societies described in the genre. I want to show here how two respected science fiction writers, one of them a radical feminist, perpetuate perceptions of Arabs and Arab society in their novels in a manner which Edward Said has characterized as "Orientalist." Such writings, while different, continue to deliver one-dimensional and stereotypical notions of Arabs and Arab society to a wide readership. Because of the genre's enormous popularity, they can be seen as a significant cultural mechanism that helps to create a context which the U.S. government can continue to assert its hegemony, convincing its citizens on an ideological plane that its actions towards Arabs at home and abroad are justified. Popular forms of entertainment not only passively reflect current social prejudices, but also actively work to shape viewers' and readers' worldviews.

Frank Herbert's *Dune* series became a classic in science fiction.* Critics and readers alike reveled in the densely textured detail of a nomadic culture and hailed Herbert's imaginative achievements as unparalleled. *Dune* describes Arrakis, a water-starved planet whose indigenous population, the Fremen, are nomadic and deeply mystical. It is only on Arrakis that the spice,

---

* Frank Herbert, *Dune* (New York: Berkley Medallion Books, 1965).

melange, essential for interplanetary navigation, can be mined. A non-Fremen, Paul Artreides, goes "native" and marries into the tribe. He unifies the Fremen and becomes their leader. Paul is able to topple other galactic centers of power by the spread of his politico-religious movement, which to his fanatically loyal Fremen is a holy war, and by his monopoly over the vital melange. The entire galaxy is conquered and Paul becomes the god of a new religion. As the supreme godhead, Paul's rule is autocratic, with dissident politics defined as both treasonous and sacrilegious.

In discussing the triumphs of *Dune*, few critics noted the amazing parallels between Fremen and Arab societies. However, the anthropological dimension of *Dune* reveals some interesting anomalies that perhaps can only be understood fully by those familiar with Arab history, language, and society. I believe that Herbert lifted, with a few adaptations, his ideas on Fremen culture from Arabian societies. Indeed, I maintain that the general outline of the plot traces, in a broad fashion, both the rise of the Prophet Mohammad and the spread of Islam in the seventh century A.D., and the recent rise of Arab power in the world owing to the demand for petroleum resources. The similarities between petroleum and melange are unmistakable, as is the topography of the Arabian peninsula and Arrakis. And as the camel has been at the center of Arab bedouins economic and cultural social fabric, the sand worm, invented by Herbert, is a means of transportation, an economic necessity, a weapon, and an integral part of Fremen culture and ritual.

Herbert not only draws upon Arab history, ecology, and topography for *Dune*'s structure, but incorporates many other features of Arabian societies to flesh out Fremen culture. The most obvious carryover is evident in Fremen language. A few examples will be sufficient to make this point clear. Fremen believe in religious ritual or the Shari'a. "Shari'a" is the Arabic word for religious law. The Fremen believe in the coming of a "Mahdi," an Arabic word meaning religious leader. Fremen believe in evil spirits, the "jinn," in "jihad," the holy war, and in one's spiritual essence, the "ruh." All these are authentic Arabic words and beliefs used by Herbert to describe Fremen language and culture.* Herbert also uses Arabic-sounding words that are not

---

* Herbert, Frank, *Dune*, pp.101, 278, 306, 382.

authentically Arabic, but that are evocative of Arabic. For example, Herbert makes up the word "amtal," which is closely related to the Arabic word for hero, "batl."

Fremen society is closely modeled upon a romantic vision of Arab bedouin society. Fremen wear long, flowing robes, their complexion is swarthy, the men are circumcised, practice polygamy, and hold certain values dear: honor, trust, valor, bravery, and the practice of vendetta. Fremen are divided into tribes and their lives are primitive and simple, formed as a response to the brutal environment in which they live. These cultural traits existed to some extent in Arab societies in the past, and have been incorporated into the romantic construction of Arabs by pre-World War II Orientalists such as Lawrence of Arabia.

Early Orientalists found much to admire in Arabian societies and romanticized Arabs in a variety of ways. Yet Orientalists maintained that the basic ingredients of Arab society, culture, and religion were static, inferior, and essentially different from western society. Popular cultural stereotypes of Arab societies (found in the west at a time when the west ruled the Middle East and did not feel threatened by it) included the perceptions that Arabs were simple, easily manipulated, religious, fanatical, and in need of leadership, usually provided by the west. Herbert's adaptation of Arab society unwittingly incorporated this earlier, and perhaps more benign, form of Orientalism. In *Dune*, Paul and other non-Fremen provide the vision and leadership for Fremen, while the Fremen are the subalterns for the hero to manipulate as he sees fit. Since the anthropological strength of the novel ultimately develops from the writer's world, it is not surprising that the relationship between Paul and the Fremen is one of exercised power, reflecting the reality of western hegemony in the Herbert's world.

Dune was published in 1965 and represents an early, unacknowledged modelling of Arab society. Although it is a more benign and romantic vision of bedouin and Arab society, it is nonetheless Orientalist and represents an interesting stage in the development of Orientalist discourse in U.S. popular culture. Such early Orientalism is still harmful in that it depicts other peoples and cultures as fundamentally different and inferior; however, when compared to the more recent discourse on Arab culture, it is benign for at least it portrays some of the social practices among the Fremen/Arabs as admirable. Herbert acknowledges in his novel the potential power the Arab world possesses because of its petroleum resources, and that he is worried about the impact a new "holy war" led by religious fanatics will have on the west. Will a new world order emerge from this new balance of power? wonders Herbert in *Dune*. Who will lead this new order? Do Arabs have the required leadership ability? These are the questions Herbert consider in 1965, when the power of OPEC had yet to be felt. In *Dune*, we see a mixture of fear for what the future may hold for the west, as well as an attraction to a romantic vision of Arab society. These real world references unconsciously incorporate the hierarchies of power and social stereotypes that flourished in Herbert's society, and they inform the structure and content of Herbert's imaginary world.

I will now examine Joanna Russ' novel, *The Two of Them,** published thirteen years after *Dune*, and ask whether a balanced picture of Arab society can be found among feminist science fiction writers. Russ, a committed and radical feminist, understands the political importance of literature and seeks to transform her readers' views through her writings, which often describe alternative societies supportive of women.

The Two of Them depicts a recently formed, Arab-type misogynist society on the planet Ka'abah (which is the name of the holiest shrine in Islam). Ernest Newmann and Irene Waskiewicz work as a team for The Gang, a mysterious, galactic, intelligence-gathering organization that wields enormous power. Irene joined The Gang because she wished to flee her oppressive mid-1950s suburban U.S. home. She and Ernest are lovers and enjoy a seemingly egalitarian relationship. They come to Ka'abah to spy, and they are hosted by a family whose youngest member, Zubeydeh, is a twelve-year-old girl who wants to be a poet. Much of the early part of the novel depicts oppressive family relationships on Ka'abah, which are particularly brutal for women. Zubeydah's aunt has been declared insane and placed in solitary confinement for attempting to be a poet, and Zubeydeh's mother is on constant medication. When

---

* Joanna Russ, *The Two of Them* (New York: Berkley, 1978).

Zubeydeh is punished for writing poetry she appeals for help, and Irene responds by kidnapping Zubeydeh and taking her back to Earth and freedom. Ernest, a likeable and liberated male, does not understand Irene's visceral reaction to Ka'abah, and the latter part of the novel is spent describing Irene's gradual realization that her relationships to Ernest and The Gang are sexually oppressive. Irene determines that she has to break away from both to be free and, indeed, kills Ernest in her attempt to liberate herself.

Russ consciously chooses to use the model of a Middle Eastern misogynist society (replete with male homosexuality and segregated women) to depict a society where the oppression of women is extreme. Her images of Ka'abah include harem women who have to make themselves beautiful, wear make-up, undergo cosmetic surgery to remove ribs, and wear jewelry that impedes free movement, such as toe-rings. Absolute male patriarchy makes women insane or unable to deal with this reality without the help of tranquilizing drugs. Ka'abah women are portrayed by Russ to be complete victims of this patriarchy.

Initially Russ poses a dichotomy between women in the western world who have freedom of movement, enjoy freer sex, and have career and educational options, and Ka'abah women, who enjoy none of these freedoms. A real strength of the book is that Russ allows Irene to realize that all women, regardless of culture, suffer from similar sexual discrimination and oppression, even western women. Russ' solution to this problem is an extreme one—to do without men, even to the point of killing them.

Notwithstanding Russ' final and more complete understanding of the global nature of sexual oppression, it is significant that Russ modeled her vision of a future misogynist society upon current myths and stereotypical perceptions of Middle Eastern society. Her description of women's oppression on Ka'abah reflects how Orientalist assumptions have been integrated into feminist discourse and popular culture. The position of women in the Middle East has been used as a way to define the flaws of Middle Eastern societies and condemn an entire civilization. Interestingly, western male imperialists in the nineteenth and early twentieth centuries used similar aruguments to justify interventionist policies in "their" colonial possessions.

In many feminist circles, it is popular to view Middle Eastern women as being the most oppressed women in the world. Western feminists have ranked women's oppression globally, and more often than not, western women emerge from this ranking as the most liberated. I feel such ranking to be invidious and paternalistic, and as a woman whose origins are Middle Eastern, I resent the constant portrayal of Middle Eastern women as absolute victims. Such condemnations present a view of Arab society that is static, erroneous, and Orientalist. Current feminist research written by many women in Middle Eastern Studies indicates that Middle Eastern women have not been passive in the face of sexual oppression, but that they have launched many movements to achieve social justice as they have defined it.

Since the publications of *Dune* and *The Two of Them,* we have witnessed the emergence of a different and more vicious depiction of Arabs and Islam in popular culture in the United States. The acceptance of these Arab and Islamic stereotypes promotes and permits the constant violation of the human and civil rights of Arabs abroad and Arab-Americans domestically. The most graphic example of the former is the total dehumanization of the Iraqi people during Desert Storm by much of the media and the general populace. Orientalist discourse helps to legitimate such atrocities.

I think it is important to note that all such Orientalist interpretations of Middle Eastern societies—romantic, feminist, or otherwise—are made possible by the imbalance of power between the west and the Middle East. To eliminate such stereotypes finally and completely would entail the dawning of a new respect for Arab political power on the part of the west. Only when Arabs and Arab-Americans can command the necessary power and influence internationally and domestically will these stereotypes begin to disappear. In the interim, it behooves Arab-American women involved in the U.S. women's movement to point out the errors of assuming that all women's movements share the same priorities and goals of the U.S. feminist movement. We must remind them as frequently as is needed, as other women of color have done, that the U.S. feminist movement cannot prescribe a strategy for all women across all classes and cultures. The complexities of the world must be reflected in our own political discourses and we must struggle to inject these complexities into a national mood that is on the way to considering Islam, Islamic fundamentalism, and Arab societies as the most dangerous threats to western hegemony in the 21st century. Our heritage demands no less.

V

Grapeleaves

Tangled Identities:

Claiming Ourselves

Grapeleaves

Grapevines grow throughout the Arab world. While the grapes are picked for eating and wine-making, the leaves are also picked; stuffed with rice, herbs, lemon and oil; and cooked. Since grapes also grow in North America, many of us went grapeleaf-picking with our grandmothers. The image of that plant, a tenacious survivor, tangling and weaving its way wherever it finds an opening, fits well with this section, since our identities are not clear-cut or easily defined. They are complex and layered, tangled and contradictory.

◡ Vegetarian Grape Leaves ◠

1 c. canned garbanzo beans (or if dry, soak overnight and remove skin)

1 c. olive oil

2 c. rice, washed

2 bunches parsley, leaves only, washed and chopped

1 bunch mint, chopped

1 yellow onion, chopped

1 bunch green onions, chopped

dash of cayenne

1 large can whole tomatoes, chopped, or 1 1.5 pounds

fresh tomatoes, skinned and chopped

1 jar grape leaves

2 c. water

lemon juice and salt and pepper to taste

Mix all of the above ingredients together except the last four. Rinse and roll out grapeleaves, and stuff with a spoonful of the above mixture. Roll leaves tightly, folding ends of leaf before the final roll. Arrange leaves side by side and on top of each other in covered kettle, adding any leftover juices from the stuffing mix. Over top of grape leaves, pour canned or fresh tomatoes and their juices with 2 cups water. Steam over low flame until done (approx.1 1.5 hours). When cooked, add a little lemon juice to taste. Serves 10.

◡ Source : Therese Saliba

A Lunatic From Libya, One Generation Removed

LILITH FINKLER

*Lunacy: intermittent insanity once believed to
be related to phases of the moon*

In the synagogue of the Ashkenazim,*
I ululate at night,
A lunatic from Libya,
One Generation removed.

I am the kaddish, a prayer of mourning.
I ache for the Jews of northern Africa,
living among white-skinned peoples.

I am the yarzheit** candle
Europe will not light.

I am the unexpressed
guttural sounds of a
youngster, unsure of
her mother's voice.

I am the lost liturgies
of the desert winds,
the frayed edges of a tallit***

---

* Jews of European Origin.

** a candle lit annually to commemorate the death of a loved one.

rustling, shaking furiously.

I am the fear of the Arabic
that resides within me.
Of the shrill curses
shouted in desperation.
Of the foods I craved,
the lentil soup and couscous
my mother never cooked.
Of the darker tone of skin,
olive shades,
black eyes and hair.

Who taught me this fear
of my other self,
the lunatic from Libya,
the hidden one, couched
in Sabbath prayers,
with the tunes of Europe
to comfort me,
lullabies providing no solace.

I am my mother's daughter,
But I wear my father's skin,
A thought process I can hide in.

I am the lunatic, a moonbeam away
from the fear of my own darkness.

*** Ritual shawl worn by Jews at prayer

Going Home

BOOKDA GHEISAR

I have lived in the United States for thirteen years now and have struggled to make this place my home, but often I have had no idea what creates a sense of belonging and being at home.

For the first six years I tried very hard to assimilate and look, act, and sound like everyone else. But then I became confronted with the fact that I had lost myself, and instead of a sense of self, I had gained a deep shame about who I was. Now, on a daily basis, I try to undo that shame and I continue to search for a place where I can belong.

I am in the Toronto airport at the immigration lines. It's 11 p.m. and I can't wait to see my family. It's been five years. Now they are waiting on the other side of those walls. But suddenly my hands shake, my heart beats rapidly, I sweat. I try to reassure myself because I have all the documents they might want to see and I am a permanent legal resident of the United States, yet I continue to feel terrified as if I have done something wrong and they are going to find out about it. I look around me and everyone is holding their blue passports in their hands. Mine is dark red. This simple fact seems to make us so different from one another. When it is my turn, the immigration officer takes my passport and looks at it and asks where I am from, even though it's written on my passport that I am an Iranian citizen. Then he takes my green card and looks at it in silence for a long long time and keeps checking out my face. I feel humiliated and uncomfortable and look around me to see that many blue passport holders have come and gone and a lot of people who have grown impatient standing in the line behind me have given up and moved to other lines. Then he simply says, "You are going to have to go in the immigration room and talk to someone there." I walk into the room and see a lot of brown people sitting around the waiting area so I join them. Everyone looks scared. I feel sure that I have done something wrong and just can't recall what it is. After one and a half hours of waiting they call me in for an excruciatingly painful "questioning," where they keep asking me questions like, "Have you ever been to Canada before?" Then they tell me I am lying because their computers show that I have never been to Canada and I do not have a family in Toronto. Later they decide to bring in my father, who does not speak any English, and question him. My father enters the room and we look at one another for the first time in five years but these strangers order me not to speak to him in Farsi. Finally they let us go at 3 a.m. My father tries to comfort me by telling me that these kinds of things happen to him and our other Iranian friends all the time.

I came to the United States in 1978, unable to speak English, completely unprepared for life here. At the time Americans exoticized Iran and when I told people about my birth place, the common reaction was, "Oh, that's where Persian carpets, Persian cats, lots of oil, and the Shah come from. How exotic." Of course, I was shocked to discover that half of the people who talked to me did not even know where Iran is. It seemed Americans' knowledge of geography did not extend beyond their own country and it was even more shocking to find out that they had forgotten their own history.

Then we experienced the hostage crisis and the fall of the Shah and a new government. People's comments changed to "Oh, that's where the Ayatollah is from, they are holding our hostages there, and chopping people's arms off for stealing things." Suddenly, in my small town, I went from being coveted and exoticized to being despised and hated. The anti-Iranian hostility rose at a frightening pace. Then for the first time I heard someone yelling at me, "Go back home to where you belong." To this day, after hearing that command thousands of times, I still feel much pain, sadness, and anger. "Go home." I want and dream more than anything else to regain a sense of belonging to somewhere; a sense of being at home.

As a young Iranian during the 1960s and 1970s, I was exposed to the media lies about the west. We saw American movies and tried to act and dress like those people. We ate at McDonald's and Kentucky Fried Chicken, watched Gilligan's Island and the Brady Bunch, and said "ok" to each other. We were crazy about the west and dreamed of it everyday. Meanwhile, the government of Iran did its best to wipe out our history, our treasures, and our past, moving the country rapidly toward westernization. We heard about the wonders of the United States all the time. I remember on family road trips, while our car bumped up and down on the potholes, my father always said, "They don't have roads like this in the U.S. I've heard the roads there are as smooth as the palm of your hand." I spent months daydreaming about this land of opportunities and tried to imagine my life in America. Of course, I could not imagine the pain and loneliness and alienation that I would feel years later in this country of my dreams.

I am going to Iran for a visit. A white feminist friend of mine asks me if I am scared for my life. She is so glad that I live in this country where women are free and safe. It's true that as a child I heard the American woman is free. She can wear whatever she wants, go out in public with practically no clothes on, and she has opportunities to do anything that she wants. Years later, I would find out that in the United States a woman is raped every three minutes, a woman is beaten somewhere in the country every eighteen minutes and one of every three young girls sexually abused before the age of eighteen. Then I learned that two in five women who are murdered are killed by their husbands and almost half of all "domestic incidents" against women are not reported to the police. I also found out that the American woman is free to wear what she wants, but that she will always be blamed, on account of her clothes, when she is raped, battered, and murdered. I saw one news story in which the mother of a five-year-old girl had taken the child's father to court for sexual abuse. The judge ruled it was not the man's fault, rather the five-year-old was a very seductive child who always wore short dresses. I had not seen any of this in the movies.

As a young adult I tried to adjust, to do the best I could to live here and finish my studies. After the hostage crisis and during the Iran-Iraq war, the American hostility, pity, and ignorance continued. I slowly came to the realization that I was ashamed to name my heritage. People who met me often assumed I was Chicano/Latina, and I avoided conversations because I dreaded the painful, and often idiotic, questions that would follow. It seemed my choice was to stay silent or to start a long process of educating people about what it means to be an Iranian.

I was more and more drawn to people of color and other immigrants because it felt comfortable and easier to be myself. During my thirteen years here, I learned to be respectful of my friends' ethnic origins. However, I so internalized my shame and oppression around my identity that I never expected the same treatment from them. I recently realized that most people I know have never attempted to educate themselves about my background. A good friend of mine recently asked me, "Now, I forget if you are from I—ran or I—raq." It's gotten to the point where I am shocked when I meet someone who pronounces the name of my country correctly!

Of course, sometimes I meet people who seem interested in learning about me and my background, yet I find that even their positive attention continues to set me apart and reminds me that I am unlike them and therefore an object to be exoticized.

> *I am a member of a feminist book discussion group. We get together for an evening and there are many new women among us. I am quiet through the first half of the meeting until I say something that sounds intelligent to a few of the new women. Many turn to me and one white feminist asks, "Where are you from?" I am somewhat confused because I thought we were discussing the book but I answer, "Iran." Then she asks me if I would say something in my language so she could just hear how it sounds. I get a picture of monkeys in the circus being ordered by their master to perform new and exciting tricks.*

During the U.S. war against Iraq, I felt sure that I was going to lose my sanity. Everywhere I went the message I received, more loudly and clearly than ever before, was that the United States is not my home; not now and not ever. I felt so much rage. I also felt unable to clarify myself and find meaningful English words for these feelings. I often wish I could be at home, where language is easier for me. Every time someone yelled at me to "Go home," the last thirteen years flashed before my eyes.

I often think about the future and what country will be my home. My family immigrated to Canada three years ago and sold the home where I had been raised. So, where is home? Is home where my loved ones are? Is home where I live? Is home where my mother was buried? Is home where I spent the first half of my life and where I know the traditions and values? Is home where I spent the second half of my life?

The trouble with looking for a home in the United States is that the mainstream patriarchal and racist culture will never allow me to make this my home. I am not allowed to be angry or criticize the American system because then someone will always say, "If you don't like it here, why don't you go back to where you came from?" And it is so extremely painful to have no answers to these questions and to consistently be reminded of being an outsider and not belonging.

I apply for a job as the clinical director at a new organization, which is supposedly radical and progressive. During my interview I tell the white gay man (who would be my supervisor) that what I want the most is a job that allows me to be creative. He nods and says, "You can do whatever you want in this job, you can even cook ethnic food for us if you wish." As I hurry outside to get some fresh air, I notice that in the waiting area there are two separate lines for people seeking employment. One line is for kitchen staff and another for mental health professionals and I notice that everyone in the kitchen line is brown or black and quietly keeping to themselves, and everyone in the other line is white and looks like they belong there and has already gotten the job. I realize the threat he must have felt about me and his obvious desire to put me in my place before I even begin.

I consider myself lucky because at least I spent half of my life not feeling oppressed and knowing what belonging feels like. It would be easy to give up, considering all the violence, oppression, wars, and injustice that surround us everyday, but I continue to find my power by connecting with other people of color, writing, and finding my voice. And I continue to follow my heart to a place where I can fully belong.

What's Not in a Name

MARILYNN RASHID

Arab-American

Although I am married, I call myself Marilynn Rashid, "to keep my own name," I say. But, of course, it's only my father's name, so this partly defeats the purpose—the patriarchy can't be broken this way. It's small solace, a partial solution, no solution. So I should add my mother's name, Philipson (son of Philip?). But, of course, that wasn't her mother's name either, just her father's. So I should use Manders, my grandmother's name as well. But I know that name carries the same half-weight. Marilynn Manders Philipson Rashid. What's in a name? A lot, but somehow not enough.

These names hearken back to Lebanon, Ireland, Luxembourg, places of origin of people lost to me, places with which I have little or no connection, places that were distant shadows even for the ones who held the names and passed them on. I am a piece of the cultural entropy of the age, forever falling away from many centers.

If we truly knew who we were, our names would not be such a problem. It is difficult to find one's way in a world divided not only by war and racism, but by freeways, television, and the technological projects of so-called progress. If we could, in fact, go back where we came from, as some would like us to do, we would still not find ourselves, for those places are changed or destroyed or occupied or part of the same industrial grid we find ourselves in here. And also, some of us, many of us, would have to cut ourselves up in twos and threes and ship pieces of ourselves all over the globe. And surely that wouldn't help our sense of fragmentation.

So we stay where we are, at least for now, and we know it as home. We stick with the names we've been given and we ask a lot of questions of the old people, if there are any left. And we listen carefully so that we can tell others. The details are important.

---

* These excerpts are from a work-in-progress.

Names do limit meaning and delete important details. Yet the naming often comes from a need to make links and find common ground, to facilitate communication. This is how the term "Arab-American" came into being. Yet I must admit I have never called myself an Arab-American. Such a weighty term speaks for large abstractions, and I am uneasy in its midst.

When I think of the word "Arab," I think of Arabic, the language which is, in my mind, one obvious thing that links most Arabs. Having studied English and several Romance languages, I know well the importance of language to a genuine understanding of a culture. But, except for a few wonderfully scatological and off-color words my Uncle Frederick taught my sisters and brothers and me, except for the names of certain Arabic dishes and a few endearing terms my *siti* used with us, and except for the sayings my father forever repeats to us, regrettably, I do not speak the language of my father's family. And I feel somewhat awkward calling myself Arab or Arabic.

I am also hesitant to call myself American or identify myself as a citizen of a nation-state that claims this continent's name as its own. I am not at all proud to be an American; with military power and the cloak of legitimacy, "America" selectively condemns and fosters violence here at home and in other places. I wave no yellow ribbons, no flags, because they speak for the forces of empire and its institutionalized violence. It is through slavery, plunder, and murder on this continent and abroad that "America" has become the most powerful nation in the world. How to rediscover a toponymy that leaves the symbols of empire behind, a naming rooted in nature, one that helps to link us intrinsically to the places where we were born and the places where we live?

Instead of Arab and American I'd rather deal with words of smaller places or regions you can see and smell, places you can imagine or realistically get around in. Michigan, where I was born, or Michigami, as the original inhabitants called it, the imprint of the hand of the great spirit; and Lebanon, the Lebanon, Marjayoun, J'daidit; and Detroit, the straits. We can see why these places were named the way they were. We know of the hills, the valley, or the mountain. We can see the river.

I am most comfortable, I suppose, defining myself as a Detroiter, since this is where I've spent most of my life. In spite of its many social problems, or perhaps even because of them, I am proud to have survived here, to have made real connections with others. I am proud to have, in small ways, spoken out against racism and ecological destruction and for community here. Place, after all, is crucial to our understanding of who we are, and I must acknowledge that this fractured urban landscape has had much to do with my sense of the world and my place in it.

Semites and Anti-Semites

Identifying himself as "Lebanese" was problematic for my father early on because when my *jido* and *siti* came to the United States at the turn of the century, the region they had come from, called "the Lebanon," was considered part of Syria. It had also been occupied by Egypt for a time, controlled by France, and invaded by the Turks. In fact, it was to avoid conscription in the Ottoman army that my grandfather came to this country. With such a history, I imagine that the concept of national identity was somewhat peculiar and arbitrary for my grandparents' generation. So my *siti* occasionally forgot about the state of Lebanon and would sometimes give her nationality as Syrian, since that's the way things seemed when she left.

When we were children, my father told my brothers and sisters and me that we were not only Lebanese or Syrian, but Semitic, and he told us stories about the Semites and Phoenicians who travelled the seas, all over the world, trading their wares. He was proud of these names and histories, and it seems to me now, looking back, that he told us these things to help us find our way in a world so far from the places that shaped his parents' families and their lives. And we could make small links to tales from far away and long ago. He explained that "Arabic," the language he and his family spoke, is a Semitic language, and that the Phoenicians were merchants like him. For my father, being a merchant was a skill, handed down through generations.

The word "Semitic" captivated me so much that for a time I incorporated it into my sense of self. I remember once in grade school filling out the "other" blank on a form requesting race or nationality with the words "half-Semitic." I had passed up the boxes marked "Caucasian" and "Black" and had filled in my own special race. When someone later told me that I could check the box marked "Caucasian," I was very disappointed.

My first year in college I met a young man named Paul in an English class. We went for coffee a few times after class and seemed to have a lot to talk about. One afternoon he told me he'd spent the summer on a kibbutz in Israel. He became very animated, explaining the details of his daily routine there, the comradery, the cooperative spirit that fed the survival of each kibbutz.

At nineteen, I was not very worldly or politically aware and at first I was genuinely impressed. But then he told me about one of the rotated duties to which he had occasionally been assigned, that of keeping watch at night with a rifle at kibbutz perimeters. He said that "Arabs" would occasionally try to get in. They posed a threat to the peaceful existence of the kibbutz, he told me, and they were "anti-Semitic." Confused, I asked him what he would have done if an Arab had approached his guard post. "I'd have blown his head off," he announced with pride and conviction. I then asked him if he knew that I was half-Lebanese, half-Arabic. I wish I had said "half-Semitic," but I had long since dropped that term from my self-description. An awkward, embarrassed pause followed. He changed the subject. We parted quickly and he never really spoke to me again, always avoiding situations in which we might have to look at each other.

There is something terrifying and yet utterly enlightening in the experience of being recognized on a street by a familiar face in a split second of eye contact and then immediately, mechanically rejected, with head shifting angles fast, pulling the eyes hard to avert your persistent gaze. It is the smooth cold gesture of denial, a small but clear admission of disavowal or hatred, a bold repudiation of past human connections. If such experiences don't break you or occur too frequently to harden you to similar hatred, they can serve at least to jolt you from complacency, to make you question and help you understand your place in the world. They also alert you to similar and more extreme actions exhibited against others around you, and you begin at least to consider the world in ways you never did before.

Initially, Paul's use of the term "anti-Semitic" disturbed me most because it tugged at, twisted, and forked some trail, some vague path not only to my past and my father's past, but to my faith in his words and stories. How could Arabs, who are Semitic, be anti-Semitic? But ultimately more than the confusion over terms, what plagued me more was the realization of the need that many people have to hate...and then to feed and cultivate their hate, to hold it tightly close to their hearts, to defend it, brick it in, to count on it, to sleep with it and dream of it, to weave it in with their breath carefully, methodically, intricately until it captures the openness that once guided them when they were children.

I came to understand that when a nation-state seizes land, it confiscates identity. Just as the United States conquered, colonized so many words in "America," so Israel had annexed, appropriated the term "Semitic." But not according to everyone, of course; Semitic is one thing, anti-Semitic something else. I had to remind myself, before I became too deeply immersed in the argument, that language is not always logical, that words do limit meaning, often leaving large gaping holes in their echo.

I have always been horrified and outraged by the massive torture, brutalization, and genocide of the Jews in Europe. So, I asked myself, if I am opposed to both subtle and blatant acts of racism against all peoples, why should I mind if the term "anti-Semitic" helps expose hatred against Jews even if it absents Arabs?

While struggling with these ideas, I met Fredy Perlman, a man who not only had lived through the consequences of one of history's most terrifying campaigns of institutionally-imposed racism, but had thought about it a lot and become acutely aware of the insidious and pervasive character of many forms of oppression of many peoples. One of his essays, called "Anti-Semitism and the Beirut Pogrom," was crucial to my growing understanding of racism and, in many ways, inspired me to grapple with similar questions in the context of my own life through my writing. The essay, prompted by the Israeli bombing of Beirut in 1982, has a simple and cogent message: people who are victimized often become victimizers, use their victimization as a tool, and as a rationalization for the hatred, torment, and oppression of others. Reading this essay for the first time, I sensed a strong and urgent imperative addressed to the reader, to humankind, to break the cycle of this deeply ingrained psychological tyranny. Fredy was not only referring to flagrant atrocities committed against different peoples throughout history; he connected them to those smaller daily acts of racism, to the routine that bolsters an entire political or economic system and he used the experience of people in his own family to exemplify it.

While most of Fredy's extended family died in Nazi concentration camps, his immediate family and several relatives escaped and found themselves in Bolivia, where he observed a relative cheating the Quechua Indians and speaking disdainfully of them; she later became a promoter of Israel and turned her hatred against Palestinians. Learning about Fredy's relatives led me to consider my father's family. In the small Illinois town in which they settled, my grandparents and their children were often singled out and ridiculed as dirty foreigners who didn't speak English. The experience did not make them more understanding of other cultures. On the contrary, after moving to Detroit, several uncles became vehement racists who moved their families to various white suburbs as soon as they could afford it and then refused to come into the city to visit us for fear, they'd say, of blacks.

Fredy's discussions helped me to see connections between my life and the lives of other children of immigrants, between the political turmoil of the present and that of the past. He explained how the force of nationalist fervor had created exiled refugees, like the central European Jews, in places all over the globe, and he made links between the oppression of indigenous populations in the Americas and in Israel. Fredy was the first person I heard who turned the term "anti-Semitic" on its head; he used it to describe the actions of the state of Israel against the Palestinians, knowing that the ancient Hebrews, Arabs, Akkadians, Phoenicians, and Ethiopians were all Semitic because they came from the land of Shem, the Arabian Peninsula, and had spoken the language of Shem.

Though we might know that words are consciously chosen and language deliberately manipulated for political and ideological purposes by those in power, we rarely realize the inevitable deleterious effects they have on our own consciousness, our own self-conception. One would hope that in their linked origins and histories of oppression, a sense of kinship and understanding would arise among Semites and descendents of Semites. This will not happen through the bureaucratic processes of nation-states, but it can happen between individuals who have learned to value and respect each other and each other's pasts, their visions, and their hopes for the re-emergence of community. We rediscover the openness that once guided us when we were children and so affirm the "other," the refugee, the exile, the immigrant, in each other, in ourselves. An unremarkable statement, perhaps, but it says something about who we all are and who we must become.

Browner Shades of White

LAILA HALABY

Under *race/ethnic origin*
I check *white*.
I am not
a minority
on their checklists
and they erase me
with the red end
of a number
two pencil.

I go to school
quite poor
because I am *white*.
There is no
square to check
that I have no
camels in my backyard,
that my father does
not have eight wives
inside the tents
of his harem,
or his palace,
or the island
he bought
with his oil
money.

My father is a farmer.
My mother is a teacher.
I am *white*
because there is no
square for *exotic*.

My husband
does not
have a machine gun,
though sometimes his eyes
fire anger
because while he too is *white*,
his borders have long since been smudged
by the red end
of a number
two pencil.

My friend who is black
calls me a woman of color.
My mother who is white
says I am Caucasian.
My friend who is Hispanic/Mexican-American
understands my dilemma.
My country that is a democratic melting pot
does not.

On Language and Ethnicity

MARGARET SALOME

I've studied and written about the status of Arabic in the United States and factors that encourage and hinder its use. As I developed the topic, this chapter became more personal, less a sterile presentation of data and analysis. This happened partly because I interviewed people and partly because my research brought into focus the powerful effect our concept of ethnic identity can have on our actions and feelings.

This work began when I found an article arguing that gaining access to U.S. socioeconomic institutions has lead to the erosion of the use of Arabic here. When I found the article, I became excited, and soon I had filled my apartment with bibliographies on the status of minority communities in the United States. My paper changed frequently during the time I worked on it. It started out as a survey of literature documenting the way feeble attempts at retaining Arabic through small community-based projects like church and mosque schools had floundered in the face of the overwhelming pressure to learn English. Then I noticed a pattern; most efforts to retain the use of Arabic, failed or not, seemed to be fueled by ethnic pride. I began to realize that only individuals could stem the loss of language, individuals who must work against the daunting power of our economic and social institutions.

I examined material by Elaine Hagopian and Bader S. Dweik. Hagopian found that members of Boston's Lebanese Christian community did not consider themselves Arabs because they identified Arabs with Muslims. Dweik, studying Lebanese-Americans in Buffalo, found that as they gained economic success and moved to the suburbs, they stopped speaking Arabic.

Dweik also studied a Yemenite community in upstate New York that had a high retention of the use of Arabic. Members of that community became laborers with low levels of income and education. Therefore, the socioeconomic homogeneity formerly shared in Yemen continues in the United States; it encourages isolation from mainstream America, and makes it easier for members to retain language, culture, and traditions. Although Dweik does not directly point out the connection, it is probable that the Yemenites' low socioeconomic status contributes to their homogeneity, or lack of assimilation. It is likely that many in this community do not have the time or resources to learn English.

There is evidence that minority communities with large numbers of speakers are also very successful at keeping their languages. Miami's Cuban community is a good example, and one that I am familiar with, since I grew up in Miami. The Cuban community is large and has lots of political clout. They also have a thriving business sector. You can spend your life in this community, go to work, run a business, and never speak English.

Similarly, in Dearborn, Michigan and Chicago there are large, concentrated Arab and Arab-American communities. It would be interesting to see how language retention in these large communities compares to that of smaller, more dispersed ones. It would also be interesting to see if an Arab-American community with a large number of elected officials could improve its retention of Arabic.

Although low socioeconomic status and sheer numbers of speakers help in the preservation of a minority language, people are also driven to preserve Arabic in the name of ethnic pride. I talked to my sister, Mary Salome, who started learning Arabic at age twenty-four. Like me, my sister grew up eating Arabic food and listening to Arabic music. Like me, she didn't learn any Arabic as a child, with the exception of names of food, greetings, and terms of endearment. Mary began studying Arabic because she wanted to be more connected to whatever it means to be an Arab.

On a 1988 visit to Israel, my sister had to come to terms with her identity as an Arab-American because the ambiguity of her identity aroused anger in Palestinians and Israelis. Her ability to speak Hebrew disgusted Palestinians and caused suspicion among Israelis. Mary wanted to talk to Palestinians, but felt frustrated that she could only do so in Hebrew. She felt thrust into the Palestinian-Israeli conflict and wanted to "choose sides."

I also talked with Silvette Boyajian, coordinator of an Arabic-language school in Seattle, Washington. Members of the Arabic-speaking community are committed to the school; it's part of a larger project involving the creation of an Arab cultural center. Community members believe a primary benefit for their children will be a sense of pride in Arab culture and heritage. Parents want to foster ethnic pride in their children because of political turmoil in the Middle East and the negative image of Arabs in the U.S. media. Silvette believes Arabs and Arab-Americans in Seattle are "fed up" with the "[recent] history of failure" in the Middle East and the focus on negative aspects of Arab politics in the American press. The newly established Arab Center and the language school will focus on food, music, and language to celebrate culture and heritage.

When I think about the fact that I didn't learn Arabic growing up, I feel frustrated, because I believe it would have helped me in my travels in the Middle East and with projects I have done on the Arab linguists of the Middle Ages. I also think knowing Arabic would make me more "legitimate" as an Arab-American. At the same time, I understand that there was no way my father could have taught me Arabic. When I was a child, he barely remembered it. My father had lost most of his Arabic because he had no occasion to use it after his grandparents, who never learned English, died.

I can see that my family fits Dweik's formula for language loss. My father moved away from the people he spoke Arabic with, got a good job, and now, we don't speak the language. Yet even though this project has been a very personal one, professionally, my research into the sociopolitical aspects of language use has been a real departure for me. This is because most of my research involves syntactic theory. As a student of syntax, I have been trained to use theory to discover what mechanisms are responsible for letting us form sentences. Therefore, in the course of my research, I didn't look at language in any sociopolitical context. In fact, I often found myself thinking that the outcome of such "sociolinguistic" research would be obvious, and thus uninteresting.

My research for this chapter taught me that the relationship between minority language retention and sociopolitical factors is not as straightforward as I once thought. In fact, minority communities retain their languages through diametrically opposed processes. In the case of the Yemenites, use of Arabic was maintained through sociopolitical disempowerment. Many Arab-Americans, however, empower themselves by teaching their children Arabic in order to encourage ethnic pride. Furthermore, Miami's Cubans have maintained and even spread the use of Spanish through political clout and business acumen. It is this paradox that intrigues me, and points to the fact that far from being obvious and uninteresting, the topic of minority language retention deserves even closer scrutiny.

Mocking Civilization

PEARL DAVIES SAAD

I watch the Palestinian girls on TV
and my heart breaks.
Their dark eyes
light-brown/dark-yellow skin
thick hair and
passionate voices.
They wear short-sleeved white blouses
and talk about self determination.
They are beautiful.

I know only what they told me:
I am dirty, ugly, not white enough.
Too yellow, too green,
hairy arms and legs.
A barbarian,
a girl mocking civilization.

I should hide,
hold myself in.
Do as I am told and
pledge allegiance
step on a crack.
I come home from school,
always on time.
I play jacks
while my mother speaks
Arabic on the phone.

~~~~~~~~~~~~~~~~~~~~~~~~~~~

Pulled

ZANA MACKI

In loving memory of HajHamood Macki, August 5, 1992

I began working as an activist in our community partly as a way to deal with the way I felt pulled in so many directions. East versus west, conservatism versus liberalism, family and religion at odds with individual needs and wants. I found emotional replenishment for this mixed bag—myself—working in the community. I eventually took on a staff position at the Detroit office of the American-Arab Anti-Discrimination Committee (ADC).

I was on the staff when the U.S. went to war against Iraq. While ADC took the position that Iraq should not have attacked Kuwait, we also publicly denounced President Bush for his invasion. The sanctions should have been given more time. ADC took the moral and just stand, even though we were heavily criticized for it. One of my Chaldean friends called me and said,"Zana, this is crazy! Now I know exactly how you felt during the TWA hijacking while working at Channel 56. They just want to blame someone." Immediately, she and other women formed Victims of War (VOW), networking in the living rooms of each other's homes.

Reporters from around the world went through our ADC office. Japanese, Dutch, and British TV, *The New York Times,* a Swedish newspaper, all kept calling for the Arab story. Once again, many wanted to go through the south and east ends of Dearborn. Sometimes I think, why not make these Middle Eastern neighborhoods into a backlot movie set for the press? Many reporters didn't seem to know there is great diversity in the community, from third-generation Palestinians in Livonia, to immigrant Lebanese, Palestinians, and Yemenites in the south and east ends of Dearborn. Hell, they didn't know that Iranians are Persians and not Arabs. And contrary to popular belief, we are not all Muslims.

The Detroit press overall is more sensitive to the community, because of our hard work over the years. Groups such as the ADC met with editorial boards to discuss issues and raise our objections about Arab stereotyping. However, the U.S. coverage of the war was very problematic. The President of the United States made Saddam Hussein larger than life by comparing him to Hitler. It didn't surprise me when more racism surfaced. It was predictable. Whenever there is a Middle East crisis abroad, somehow our community pays for it at home. I saw stickers saying, "I'd fly 10,000 mile to smoke a camel." A bedouin man dressed in traditional garb with the caption below it, "Make my day… I want to kill a Shiitthead (Shiite)." Children came home from school asking, "Mom, am I bad because I'm Arab?"

One FBI agent who came to the ADC office, Michael, came to pick up some equipment used to track down someone who was making threatening phone calls. I threw a pencil at him because I was angry that the FBI interrogated people in the community to see if they knew anything about terrorism. Congressman John Conyers Jr. (D-MI), a senior member of the Judiciary Committee, criticized the FBI for targeting 200 Arab-American business and community leaders as possible sources of information about terrorist activity simply on the basis of Arab ethnicity. They asked, "What are your political beliefs?" and "Do you know of any plans to destroy the Federal Building?" They interrogated my sister.

Overall, the war situation was taxing. Mostly the press did what the U.S. government wanted it to do, and only reported what this country wanted reported. It was either that or no instantaneous pictures beamed around the world. This coverage was different from Vietnam, because this was a "feel good" war. Flags were brought out, families were interviewed. The last thing I wanted to do was wave the American flag when so many innocent lives were destroyed. I felt I lived in a country where the state dictated what would and would not be seen. Reporters used words like collateral damage and many people convinced themselves it was a bloodless war. America would be victorious, and no one would see maimed bodies charred in an inferno.

During the midst of the Gulf War, Bob David, a U.S. Congressman from Michigan, made an anti-Iraqi joke at a Republican fundraiser: "What's the difference between catfish and Iraqi women?" The answer: "One is a fish and the other has whiskers and smells bad." Jessica Daher, my ADC co-worker, and I were angry and vowed we would get even. We decided to help Congressman David understand the difference between women and catfish. Jessica called an Arab fish market and the owner donated 15 pounds of catfish. We sent out a press release and the following day held a press conference at the Federal Building. The photographers wanted a picture of us with the crate of fish. The slimy fish kept slipping through my fingers until I used some newspapers as a buffer. The story got on the wire services and later I heard Sam Nunn and the heavyweights on the Hill got a big chuckle out of the story.

After the war ended in just 40 days, it didn't take long for the patriotic attitude to disappear as well. Yet our community continues to have fundraisers for Iraqi casualties. I remember seeing a Chaldean friend, who, for the first time, felt ashamed to be an American. My friend still worries that someday the U.S. will renew its war against Iraq. He said he wasn't worried about himself, but about those who couldn't fend for themselves. I remember thinking if there is a crisis in Palestine, Lebanon, Iraq, or any other Arab country, we will speak out as Americans committed to ending bigotry and racism.

Abyss

DORIS SAFIE

1.

New Hampshire flies
are so stupid
they sit on your
> plate
> hand
> nose
just asking for trouble.

Like the words on a T-shirt I saw
cresting across the pectorals and deltoids
of a strutting skinhead
they shout
> No Brains, No Headaches!

As if that weren't enough
they buzz in stereo
in case you don't get the message.

Deadly they rattle at windows
bang at walls
fuzzing nostalgia with hope.

2.

Once on a yellow island
when immortality was still true
I gathered shiny black pebbles

that lay on the beach where we lay
and offered them to you,
you of the shining black eyes.

They're goat droppings, you fool!
Throw them in the water!
Wash your hands! They're dirty!

As I stood wondering at this change in you
that was no change but truth hidden
at what spies and torturers call the Third Level
you tossed them into the blue blue sea
and for a moment I saw the impossible,
a fourth primary color.

3.

Picture a stand of five young birches
lit by the singular light of winter-becoming-spring
and encrusted with ice,
weighed down by their own glory.

Imagine talking to them, loving them,
using words meant to drive you crazy with lust:
>   *ebullition*
>   *leek*
>   *cerulean*
>   *comma*
and *scythe* and

the Arabic *silsila*
a chain, a link
with the past so you know

who you were
so you know who you are.

4.

Say you'd been watched
and the niddering voices at dinner
take you down to the Third Level
where goat droppings in the sea
and dead flies on the sill
pulse with new color
and come up the color of acid.
Now she's talking to trees!
Imagine that! Dreamer!
Majnooni! Crazy girl!

You think this is how it isn't,
that words are just rumors
looking for spaces to fit into,
that suspicion thrives
among miscellaneous people. You think
there's no hope for the human race. In moonlight

I have two shadows,
one behind and one in front.
I can smell the breath of paradise.
I know there are people
who don't deserve their children.
But if I don't celebrate them
I must die.

Two Women Drinking Coffee

LAILA HALABY

They sit in jeans and drink their coffee, black
As kohel on their eyes. They pour their tales
Of broken romance through a sieve: the words,
While cardamom in flavor, are in English.
Today they've met outside of a café;
Their work is done and each is going home.
It's here they punctuate each other's day
With stories, lively jokes, and cigarettes.
The mood is soft, the laughter not so strong.
The talk is dominated by their thoughts
Of home, to which there's no return: like love
That's lost and leaves a stinging sadness there
To bite the heart without a kind of warning.
The one who's lost most recently then sighs.
Her hands are silent, her head turned away
As she speaks in words with orange blossom scent:
The angel I believed was always here
Has flown to heaven and I now must cope
Alone with love that's in a different tongue
I understand too well to misinterpret.

In Search of Home

CAROL HADDAD

The recurring nightmare: my ten-year-old self walking down our sterile suburban Detroit street, lined with Malvina Reynolds' "little boxes." I cannot distinguish my family house from the others on my return trip from the corner drugstore! Unable to find my home, I am lost in a hostile world of neighbors who don't speak to us. I walk with eyes straight ahead, heart racing. Morning arrives, and the sounds of summer dance in through my open window, ending the nightmare. I am home again.

Little did I know then that my search for home would be a lifelong quest. Each time I left the security of my family house, I experienced the oppression of being darker and different. Sometimes I did not know whether people stared at my family in public because of our exotic good looks and the fashionable clothes that my mother sewed for us, or because they considered us "niggers"— a barb once hurled at me in an argument with a Polish-American boy who lived on my block. When in 1955 we first moved into this lower-middle-class Irish-German-Polish neighborhood, the same boy's mother inquired of my mother, "Is your husband Negro?" after seeing him, tanned and shirtless, mowing the front lawn one day.

Irish- and German-American kids on our block taunted us for "eating leaves" as we picked them young and tender from a nearby grapevine in early summer. Knowing we would soon feast on this delicacy that Mom would stuff and roll with fresh ground lamb, rice, spices, and lemon did not erase the hurt of ignorant insults. And the teasing I experienced from these same parochial schoolmates for being a "hairy ape" was enough to entice me to endure the torturous process of bleaching my "moustache" and forearm hair with a burning solution of hydrogen peroxide mixed with ammonia. My skin developed a sore rash each time but the resulting blond hair was worth the pain.

Although my parents were U.S.-born of immigrant parents, they retained and took pride in their culture. Each summer we visited our long-distance grandmothers, cousins, aunts, and uncles, and felt a sense of community and belonging as we attended *haflis* (picnics) sponsored by the Melkite Catholic church. At home my parents frequently threw large dinner parties, replete with Arabic food, music, and dancing. Often relatives or friends from the Middle East visited, and I learned from the long discussions about the theology and politics that my father was so fond of.

As the 1960s rolled in, I realized that despite the prejudice we faced, we had enough white-skin privilege to live in a neighborhood where black families would never have been allowed. Although my darkly-tanned family was once refused restaurant service in a resort town in the *White* Mountains of New Hampshire, I learned that this was a daily occurrence for African-American people. In our own white suburb of Detroit, residents armed themselves with rifles during the 1967 riot, vowing to "kill any niggers" who tried to set foot in our neighborhood.

Outrage over those incidents was one strand in my growing political consciousness. My parents instilled in us a sense of the importance of working for social justice, and this was another strand. Once at university, I found myself drawn into a peer group of countercultural musicians and artists, a public interest research group, and the burgeoning women's movement. And of course, I took part in peaceful demonstrations opposing the Vietnam War.

Arab issues did not surface in any visible way for me again until 1973, when my housemate's Jewish and staunchly pro-Israel boyfriend challenged me to frequent debates about the Arab-Israeli conflict. I did not know much about the subject, and began reading. The more I read, the more outraged I became. The injustice perpetrated upon the Palestinian people and the seeming indifference of the world toward their plight was shameful. Their displacement from their homeland and the attempts of the Israeli government to eradicate a culture and a people seemed a modern-day replica of the United States Cavalry's treatment of Native Americans. The more conscious I became of events in the Middle East and the role of the U.S. government in shaping them, the more I found myself in a state of anger and depression. The efficacy I had experienced during the anti-war years slipped into a sense of powerlessness. How could one be aware of these issues and feel otherwise? It seemed that our government and media colluded to keep negative information about Israeli actions out of the news, and to place stories about Arab "terrorists" in the headlines. The Johnson administration's hush-up of Israel's bombing of the U.S.S. Liberty in which thirty-four American navymen died is only one example many.*

Finally, at the 1981 National Women's Studies Association (NWSA) Conference in Storrs, Connecticut, I met my first Arab-American feminists, and I took several important steps toward finding home. During an exercise in which we divided ourselves into groups of "women of color" and "white" women, I went to the white women's workshop. When I later encountered one of the Arab-American women, she asked me why I had not attended the women of color group. Somehow, despite all the racism we Arab-Americans experienced, I had failed to regard myself as having a legitimate claim to that identity. In the communities in which I had lived, races were primarily black or white. I had not yet been exposed to the full spectrum of the rainbow—African, Latina, Asian-Pacific Islander, and Native American.

I took several more steps toward home in 1982, when Israel invaded Lebanon. Anger, outrage, and powerlessness came pouring out. The noticeable silence from the left, and from feminist and lesbian communities, compounded these feelings. Approximately one week after the invasion had begun, I found myself at another conference of the NWSA. The Third World Caucus brought forth a resolution condemning the invasion. We were not prepared for the hostility and parliamentary maneuvering we would encounter from a handful of Zionist attendees, and the resolution was watered down and effectively defeated. Not all was lost, however, for I had earlier been granted a spot on a panel featuring some of the most prominent women of color in women's studies circles.**

The speech that I gave, "Arab-Americans: The Forgotten Minority in Feminist Circles," received acclaim and some criticism.

* The story of this bombing attack is documented in a book written by a former ship's officer who was on board at the time. See James M. Ennes, *Assault on the Liberty: The True Story of the Israeli Attack on an American Intelligence Ship* (New York: Random House, 1979).

** The other panelists were: Chela Sandoval, Carol Lee Sanchez, Rosa-Maria Villafane-Sisolak, bell hooks, Nellie Wong, and Gloria Anzaldúa.

In a subsequent report on the conference featured in the October 1982 issue of *off our backs*, writer Jeanne Barkey singled out my presentation for critical editorial comments. She also misidentified me as another Arab-American who had also spoken at the conference. As a ten-year reader and supporter of *oob*, I complained and extracted an editorial apology, which included printing my speech, a copy of June Jordan's poem "Apologies to All the People in Lebanon," and a preliminary statement of purpose for the Feminist Arab-American Network (FAN).* Out of the isolation we had experienced was born a new organization that we could relate to as feminists and as Arabs. Our statement of purpose discussed the need for us to increase public awareness of issues affecting our lives, to work toward eliminating negative stereotypes of Arabs, to work in coalition with women in Arab countries, and to support each other. Part of the statement read:

There is a critical need for Arab-American feminists to be visible in the feminist community. The U.S. feminist movement exists within, and has rarely challenged, a larger American culture which has historically and systematically suppressed information, news and research about the Arab world and Arab-American culture from an Arab perspective. The result is the portrayal of Arabs in negatively stereotypical ways, without regard for the wide range of cultures, religions, classes and political affiliations in the twenty-one Arab states.

Similarly, Arab-American feminists need to work within our Arab-American communities and institutions to eliminate sex-based prejudices and discrimination and to promote discussions of social, political, economic, and cultural issues from a feminist perspective in Arab thought and debate.

FAN had more than enough issues to respond to. *Ms.* Magazine published an article entitled: "Anti-Semitism in the Women's Movement," which insulted Arabs and progressive Jewish and non-Jewish feminists by suggesting that critics of Zionism and Israeli aggression are "anti-Semitic,"** a curious term to level at Jews and Arabs, who are, in fact, all Semites. Although none of the critical letters sent to *Ms.* by FAN members were printed, some letters from non-Arabs

* These appeared in the March 1983 issue of *off our backs*.

** This article, authored by Letty Cottin Pogrebin, appeared in the June 1982 issue of *Ms.*

were published. We were outraged, but not surprised. It was common practice for Arab feminists to be denied a public forum, or to be featured in an article or panel discussion only when the Arab viewpoint was "balanced" by a Jewish one.* We decided such erasure would not take place at the 1983 NWSA Conference, to which we came well organized and well represented. Azizah al-Hibri, founder and former editor of *Hypatia: A Journal of Feminist Philosophy* and one of the original members of the FAN collective, delivered an address entitled "Unveiling the Hidden Face of Racism: The Plight of Arab-Americans" at the plenary session on racism and anti-Semitism in the women's movement. We conducted two conference workshops as well, and continued this work at events and in publications across the country. The more we spoke and published, the more feminist publishers and conference organizers

---

* Even non-Arab academics and artists who publicly spoke out on behalf of Arab interests faced severe consequences. For example, the African-American poet and writer June Jordan was removed as an op-ed writer for the *New York Times* following the *Village Voice's* publication on July 20, 1982 of her poem "Apologies to All the People in Lebanon," in which she reacted to U.S. complicity in the Israeli invasion of Lebanon. She was also jeered by some feminists at a poetry reading she delivered at the 1983 National Women's Music Festival. British actress Vanessa Redgrave experienced the 1982 cancellation of her contract and scheduled appearance with the Boston Symphony Orchestra to narrate *Oedipus Rex,* as well as a near decade-long boycott of her work by U.S. producers and directors because of her outspoken support for the Palestinian cause. Professor Elizabeth Fernea was attacked by the Anti-Defamation League of B'nai B'rith for a 1981 film she made (*Women Under Siege*) on the lives of Palestinian women living in the Rashidiya refugee camp. Although the film was a finalist in the 1984 American Film Festival, the B'nai B'rith denounced it and demanded that the National Endowment for the Humanities withdraw the funding it had granted to her. Fernea was not the only American academic to incur the wrath of the B'nai B'rith; in 1983 the New England Regional Office of the Anti-Defamation League compiled and sent a list of "anti-Israel, pro-Arab" academics and organizations to student leaders on American campuses. See Karen J. Winkler, "Political tensions of Arab-Israel conflict put pressure on scholars who study Middle East," *Chronicle of Higher Education,* March 27, 1983, 5; and Paul Findley, *They Dare to Speak Out* (Westport, CT: Lawrence Hill, 1985).

sought our viewpoints. Although scathing attacks and even threats continued, our voices began to be heard—and affirmed.

Ultimately, we lacked funding to bring members together for a meeting and to obtain clerical support, and FAN withered on the grapevine. When it began, FAN occupied a lonely spot on the feminist horizon. Now there are many organizations of Arab women,* and Arab voices and perspectives have begun to be represented in the mainstream women's community; for example, Hanan Ashrawi spoke at a 1992 National Organization for Women (NOW) conference. Still, FAN served a critical need for women who sought to connect their feminism with their Arabness, and for this reason, it has been revived.** It was through FAN that I found home, and it is my hope that its renewed presence will help Arab sisters find the strength of spirit to continue their long journeys.

---

* These include: The Union of Palestinian Women's Associations in North America, The Institute for Arab Women's Studies, and the Association for Middle East Women's Studies. Addresses for these organizations appear at the back of this book.

** For more information, write to FAN at P.O. Box 38-1843, Cambridge, MA 02238.

Hairless In Gaza
(or plucking the lines of gender difference)

HODA M. ZAKI

Sweaty thighs and knees
on a hot and sticky day.
Numbing pain endured.

But we bear it.
The price of sugar goes up.
But sugar and lemon will be cooked
to make a glue to bind all women.

Bikini lines were known long ago here
although we never wore them.
"Do your arms too" they urge
"Inti aiza tibi zay el ragel?"*

Each of us has a recipe she touts as a success:
Use molasses instead of sugar
Aspirin in lieu of lemon
And leave the water out.

When did it begin?
With the Ancients? Did Nefertiti
grimace too on a hot, cloudless day?

---

* "Do you want to be like a man?"

We are amused at the national debate
in the style sections of the *Post* and *Times*.
To wax or not, to shave or to use the new
Israeli Epilady that takes the hair out by the roots.
See, we say, how the Israelis exploit our culture.
And using it, I bend over. It circles my legs and
I hear its sound and I remember Uzis and cluster bombs.

After it is over
Satin limbs gleam softly
Our onoutha * asserted
And we are ready for anything.

* femininity

Blood

NAOMI SHIHAB NYE

"A true Arab knows how to catch a fly in his hands,"
my father would say. And he'd prove it,
cupping the buzzer instantly
while the host with the swatter stared.

In the spring our palms peeled like snakes.
True Arabs believed watermelon could heal fifty ways.
I changed these to fit the occasion.

Years before, a girl knocked,
wanted to see the Arab.
I said we didn't have one.
After that, my father told me who he was,
"Shihab"—"shooting star"—
a good name, borrowed from the sky.
Once I said, "When we die, we give it back?"
He said that's what a true Arab would say.

Today the headlines clot in my blood.
A little Palestinian dangles a toy truck on the front page.
Homeless fig, this tragedy with a terrible root
is too big for us. What flag can we wave?
I wave the flag of stone and seed,
table mat stitched in blue.

I call my father, we talk around the news.
It is too much for him,
neither of his two languages can reach it.

I drive into the country to find sheep, cows,
to plead with the air:
Who calls anyone *civilized*?
Where can the crying heart graze?
What does a true Arab do now?

VI

Mint

Moving Beyond Survival: Celebrating Who We Are

~~~~~~~~~~

Mint

When I bite into a mouthful of well-made tabouleh with a strong mint flavor, I am flooded with thoughts of my grandmother. That sharp mint flavor adds so much to many Arabic dishes, gives so much distinction to particular foods. Mint is a common, tenacious plant that grows wild in the Arab world and in North America, and it can't be held down. Prune mint—a large quantity will grow back. Uproot it—some of it will manage to keep a root-hold and return. Put some in water—new roots come forth and you can plant it almost anywhere and it will flourish.

↫ Tabouleh Salad ↬

1 cup cracked wheat, known as bulger. Fine bulger is best
2 large bunches parsley
4 tomatoes
a few radishes
cucumber
1 bunch mint
garlic
1 bunch scallions (green onion)
1 or 2 lemons
1 c. olive oil
salt and pepper to taste.

Fill bottom of bowl with wheat. Soak with hot water until soft, drain. Chop parsley, scallions, and mint fine. Chop tomatoes, radishes, and cucumbers into chunks. Mix together all of the above and add salt and pepper.

Either squeeze the juice out of the lemons, or microwave lemon halves and remove seeds, using juice and pulp (the microwave makes the whole inside of the lemon come out in one piece). Mix in lemon, crushed garlic, oil. Taste. Adjust for salt, lemon, or oil.

↫ Source: Anne Mamary, and from various family members.

ABC/ابت

PAULINE KALDAS

Child, open your black eyes
follow your brown skin to this sound خ —
      deep from your throat
            bring it out like a cough

    ع — in the center below your heart
      pull to a tone like a cymbal

as your grandparents choked their last
        Arabic signature   bought
you a ticket to America

   ح — walk in a desert
           till your thirst becomes sand

   ه — walk longer till the air feels of water

like your great-grandmother's face melting into the sweat
    from her hand pushing the dough   down   to rise

    ق — begin to swallow your tongue

your orphan great-grandfather died
taking in a breath   rubbing
    the pain in his arm   ث —

hold your tongue in your teeth
        snatch the air

Five Steps To Creating Culture

JOANNA KADI

I perch on a chair in her small kitchen and watch my grandmother make laban. She pours milk into a pot, and although she does not measure it, she knows exactly how much to put in. Slowly she brings the milk to a boil and I smell it as it warms. Once the milk boils, she takes it off the stove and sets it on a wooden board. After a few minutes, Gram puts in her little finger and counts to ten. That means it has cooled the right amount. I never saw her put her finger in before just enough time had passed. Then she stirs in the laban from the previous batch; that is, she adds the culture. She wraps the bowl carefully in several towels and leaves it to sit overnight.

There are many places Arabs can go to find our cultural achievements—bookstores, museums, art galleries, music halls. We can also stay home. At home we make Arabic foods, we hear traditional rhythms played on durbeckes, we tell jokes that reflect Arab humor. All of that is our culture surrounding and sustaining us. Our culture is common, easily recognizable, and re-created daily. That common-ness and daily-ness does not take away from its power, beauty, and historical meaning.

Our foremothers were often the ones who handed on our culture; mothers, grandmothers, and aunts who carried out daily tasks in the kitchen, who passed on baking rituals and cooking rituals and singing rituals and dancing rituals and storytelling rituals. Most of their cultural achievements are not recorded in any tangible form. But those achievements are every bit as important as books and pieces of art, they carry as much wisdom, sustenance, beauty, and meaning.

When I pondered our grandmothers' activities I realized we have not often noticed them. They are not what springs to mind when we think of cultural achievements. There may be several reasons for this; let me name two that I think are important. First, our community has not always noticed or affirmed women and the things we do. Second, these parts of our culture are so common and so present that we tend to overlook them. When you watch someone make laban once a week for years and years, you may not notice the importance of what they are doing.

I did not sit in that kitchen smelling warm milk and think to myself: My grandmother is engaged as a cultural worker. But that is what she was. And since I am now a cultural worker, in a different medium, I believe there is much meaning for me in analyzing my grandmother's process of creating.

My grandmother lived with her eldest daughter, my aunt, in a small house around the corner from me. Another aunt and uncle and group of cousins lived a few blocks away. We were the only Lebanese, the only Arabs, in our white, working-class neighborhood. Sometimes our neighbors ignored this fact, sometimes they emphasized it in racist, cruel, and hurtful ways. As a child this confused me, but then so did many other things.

One point of my confusion had to do with what it meant to have culture. Growing up, my only understanding of culture was what white, middle- and upper-class people achieved and did. I could not translate that understanding to my identity as Arab and as working-class. So, although my family listened to Arab music, danced Arab folk dances, and ate Arab food, I did not perceive any of this as culture. Perhaps if we had not been so isolated from a larger Arab community things would have been different. But as it was, the people around us, and society generally, perceived our music and our food on good days as a series of weird, isolated, and exotic behaviors that for some reason my family engaged in. On bad days they perceived it as disgusting as well as weird.

It is only now with the benefit of hindsight that I understand I grew up surrounded by Arab culture. It is only now that I understand what happened in my grandmother's kitchen. It is only now that I perceive the connection between what I do as a cultural worker and what my grandmother did when she made laban.

Gram is making laban. As is always the case when she cooks and bakes, there is no recipe. No directions, no reminders. Still, she knows exactly what to do. The knowledge is inside her. She carries this important knowledge of how to sustain family. She learned it in the hills of Lebanon; now she repeats those same acts, carries out those same steps. It comes from within. It has been passed down from so many generations back that I cannot conceive of our numbers. She knows how to create things that allow her loved ones not only to survive, but to flourish.

I am a cultural worker. I want to create things that allow my loved ones not only to survive but to flourish. But there is a big, big difference between my grandmother and I. The knowledge is inside her; the recipe she needs has been handed down, one generation to the next. She is secure in the knowledge of what to do. I am not. I am foraging for a recipe, a tradition, one that originated in the east and will serve me well in the west. I have no previous generations to tell me which stories to write and how and why. So I am floundering, looking for recipes that will serve us, looking for recipes that let people know the place from which we came and the place where we are now, trying to mix the old and the new, never an easy task. I'm trying to create, I'm trying to sustain my family.

For Gram, making laban is easy. Each step is ingrained in body memory. Pour the milk into the pot. A measuring cup is not necessary. You will know how much you need. Bring the milk to a boil, slowly. You cannot rush these things. Let it cool. You will know when it has cooled because you will be able to place your little finger into the milk and count to ten. That's when you add the laban from the previous batch; that's when you add the culture. Wrap carefully in towels. Let sit overnight. Eat.

This ritual happened so many times that simply thinking about it brings back smells and colors and a cozy feeling of being home. I am sitting, feet drawn up, hands hugging knees, on one of the vinyl chairs in Gram's kitchen. The rain beats soothingly on the window. We are comfortably silent together, and then we talk. The kitchen smells faintly of my Aunt Rose's cigarettes. Also of coffee, and Gram's own aroma of sweat, plain soap, and hard work. I am four years old, eight, fifteen. I know her kitchen as well as I know the one at my house.

Making Laban/Writing Stories

Step I. Heat the milk and let it reach the boiling point. Reach the boiling point. I have reached the boiling point many times. I know about Lebanon's suffering, Palestine's dispossession, Iraq's devastation. I know how many times I have been called names, how many Arabs have been beaten on American streets. I know how imperialism and colonialism ruptured the Arab world, carved it up, broke it down, forced us to leave. Now we live here where we are called names as we walk down the street. Where our restaurants are burned down. Where the FBI harasses us. Where our mosques are vandalized. All of this knowledge is what leads me to the boiling point. It makes me angry. And I think it is good for a cultural worker to be angry, not with the kind of anger that poisons our insides and drives people away, but with the kind of anger that gives us momentum and courage, pushes us forward, the righteous anger that allows us to say no, to fight back, to get out of bed on days when the pain is overwhelming.

Step II. Check to see if the milk has cooled enough. When you can keep your finger in the milk for ten seconds you will know it's the right time. The knowledge resides in the bone, in the body. The knowledge of which story to tell and when to tell it resides in the bone, in the body. There's an internal temperature gauge. It's always better to wait until the temperature has fallen before I sit down, pen in hand, use these fingers, just as Gram used hers. I wait to write, wait until the time is right, until anger is not the most overwhelming emotion. The time is right only when thoughtful reflection, love and humor catch up with anger so that they all mix together. When we are at the boiling point it is not the best time to make stories. Wait until the temperature has fallen.

Step III. Add the culture and stir. Take the laban left over from the previous batch and add it to the milk that has cooled. This culture travelled a very long way. It left a trail from the mountains of Lebanon. Somehow it survived a passage across the ocean and several transplants in a cold new country. It survives and it continues to offer sustenance and nourishment. It gives, over and over again.

Add the culture and stir. To be a cultural worker is to give life, to give back to the community, to tell our stories, to pass on recipes, to tell us who we are, to mark a trail that curves east to west to east to west. To be a cultural worker means to give life, to offer sustenance and nourishment, to give, over and over again.

To be a cultural worker carries many responsibilities. Add the culture at the right moment. Make sure the culture is grounded in the community, that it does not exist in an individual void. Add the culture in the hope that it gives something back to all of us, whether resistance, laughter, grief, celebration, or pride. That is what the cultural worker must offer.

Step IV. Wrap carefully in towels and let sit overnight. Only then does the milk become laban. Only then does the culture do its work.

As a cultural worker it matters how I do things. It's critical that I treat the work carefully, wrap it well, protect it, keep the warmth in. The conditions must be right for growing. If the warmth is there, and the timing is right, and if this fragile entity has been carefully encircled with protective wrapping, then this batch will sustain many people.

I need to be careful about every batch. There is power in the written word and power in the published word. Who am I speaking for? What are my underlying beliefs? Who am I accountable to? Whose stories get told and whose do not? Do I tell the stories of Arabs who have made it in the white man's world, or do I tell stories about Arabs who are single mothers on welfare, or gay men dying of AIDS, or young drug addicts on the street, or old people whose hearts are breaking of loneliness? Whose stories are necessary to us? Whose stories get told?

Let the words sit, let the stories be. Everything of importance needs time to grow, and that includes culture. Words need to be left alone so that they settle properly, so that certain things can come to the surface and others go deep. Allow time to settle, to see if the words are right, to see if they make sense. Re-read the words.

Examine them carefully. Make sure they are the best to serve at this moment in time.

Step V. Eat. I returned to my grandmother's house the day after she made laban because I love eating fresh laban. I love its cool, slippery texture, its strong, thick taste. It slides gently down my throat. I know my grandmother made it not out of a sense of duty but with love and tenderness. Her love and her tenderness added so much. "Eat," she said to me, and I did. Huge quantities of laban, grapeleaves, kibbeh, tabouleh, and all the other wonderful things she made.

"Eat," she said to me, and what she meant was, Let me sustain you, let me nurture you, let me help you not only to survive but to flourish, you are my loved one and I want to give this to you. "Eat," she said to me, because it was absolutely essential for my growth and development that I did.

I am a cultural worker. I write stories and essays. Each one comes with a different taste and texture, and I want you to feel each one and taste each one, to let the words slide into bodies, to know with certainty that my words are written not out of a sense of duty, but with love and tenderness, anger and passion.

Eat, I say to my loved ones, and I hope you will, huge quantities of laughter and tears and hope and grief and anger and healing. Quantities of words that I have written, that others have written with the same amount of love and tenderness, anger and passion. Eat, I say to my loved ones, and what I mean is, Let me sustain you, let me nurture you, let me help you not only to survive but to flourish, I want to give this to you. Eat, I say to my loved ones, and what I mean is, Culture is absolutely essential for our growth and development. As necessary as food. As critical as water. As mandatory as air. As indispensable as sunlight and moonlight.

We have always known this. We have always sustained ourselves, through hard times and through good times, with our jokes, our stories, our laughter, our food, our music, our art. We have woven these things into our everyday life. They may have become common activities, they may be so much of our daily life that sometimes we fail to notice them. But their common-ness and daily-ness does not take away from their power, their historical meaning, and their beauty. We owe it to ourselves, our ancestors, and the ones who come after us to celebrate our wonderful culture, whether we find it in the laban we eat or the stories we read.

Camel Girl

EILEEN KAADY

Riding leisurely
swaying and singing loudly
between the humps of my Camel Girl.
She is my joy, my companion, my help-mate.
I daily pamper her, and groom her
copper tone fur.
My body flows,
responsive to her lumbering movements.
I see all, from my perch on her rounded back.

The muffled jangling from the saddle bag
reveal bronze and silver utensils, and a
copper drinking cup.

In a special pouch are my
endeared feathers, stones, shells and
small worn-smooth wooden pieces.
For my symphonies with river and wind
I carry bells and derbeke.

I have taken great care in planning for my comfort,
and for welcomed guests on my journey:
blanket rolls, pillows, candles,
orange blossom water and gentle soaps,
herbs for soothing the organs.

My diet is bread, almonds,
pomegranates, dates and figs,
assorted cheeses and olives,
spring water.
I am grateful to discover fresh fruit and
vegetables and mint and breads
along the way.

When I lay down under the
obsidian desert sky
my reflection in the firelight has been
captured in the bright, loyal eyes
of Camel Girl.
We breathe the immense night into our new day.

New Country Daughter © L.A. Hyder

Artist

HAPPY/L. A. HYDER

I believe I always wanted to be an artist, even before I knew the words for it. Sometimes I wonder how I kept, or even found, that image of myself. Growing up in my working-class, ethnically Eastern European and Mediterranean neighborhood did not offer that option. At the age of forty-six, known as an artist and director of an arts organization of my own making, I am grateful I did.

My years in college (as an English major) coincided with the realization of pop art and psychedelic art. Both were easy to grasp, concerned with the present moment, often political, and exciting to see. "Finding" women artists gave me another sense of my possibilities as an artist and fostered my feminist streak even before I could recognize or articulate it. The mystique of making art surrounded me as the accessibility of pop art made my mouth water.

I moved to San Francisco in 1969 and circumstances were such that within a year I had a 35 millimeter camera in my hands—instantly calling myself a photographer and jumping into it. Printing a picture from film I had taken was the most exciting thing I could imagine.

Photography allows me to record what I see and have it come alive in the richness of black and white. My sense of a good photograph is based on those which first excited me. They came from *Life* magazine and such artists as Margaret Bourke-White and Eugene Smith, both masters at their craft and innovators in photography.

I combined my art with my emerging activism in the 1980s as a founding member of Vida Gallery in the San Francisco Women's Building and became part of a world populated with feminist activists. Vida Gallery featured the work of international women artists from 1981 to 1986; not a radical concept although often taken as one.

It was during these years I first began using art to express my Arabness. It opened another part of myself as I used my strongest link: my own face in the mirror. My photograph, "New Country Daughter/Lebanese American," came in response to a Vida exhibition titled "Women of Color and Vision." The many doors in my apartment hallway and the fact that my upbringing held both old country and new country ways is where I got the idea for this photograph. I was in a new apartment, part of an art collective, coming out as a lesbian, stepping into a new world and surrounded by possibilities.

Meeting Arab-American women who have seen this photograph and who tell me how exciting it was to find this image *of us* is one of my highest moments as an artist. It is now a part of a set of postcards I produced—a perfect, affordable way to bring our images into the world. Although "New Country Daughter" has come to symbolize the experience of many of us, as I took the two photographs that make up the image I was thinking specifically about myself.

Making art that speaks to my heritage, my background, and my political and social ideals has become an important and necessary way to use my gift.

My work as artist and activist has continued. In 1989, I produced the exhibition "Dynamics of Color: Works by Lesbian Artists on Racism." It accompanied a conference addressing racism in the lesbian community where I spoke about anti-Arab racism. While the exhibition had many functions, for me the most important were including lesbian artists from racially diverse backgrounds and showing our activism in the struggle to end racism. The inclusion of my own three-dimensional box construction "Tadamun/Solidarity, dedicated to my Lebanese and Palestinian sisters," made Arabs visible in this struggle.

Shortly after this experience, I founded LVA: Lesbian Visual Artists, a promotional and networking organization. Its purpose is to make lesbian artists and imagery more visible. In founding LVA, I used the same premise as in my art. It is important for our identities to be seen clearly. Images of lesbians seen in the papers are generally distorted or sensationalized...and are most often not made by lesbians. The same, it seems, is true of images of Arabs worldwide. We are either romantiziced or villainized.

Making art is not easy. There are no ways to learn how to make a powerful image, only to gain technique. As a self-taught artist, I must overcome the unease of self-doubt whenever I try something new. I am at my strongest when I embrace the throes of creative energy. This energy comes when I am most firmly rooted in my self and remember there are no rules that say who can and who cannot be an artist.

Today I can connect my evolution as a feminist, activist, and artist. Whatever the situation, I find it imperative to say I am Arab in the same breath I say I am lesbian and all of the above.

A Blessing

ADELE NE JAME

for my daughter

Silence was Thoreau's proof against cynicism.

—William Bronk

Outside your window the morning air is a whirl
of blossoms and rain as if working furiously
towards some gladness—and you asleep
as I watch, working out some dream
of your life—now where it is all a beginning,
paused like a diver on the highboard, balancing
all her weight on her toes, heart like a furnace
that moment before the fall into the unforgettable blue.

And what counterstatement can survive
the body's frenetic demands? At your waking
I might say, the moon comes and goes—
or mention the black angel whose wings are velvet
and always widespread—or offer instead
the story of my Father's sister, eighty years ago
a child herself, who after losing
ten brothers and sisters to the great war,
walked across the blazing desert alone
from Damascus to Beirut. Her whirling robes
like her heart, a weapon against that ruined world.

But on a morning like this when the light
gathers around you with inexpressible
grace and privacy,
the words seem somehow indecorous—
so I offer instead an unspoken blessing,
the heart's caesura, and yield again
to love's last work, its silent implosion.

Armenian/Lesbian:

Telling Our Stories

ZABELLE

Once there was and was not

The trouble with writing as an Armenian lesbian is that one so often feels like an *odar*, without community: a woman with no name. And as the poet Adrienne Rich has said, "Whatever is unnamed...undepicted in images...misnamed as something else will become not merely unspoken, but unspeakable." I begin this naming by acknowledging my debt to her and to two peoples—Armenians and lesbians—whose passion for survival against the odds is a constant inspiration.

I am deeply aware of the astonishing diversity of lesbian experience, as varied as a carpet of many glowing colors. Yet while the lives of Armenian lesbians are part of this overall design, we share with other Armenians the cultural invisibility of a small group in diaspora. Where local settlements are small, Armenian lesbians are few. Other women may be quite willing to learn about our traditions, but we must go elsewhere for a sense of ethnic community. This is one way of being an *odar*, a foreigner.

The next question, of course, is: Where do Armenian lesbians go? Answer: Wherever other Armenian women go. We are not yet priests of the Armenian Apostolic Church (although I wonder about some of the saints—not to mention the old goddesses!). We do not, so far as I know, head Armenian political parties or major corporations. On the other hand, we *are* everywhere else: linking pinkies at Armenian dances; lining up for shish kebab and tabouleh at the church picnic; winning at tavloo. We attend Armenian concerts, readings, church services, day schools, and academic conferences. Some of us speak fluent Armenian and some do not, but we all know the stories of 1915. We march against genocide on April 24 and against gynocide when we take back the night.

Yet here again we are invisible, not as Armenians but as lesbians. If, as researchers estimate, one in ten U.S. residents is gay, then there may be as many as 25,000 of us in this country. One would scarcely believe it, however, considering the silence about our lives in Armenian circles.* True, we help to maintain that silence, but when the alternatives include family rejection, social ostracism or even physical violence, the choice to stay in the closet is not a pretty one. Once again we must go elsewhere for a sense of lesbian community. This is another and more ironic way of being an *odar*.

Despite all this, every so often our worlds converge. Several years ago I walked into a feminist bookstore in upstate New York and discovered a record album, *Tattoos*, by Sirani Avedis, an Armenian woman who at that time was writing jazz-influenced lesbian-feminist music. One song which spoke to me in particular, "Rainbow Woman," contained the following lyrics:

> You've been harnessed/but you're breaking the chain
> You come from a heritage of genocide and pain
> And you fought hard/when they told you you were wrong
> And even today you sing the gutsiest song...

Perhaps, as Avedis writes, we are "not as white as a Caucasian maiden/not as black as any Afro-American." Yet as "rainbow women," Armenian lesbians can negotiate colors and cultures on our own terms. Connecting with the music of current day artists like Avedi helps me feel less like an odar, as does remembering and re-creating traditional Armenian folktales.

* When this essay was first published in 1988, the figure of 25,000 was met with some skepticism in the Armenian-American press. In 1992, however, the Armenian General Benevolent Union estimated that one million Armenians were residing in the United States, with a quarter million in metropolitan Los Angeles alone (*AGBU News,* December 1992, 2, 8). Assuming that, nationally, about 700,000 are adults, 10 percent of that number yields an estimate of 70,000 gay Armenian-Americans, both male and female. Thus 35,000 is now a more likely figure for Armenian lesbians in the United States, including nearly 9,000 in Los Angeles.

Three apples fell from heaven

In the town of Oshagan, as late as 1913, it was said that once a young village woman married the Armenian king's daughter. This is how the story begins:

> There was and there wasn't, once upon a time there was an old woman who had one daughter. Since she was an only child, the old woman dressed her daughter in boys' clothes, so that she could play with the neighbors' children.
>
> Now one day the king's daughter got lost, and was found by the old woman's daughter, who took the princess to her mother, and said:
>
> "I have found this little child. Let us keep her."
>
> So the old woman kept the girl.*

Once the girl's identity becomes apparent, the old woman informs the king, who sends out a minister to fetch her, mounted on a magical mare named Lulizar. The old woman's daughter goes back with them, for the king has proclaimed that whoever finds the princess will be granted any request. Prompted by Lulizar herself, the young woman, still dressed as a boy, asks for the mare.

"Lulizar is worth my entire kingdom," says the king. "If I give her to you, I might as well give you my daughter too." And so he does.

Complications arise on the wedding night, when the princess, who after all had been living with the young woman prior to the marriage, "discovers" the sex of her new spouse. From then on the princess plots to get rid of her by having the young woman sent off on various dangerous quests, but each time the magical Lulizar helps her to succeed. Finally she is sent to recover a rosary from the "mother of the devs,"** who curses the unseen thief with an instant change of sex—a solution which satisfies the princess.

---

* Excerpted from "Tgha dardzogh akhchike" [The girl who changed into a boy], told by Avetis Nazarian; in *Armenian Folk-Tales and Fables*, trans. Charles Downing (London: Oxford University Press, 1972), 83.

** A dev is a supernatural being similar to a European ogre.

I believe it is time for a new telling of the story, one in which the women have names, the mother of the devs cures the princess of her homophobia, and Lulizar receives the freedom that is her just reward. Then everyone can live happily ever after.

Three apples fell from heaven: one for the teller, one for the listener, and one for those who heed the tale.

≈≈≈≈≈§≈≈≈§≈≈≈≈

Mint, Tomatoes, and the Grapevine

ANNE J. M. MAMARY

*MINT** *akin to OE gemynd mind; memory*—Delicious, fragrant mint, always spilling over the edges of the garden box, growing in the cracks of the back walk, up the side of the chipped cinder block garage. Cover it, cut it down—you can be sure tough tenacious mint, with roots deep beneath the cement will survive, redolent.

(mint) n. 1. Any of various plants of the genus Mentha.

Spearmint, peppermint, would you girls run out back and bring back two big hands full of mint?

(Mountain Mint—any of various aromatic North American plants of the genus Pycnanthemum, having clusters of small white or purplish flowers)

Wintergreen, Aunt Mary's living room is fragrant with bunches of fresh mint, tied together with ribbons, fluttering like summer wild flowers; she hangs them upside down to dry and we'll have green this winter, cool refreshing summer mint, dark inviting winter mint.

Many species are cultivated for their fragrant oil, used for flavoring.

Wash mint chop, rinse wheat, dice tomatoes, chop parsley, lemon juice (not too much, Jiddu doesn't much care for lemon juice—he's sour enough already), olive oil, scallions, radishes (our Mary's secret ingredient), more mint, always more mint (Is there enough mint? what do you think, einou?)

---

* *American Heritage Dictionary,* (Boston: Houghton Mifflin, 1982).

Characteristically having aromatic foliage and two-lipped flowers.

Mint plants speak to a place nearly forgotten, never forgotten, whispering two-lipped foliage, singing kiss of mint, I kiss her two lips, clusters of small purplish flowers, aromatic two-lipped flowers deliciously, delicately remind...

Mint brings on memories of an old woman. My Sittu died the spring before last. Minty, my memories of her. And her own memories—did I listen often enough? The daughter of Syrian immigrants, my grandmother did not learn English until she went to school. When she was fourteen her mother died, leaving Hannah, my Sittu, in charge of raising the younger children and protecting them from their violent, abusive father. Married at seventeen to my Jiddu, she soon had two sons and a husband not unlike her father. He worked in factories, drove trucks and later became a mechanic; she raised her three sons, the youngest coming seventeen years after the second. The middle child, my father, spent Saturdays at home scrubbing baseboards, beating throw rugs, dusting and scrubbing to ward off accusations of "dirty Syrian." He ate boxes of cookies to gain weight; his slenderness, she worried, would reflect poorly on her abilities as a mother. She also ironed shirts in a factory, took care of elderly parents, sisters' children, and anyone who needed a place to stay and a good hot meal.

At the funeral the priests talked about my grandmother as generous and devout. About how she welcomed them into her home and fed them well, and about what a good christian she was. Good daughter, good wife, good mother, good grandmother, good christian, good neighbor, good churchwoman. Under the watchful eyes of the painted saints looking out of gold framed portraits and through the jangle of their swinging incense burners, the priests prayed for her soul. Through the frankincense haze, I wondered about the memories these men had of my Sittu. They had made her into someone I never recognized—into a handmaid for their projects and needs. The priests' memories of my Sittu were not my memories of her. And I do not think she would have remembered herself that way either. In their righteous prayers for her soul, they missed the chance to recognize their own roles in killing—misnaming—Hannah. When the holy men closed the casket, chanting ashes-to-ashes and pleading for her soul, they missed the spiral of mint curling around the fingers of her strong gentle hand.

TOMATO Succulent hearty tomato, tickly stem of tomato, slurp up a whole red tomato. Juice running down chins, toss the seeds into the garden out back.

1. a plant, Lycopersicon esculentum widely cultivated...

Jiddu says he's trying to keep the garden like Hannah would have wanted; he planted twelve tomato plants this year, and 100 more came up, the garden a wild, uncultivated jungle of tomato vines,

2. The fruit of this plant.

cherry tomatoes, golden tomatoes, fava beans in tomato sauce bubbling, steamy red on Sittu's stove on a winter afternoon, grandchildren sneak a taste.

Edible, fleshy, usually red.

Plum tomatoes, vines heavy with round ripe tomatoes, a mouthful of tomato, warm from a summer vine, wet like a lover's blood, tomato in my blood, uncultivated fleshy memories red through my veins.

The food my Sittu prepared nourished me in so many ways. It is her food and her delight in cooking with the women in her life that link me to her and my Arab-American heritage. When I wonder if and how I can claim this connection, it is always to the food that I turn—to mint, tomato, parsley, grapevine leaves, apricot. Before the funeral my grandmother's sisters talked about their lives together. They remembered baking hundreds of dozens of cookies: anise cookies, the only vaguely sweet mamul filled with walnuts or pistachios, the sweetened messy shredded-wheat cookies, and baqlawa, which they swore was far superior to Greek baklava.

And they remembered how bright my grandmother was—how she read and thought carefully, even though she had only an eighth-grade "education." They talked about listening to news coverage of events in the Middle East so they could see if the few Arabic phrases they heard were "our Arabic." Their stories, their memories differed so much from the priests' that it is hard to recognize the same woman. The sisters' stories included my grandmother's voice weaving in and among their own voices. Sisters did not speak of sister as one who had been invented by and in the service of their needs—their stories growing wild around the potted versions the priests told at the funeral.

ARAB *   Part of me and a most distant "other" according to the lessons of my childhood, ancient mathematicians, terrorists,

waif

Depraved far-away people, my father pulled from line and frisked at JFK in the early 1970s in front of my mom and my brother and me by "security"—with his black beard and olive skin, he looked "threatening" (read Arab) to the guards.

homeless waif, dogie, stray, waifs and strays, ragamuffin, tatterdemalion, gamin, gamine, urchin, street urchin

In 1907 a congressman from Alabama declared, "I regard the Syrians and peoples from Asia minor as the most undesirable"** of immigrants. After the immigration of nearly 250,000 Arabs, U.S. immigration laws in the 1920s "lumped Arabs and Asians and Blacks and Jews and Latinos together as "undesirable races."'***

* *Roget's International Thesaurus,* fifth edition (New York: Thomas Y. Crowell, 1979).

** Elly Bulkin, "Hard Ground: Jewish Identity, Racism, and Anti-Semitism," in *Yours in Struggle: Three Feminist Perspectives on Anti-Semitism and Racism,* ed. Elly Bulkin, Barbara Smith, and Minnie Bruce Pratt (Ithaca: Firebrand Press, 1988), 203.

*** Bulkin, p. 204.

Arab, street Arab, mudlark, guttersnipe.

In the face of this anti-Arab sentiment, my family made a home in this country. This home was built with many things, including internalized hatred of Arab peoples along with the racist "relief" that we are not, in my grandfather's words, "as dark as black people." That is, his/our self-definition often came by denying and running from variously deep shades of olive skin and at the same time clinging to the power in the United States which comes from having a sense of self delineated as being "not someone else"—here not someone darker.

✄✄

You should not be talking about this, you with the blond streaks in your hair, as if you are somehow connected to it... (the words of accusing colleagues after a talk I gave on homophobia and my Arab-American and Pennsylvania Dutch "homes.")

I resent being seen as a "collector of oppressions" when I talk about my family—*my* family—as close to me as my father and a Sittu who considers me as real as her grandchildren who are "100 percent"... I have certainly benefitted from white skin privilege in this country but that is exactly why I talk about how my family made a place for itself in a country with a complex and deep racism and in a country which is anti-Arab, fiercely.

I'd like you to meet Anne, my Syrian friend. (English-American speaking to Chinese-American friend.)

While some have accused me of "stacking up oppressions like virtues," I find myself being used by a European-American to give herself legitimacy. That is, she counts me among her accomplishments—a Syrian friend, a Chinese friend, an African friend, a Jewish friend...These requests and commands prove the necessity of my speaking about Sittu, about my connection to her life and about the ways in which anti-Arab behavior affects her, affects me. Please, I already lost a grandmother to liver cancer, don't kill her again by denying my connection to her or by making that bond a feather for your cap.

My great-aunts talked about their mother leaving Haifa to come to the United States. They talked about the translations of the family's name (their father's family name) both in the Middle East and upon arrival in this country. A small Christian minority, Sittu's unmarried name was Cross. Her family was given the name Salibi (something like "Cross Bearers") by the Muslim majority. Upon arriving in the United States, several hundred years later, the name was anglicized from Salibi to Cross, undergoing another translation to fit the dominant group's world view.

My great-aunts told about the name Mamary, too. Forced to build towns for Muslims in Syria, my grandfather's family was given the name Mamary, meaning builder. Traditionally, they said, sons took their father's first names for family names. They talked about Jiddu's father not being allowed into the United States and his work on the Panama Canal while he waited to come to the United States. Upon arrival, my great-grandfather dropped Mamary and immigration listed him as Albert Elias. But instead of becoming Subrai Albert, my grandfather became Subrai Elias, as the names underwent another translation in America. Somehow, someone retrieved Mamary as a family name and my grandfather became Subrai Elias Mamary once again.

GRAPEVINE At a church picnic in a park, Hannah spots some small and tender leaves, deep olive green. She sends Subrai back to collect them in the middle of the night.

1. A vine on which grapes grow.

Dark violet, deep midnight blue, sea mist green, fleshy smooth skinned grapes hiding behind silky leaves.

Any of numerous woody vines bearing clusters of edible fruit.

Soak the leaves, measure rice, grind beef or lamb, mix in onions, special Syrian spices, rice, put a small spoonful of meat-rice mixture on grapevine leaf, fold in pointy ends and roll into small cigar in one quick motion, look, Adela, at how well she rolls the grapeleaves.

2. An informal, often secret means of transmitting information, gossip or rumor from person to person...

Secretly in the safety of the night, two, three, more, women share knowledge, love, a memory, respite, a fragment...

connected by secret word of mouth.

Women, mouths pressed together in secret words, a caress, an embrace, quickly darting tongue, smooth deep purple midnight grape, how to remember when there are no maps in this night sky...

My grandmother's sisters talked about the transmissions and translations of the men's names, and the men's lives from the Middle East to the United States. No one told me how daughters were named. Would I be Anne Janet? And she Janet Pearl? And then how would I name the connection to Hannah? No, no one described a system of naming or connection among the women. The naming is much more like the grapevine—a secret, informal transmission. My grandmother spoke of her sisters as "our Helen," "our Adela," her niece "our Cassie," her daughter-in-law "our Mary." She and I are connected, Anne and Hannah versions of the same name. We are connected in ways that spring through cracks like mint, or sprout up in gardens unplanned like tomatoes and in the grapevine wanderings of our imaginations.

I need this grapevine—this secret means of transmitting information, to remember my Sittu as she was to herself (and much of this I can never know) and as she was and is to me. Grapevine remembering fills the secret word of mouth, the two-lipped mint flowers, the dusky purple grapes, the fleshy red tomato with another sort of knowing as well. Though I am so glad to be included with the women in my family and I am honored every time I find myself among them rolling grapevine leaves or chopping mint or dicing the juicy warm tomatoes, I still wish these loving and lovely creations were not always in the service of father, son, grandfather, cousin, grandson, uncle, great-grandson.

I have spoken through the grapevine, in code, with my cousin Sandy. We assured each other at my cousin Mary Ann's wedding that we will be spinster cousins together in fifty years. I remember how I used to be absolutely enchanted with Sandy's waist-length, raven hair when we were little girls. I still am thrilled with the black, coarse strands in my hair which remind me of hers. By grapevine, by mint, tomato, and grapevine code, we have spoken our lesbian selves. She and I have said we need each other in so many ways. Until recently, she was the only other Arab-American lesbian I knew. She and I need each other as dykes, as Arab-American dykes, as our Sittu's granddaughters.

Tenacious, Sandy's and my connection grows like mint in our Jiddu's garage wall. Not only do she and I give each other a place, but we remember our Sittu and the way she released us like tomato seeds or a grapevine in the park.

VII

Appendix

Arab Resources and Organizations

The Image of Arabs in Sources of U.S. Culture

MARSHA J. HAMILTON

The Middle East is seldom out of the news. Civil unrest, terrorism, and volatile political personalities all reinforce many Americans' negative mental image of the Arab world, the Arab people, and Islam. In ignorance, many Americans think of Arabs, Turks, and Iranians as one ethnic group; forget that not all Arabs are Muslims; and fail to understand that peoples in the Middle East are as diverse as those found in the United States.

How the U.S. depicts other cultures may say more about our own fears and values than about the culture represented. Many American images of other peoples have their source in European, especially British, popular culture. For hundreds of years, Europeans and Americans have viewed the Arab Middle East in terms of a few unchanging stereotypical images: the wealthy sheikh, the harem beauty, the religious fanatic, or the downtrodden peasant. These images were common in colonial America; yet despite massive social change in the Arab world, they remain virtually unchanged in U.S. popular culture today.

Literature on the image of Arabs in U.S. culture agrees on two points: the images are stereotypes and the images are negative. Adjectives such as "lazy," "dirty," "backward," "oversexed," "fanatical," "violent" and "greedy" have been applied at different stages of U.S. history to groups including African-Americans, Chinese, Eastern Europeans, the Irish, Jews and Native-Americans. As each group fights the discrimination that is a direct result of stereotypes and sensitizes the U.S. public to that particular group's plight, another ethnic or social group takes its place in the role of the villain. The decline of the Cold War and the newly-polished image of Russia and the surrounding regions have been matched by a parallel increase in vilification of the Arab.

By the time children are four years old, they have begun the process of assimilating stereotypical images from television. This process is examined by Jack Shaheen in *The TV Arab*, the personal odyssy of an Arab-American in the world of television production. Shaheen asks why Arab characters are always villains despite many positive real-life role models available in Arab and Arab-American communities. This readable book discusses stereotypes in programs ranging from children's shows to prime time and follows Shaheen's discussions with statements from television spokespeople who say that America is "not ready" for positive Arab characters.

Current stereotypes of Arabs and Islam in popular literature are examined by Janice J. Terry in *Mistaken Identity*. Terry looks at the negative image of Arabs in over seventy British and American works including "instant" histories and romance, adventure, spy, and mystery novels. In *The Middle East in Crime Fiction: Mysteries, Spy Novels and Thrillers from 1916 to the 1980s*, Reeva S. Simon analyzes the plots, heros, villians, and major themes of about 620 American and British authors like John Le Carré plus some unexpected writers like Spiro T. Agnew, Marvin Kalb, and Ted Koppel. Although voluminous, Simon's annotated list is admittedly not exhaustive. Sadly, almost every title contains one or more villainous Arab characters. Suha J. Sabbagh summarizes the same subject in a fifty-seven-page monograph, *Sex, Lies and Stereotypes: The Image of Arabs in American Popular Fiction*.

Public Opinion And The News Media

The news media are often blamed for perpetuating negative images of Arabs and the Arab world. News thrives on controversy, and the images journalists use to describe events, individuals, organizations, and nations in the Arab world have been highly controversial. Several works representing different viewpoints analyze the people who bring us the news. Highly recommended is *Split Vision: The Portrayal of Arabs in the American Media*, edited by Edmund Ghareeb. This incisive look at television and print coverage of the Middle East between 1975 and 1982 includes interviews with journalists of the stature of Peter Jennings and essays on the prevalence of negative images of Arabs on television and in editorial cartoons, textbooks, and fiction. Authors tackle the sensitive subject of U.S. support for Israel and attempt to combat the belief that to be pro-Israel one must be anti-Arab. Other highly recommended collections are *Television Coverage of the Middle East*, edited by William C. Adams, and *The American Media and the Arabs*, edited by Michael C. Hudson and Ronald G. Wolfe. Both provide insight into the difficulty of reporting on complex Middle East issues.

Less information is available on the earlier history of media coverage of the Middle East. Although badly printed, Issam Suleiman Mousa's *The Arab Image in the U.S. Press* is useful for its coverage of the period 1917-1947. Richard Curtiss' excellent *A Changing Image* examines American news coverage of the Arab-Israeli conflict from 1918 to the Reagan years, concentrating on the more recent period. Montague Kern's very brief *Television and Middle East Diplomacy: President Carter's Fall 1977 Peace Initiative* can be used in conjunction with Carter's own books *Keeping Faith: Memoirs of a President* and *The Blood of Abraham*.

Two works with a Palestinian viewpoint are Edward Said's *Covering Islam: How the Media and the Experts Determine How We See the Rest of the World* and *Blaming the Victims: Spurious Scholarship and the Palestinian Question*, edited by Said and Christopher Hitchens. These works critique the media for presenting Islam and Palestinians solely in a threatening context while ignoring deeper issues and background information.

The Middle East and the United States: Perceptions and Policies, edited by Haim Shaked and Itamar Rabinovich, contains seventeen papers from a 1978 international colloquium sponsored by the Shiloah Center and the Center for Strategic Studies at Tel Aviv University, on U.S. policy and public opinion toward the Middle East. *Public Opinion and the Palestine Question*, edited by Elia Zureik and Fouad Moughrabi examines existing American, Canadian, western European, Israeli, and Palestinian public opinion polls in five essays covering the period from the 1940s to the early 1980s.

Education And Audio-visual Materials

Simplistic media views of the Middle East are accepted by U.S. audiences because they reinforce images that are already a part of U.S. culture. Many champions of multicultural education believe that stereotypes seldom survive in an atmosphere of knowledge and free access to information. What role then has the U.S. educational system played in promoting a balanced understanding of the Arab world?

Most minorities are justifiably concerned with how they are portrayed in textbooks and how their history is taught in U.S. schools. Several studies by Arab-American scholars have examined the poor representation of Arabs and Muslims in textbooks. Among these is Michael Suleiman's *American Images of Middle East Peoples: Impact of the High School*. This brief, frequently cited work is a landmark study on the effect of Arab stereotyping in the U.S. educational system. Suleiman's *The Arabs in the Mind of America* documents how the prejudices of U.S. high school teachers are transferred to students and how stereotypes enter the school system unwittingly to become part of the curriculum. Suleiman also examines the negative effect this process has on Arab-American children and on the formation of U.S.-Middle Eastern policy.

However, available works provide easily implemented programs to help identify and correct institutional gaps. *The Arab World: A Handbook for Teachers* by Ayad al-Qazzaz is a major revision of his *The Arabs in American Textbooks*. These works point out strengths and weaknesses in the Middle East coverage of specific elementary and junior high school textbooks, and al-Qazzaz includes a bibliography, list of AV materials, and books recommended for young readers. The scholarly Middle East Studies Association has also addressed this topic through its publication of William J. Griswold's *The Image of the Middle East in Secondary School Textbooks*, which looks at negative "national characteristics" attributed to the Arab and Islamic worlds in dozens of U.S. and Canadian textbooks. The work offers alternative syllabi for study of Middle Eastern culture, history, and political science and is most useful in its positive recommendations, which have been adopted by a few textbook publishers.

More assistance is available in *The Middle East: The Image and the Reality* by Jonathan Friedlander. These ten clearly written essays on teaching the Middle East from elementary to high school are presented with practical plans including a list of recommended audiovisual and library acquisitions to support teaching. Its companion volume, the *Teacher's Resource Handbook for Near Eastern Studies* by John N. Hawkins and Jon Maksik is an annotated bibliography of 828 records, tapes, books, filmstrips, and films to support teaching from preschool through high school.

There is a wealth of basic documentation on audiovisual materials about the Middle East and North Africa. However, much information is dated as many of these reference works were published in the early 1980s. In addition to those already mentioned is the *Educational Film Guide for Middle Eastern Studies*, by Joseph Greenman and Ann Joachim, a catalog of about 580 films with short annotations covering Israel, Turkey, and Iran in addition to the Arab world. *The World of Islam, Images and Echoes: A Critical Guide to Films and Recordings*, edited by Ellen Fairbanks-Bodman, is one of eight units in the Islamic Teaching Materials Project sponsored by the American Council of Learned Societies. Audrey Shabbas's more recent *Resource Guide to Materials on the Arab World*, published by the Association of Arab-American University Graduates, describes titles in a variety of formats to support instruction. *The Middle East and North Africa on Film: An Annotated Filmography*, by Marsha Hamilton McClintock, is an exhaustive annotated filmography of 2,460 films produced between 1903 and 1980 dealing with the Arab world, Turkey, Iran, and Israel. All of these guides contain distributor information.

Another resource for the educator is the local Arab-American community, which may provide speakers for the classroom or for special international day events.

Arab-American Civil Rights

A major concern of the Arab-American community has been that negative stereotypes of Arabs affect not only U.S. political policy but also the daily lives of Americans of Arab ancestry. Hate crimes against Arab-Americans increase in direct proportion to negative news coverage of Middle East events. Even non-Arab stories, such as the Iranian hostage crisis, caused hate crimes against Arab-Americans to increase.

Several Arab-American organizations work to counter unbalanced imagery and protect the civil rights of Arab-Americans. These include the National Association of Arab-Americans (NAAA), the Association of Arab-American University Graduates (AAUG), and the American-Arab Anti-Discrimination Committee (ADC). Each of these organizations has a publications office and these and other Arab-American organizations publish much material of interest. Several directories are available to help identify organizations.

Middle East: A Directory of Resources, edited by Thomas P. Fenton and Mary J. Heffron, is intended for educators. It contains lists of Jewish and Arab organizations, an annotated bibliography, and lists of periodicals and audiovisual materials on the Middle East. *Middle East Organizations in Washington, D.C.*, by Sindy Wayne and Riad El-Dada, describes 116 organizations whose focus is the Middle East. About half cover the Arab world. The third edition of the handy reference work *Arab-American Almanac* describes Arab-American organizations and serves as a state-by-state guide to religious institutions, newspapers, and radio programs directed toward the Arab-American community.

The ADC Times: News and Opinions of the American-Arab Anti-Discrimination Committee is a newsletter published ten times per year covering organization activities and lobbying efforts, as well as programs to counter anti-Arab stereotypes in advertising and the media. The publication also covers controversial political topics such as the Palestinian uprising and Israeli-Arab world relations. An example of an AAUG monograph is *Arabs in America: Myths and Realities*. This collection of fifteen scholarly conference papers covers images of Arabs in the media, immigration of Arabs to the U.S., and the question of Palestine.

Readers interested in a popular overview of the history of Arabs in the U.S. have several works from which to choose. *Arabs in America 1492-1977: A Chronology & Fact Book*, edited by Beverlee Turner Mehdi, begins with a chronology of events followed by the texts of major documents on U.S.-Arab world relations and on the Arab-American community. A personal vision of the community is provided by Gregory Orfalea in *Before the Flames: A Quest for the History of Arab Americans*. This highly recommended collection illustrates the diversity of the Arab immigrant experience through 125 narratives by Arab-Americans of varied religious, social, and economic backgrounds covering the period between the 1880s and the present. Two annotated bibliographies are Philip Kayal's *An Arab-American Bibliographic Guide* and *Arabic-Speaking Immigrants in the United States and Canada*, edited by Mohammed Sawaie. Alixa Naff's *Becoming American: The Early Arab Immigrant Experience* focuses on Syrian immigrant experience from the late nineteenth century to the 1930s and the role of peddling, transporting dry goods directly to consumers, as a route for many to assimilation into U.S. culture. This is a controversial book in Arab-American circles due to its emphasis on peddling over other trades. Written by a major figure in the Arab-American community, this interesting work also includes much information from a woman's perspective.

Other problems facing the Arab-American community are described in *The Arab World and Arab-Americans: Understanding a Neglected Minority*, edited by Sameer and Nabeel Abraham. These thirteen concise essays resulted from a project to raise cultural awareness of the heritage and needs of the large Arab-American student population in the Detroit/Dearborn school systems. Some essays focus on Detroit but many discuss the larger image of Arabs in film and textbooks and the effect these have on children and teachers. This work makes positive suggestions for organizing consciousness-raising seminars in local communities.

A visual journey through the Arab-American community is available in a 30-minute videotape by Jonathan Friedlander, *Arabs in America*, produced through the UCLA Office of Instructional Development. The tape uses photographs from archives and private collections to illustrate the history and diversity of the Arab-American community. It also addresses the issue of the poor image of Arabs in U.S. popular culture.

Arab Women

Europeans and Americans in sexually repressed mid-nineteenth-century society used the Middle East as a distant locale into which sexual fantasies could be projected and, in the case of travellers like the French novelist Gustave Flaubert, acted out. The western image of Arab women has both fascinated and angered western audiences. But how close is the image of the harem beauty, the belly dancer, or the stooped matron swathed in black to the reality of Arab women today or throughout history? The reality of women's lives may be examined in statistical works such as *Women of the World: Near East and North Africa*, by Mary Chamie; through numerous historical and anthropological studies such as *Women in Nineteenth-Century Egypt*, by Judith Tucker, or in *Land before Honour: Palestinian Women in the Occupied Territories*, by Kitty Warnock. Anthologies containing Arab women's own voices include the excellent *Middle Eastern Muslim Women Speak*, edited by Elizabeth Fernea and Basima Bezirgan, and a less-focused work, *Images of Arab Women: Fact and Fiction*, by Mona Mikhail.

But the finest single "stereotype-buster" is the highly recommended *Images of Women: The Portrayal of Women in Photography of the Middle East, 1860-1950*, by Sarah Graham-Brown. This is a detailed analysis of women of diverse socioeconomic groups over a ninety-year period, addressing both women's public and private lives. The well-researched text, heavily illustrated with period photographs, parades the richness and diversity of Arab women's history and their service in both traditional and nontraditional roles, and it slams the image of Arab women as sex objects, as so often portrayed in Orientalist art.

The concept of the harem, or separate living and working quarters for women, has also been difficult for western audiences to comprehend, especially as the term is often incorrectly confused with the idea of polygamy. Indeed, the western image of the harem as a wild sexual playground is still the most pervasive of U.S. popular cultural representations of Arab women.

The traditional world of the harem is documented in several works, including Fanny Davis' readable *The Ottoman Lady: A Social History from 1718 to 1918*. Although Davis examines Turkish, not Arab women, the description of upper-class women in Istanbul over a two-hundred-year period gives a clear picture of the activities within the harem where women performed many social and household functions. Also describing Turkish women is *Harem: The World Behind the Veil*, by Alev Lytle Croutier, whose grandmother lived in a nineteenth-century Turkish harem. Unfortunately, the text relies heavily on secondhand material, largely by European men who were seldom permitted inside a harem. A highly recommended primary source is *Harem Years: The Memoirs of an Egyptian Feminist (1879-1924)*, by Huda Shaarawi, the political activist who is remembered for being the first Egyptian woman to appear in public without a veil. This unique autobiography covers her personal life, her awakening as a feminist and her fight for women's rights and Egyptian independence.

The sinister side of colonialism and its effect on Arab women is examined in *The Colonial Harem*, by Malek Alloula. This is a disturbing collection of French colonial photographic postcards depicting nude Algerian women, cards that were openly sent through the mail from Algeria to France between 1900 and 1930. A nationalist/feminist text decries the "cultural violence" of this exploitation of women and the dehumanizing effects of colonization.

One book on women that defies categorization is *Serpent of the Nile: Women and Dance in the Arab World*, by Wendy Buonaventura. This is a delightful look at traditional Middle Eastern dance, at the role of dancers and singers in the eighteenth- to twentieth-century Arab world, and at attitudes toward dance in the Arab world and among European travelers. It contains a lengthy section on popular U.S. images of the belly dance in the nineteenth and twentieth centuries. Lavishly illustrated with paintings and photographs, this work chips away at the stereotype of the belly dancer.

The history of the image of Arabs in U.S. popular culture and its historical sources has been a sad compendium of outdated stereotypes, convenient villains, sexual fantasies, excuses for discrimination, and justification for support of particular economic or political policies. Continued U.S. involvement in the Arab world may again bring stereotypes of Arabs to the U.S. public as hurried commentators reduce to simple terms extremely complex political situations rooted in decades of conflict. It is to be hoped that Americans will be motivated to search beyond these simple stereotypes for a deeper knowledge and understanding of the rich and diverse cultures that make up the Arab world.

The caveat "consider the source" is nowhere more appropriate than in selecting source materials in Middle East studies. A critical perspective, and healthy scepticism, are useful tools when placing a work in context or in evaluating an author's purpose. Publications with differing viewpoints have the ability to teach us more about ourselves and the diverse people who inhabit the world which we all share.

Works Cited

The ADC Times: News and Opinions of the American-Arab Anti-Discrimination Committee. ADC Research Institute (October 1984-); continues ADC Reports.

Alloula, Malek. *The Colonial Harem,* trans. by Myrna Godzich and Wlad Godzich. University of Minnesota Press, 1986.

The American Media and the Arabs, ed. by Michael C. Hudson and Ronald G. Wolfe. Center for Contemporary Arab Studies, Georgetown University, 1980.

The Arab World and Arab-Americans: Understanding a Neglected Minority, ed. by Sameer and Nabeel Abraham. Center for Urban Studies, Wayne State University, 1981.

Arab-American Almanac. 3rd ed. News Circle Publishing Company, 1984.

Arabic-Speaking Immigrants in the United States and Canada: A Bibliographic Guide with Annotations, ed. by Mohammad Sawaie. Mazda Publishers, 1985.

Arabs in America [videotape]. Regents of the University of California, 1981.

Arabs in America 1492-1977: A Chronology & Fact Book, ed. by Beverlee Turner Mehdi. Oceana Publications, 1978.

Arabs in America: Myths and Realities, ed. by Baha Abu-Laban and Faith T. Zeadey. Medina University Press International, 1975.

Blaming the Victims: Spurious Scholarship and the Palestinian Question, ed. by Edward W. Said and Christopher Hitchens. Verso, 1988.

Buonaventura, Wendy. *Serpent of the Nile: Women and Dance in the Arab World.* Saqi Books, 1990.

Carter, Jimmy. *Keeping Faith: Memoirs of a President.* Bantam Books, 1982.

—*The Blood of Abraham.* Houghton Mifflin, 1985.

Chamie, Mary. *Women of the World: Near East and North Africa.* U.S. Dept. of Commerce, Bureau of the Census, 1985.

Croutier, Alev Lytle. *Harem: The World Behind the Veil.* Abbeville Press, 1989.

Curtiss, Richard. *A Changing Image: American Perceptions of the Arab-Israeli Dispute.* American Educational Trust, 1986.

Davis, Fanny. *The Ottoman Lady: A Social History from 1718 to 1918.* Greenwood Press, 1986.

Graham-Brown, Sarah. *Images of Women: The Portrayal of Women in Photography of the Middle East, 1860-1950.* Quartet, 1988.

Greenman, Joseph and Ann Joachim. *Educational Film Guide for Middle Eastern Studies.* University of Michigan, 1980.

Griswold, William J. *The Image of the Middle East in Secondary School Textbooks.* Middle East Studies Association of North America, 1975.

Hawkins, John N. and Jon Maksik. *Teacher's Resource Handbook for Near Eastern Studies: An Annotated Bibliography of Curriculum Materials Preschool through Grade Twelve.* Gustave E. von Grunebaum Center for Near Eastern Studies, UCLA, 1976.

Kern, Montague. *Television and Middle East Diplomacy: President Carter's Fall 1977 Peace Initiative.* Center for Contemporary Arab Studies, Georgetown University, 1983.

Kayal, Philip. *An Arab-American Bibliographic Guide.* Association of Arab-American University Graduates, 1985.

McClintock, Marsha Hamilton. *The Middle East and North Africa on Film: An Annotated Filmography.* Garland, 1982.

Middle East: A Directory of Resources, ed. by Thomas P. Fenton and Mary J. Heffron. Orbis Books, 1988.

The Middle East: The Image and the Reality, ed. by Jonathan Friedlander. Regents of the University of California, 1981.

The Middle East and the United States: Perceptions and Policies, ed. by Haim Shaked and Itamar Rabinovich. Transaction Books, 1980.

Middle East Organizations in Washington, D.C., ed. by Sindy Wayne and Riad El-Dada. Middle East Institute, 1985.

Middle Eastern Muslim Women Speak, ed. by Elizabeth Fernea and Basima Bezirgan. University of Texas Press, 1977.

Mikhail, Mona. *Images of Arab Women: Fact and Fiction.* Three Continents Press, 1979.

Mousa, Issam Suleiman. *The Arab Image in the U.S. Press.* Peter Lang, 1984.

Naff, Alixa. *Becoming American: The Early Arab Immigrant Experience.* Southern Illinois University Press, 1985.

Orfalea, Gregory. *Before the Flames: A Quest for the History of Arab Americans.* University of Texas Press, 1988.

Public Opinion and the Palestine Question, ed. by Elia Zureik and Fouad Moughrabi. Croom Helm, 1987.

al-Qazzaz, Ayad. *The Arab World: A Handbook for Teachers.* NAJDA, 1978.

—*The Arabs in American Textbooks.* NAJDA, 1976.

Sabbagh, Suha J. *Sex, Lies and Stereotypes: The Image of Arabs in American Popular Fiction.* ADC Research Institute, 1990.

Said, Edward W. *Covering Islam: How the Media and the Experts Determine How We See the Rest of the World.* Pantheon Books, 1981.

—*Orientalism.* Pantheon Books, 1978.

Shabbas, Audrey. *Resource Guide to Materials on the Arab World.* Association of Arab-American University Graduates, 1987.

Shaheen, Jack. *The TV Arab.* Bowling Green State University Popular Press, 1984.

Shaarawi, Huda. *Harem Years: The Memoirs of an Egyptian Feminist (1879-1924).* Feminist Press at the City University of New York, 1987. [Author also listed as Sha'rawi, Huda.]

Simon, Reeva S. *The Middle East in Crime Fiction: Mysteries, Spy Novels and Thrillers from 1916 to the 1980s.* L. Barber Press, 1989.

Split Vision: The Portrayal of Arabs in the American Media, ed. by Edmund Ghareeb. Revised and expanded ed. American-Arab Affairs Council, 1983.

Suleiman, Michael. *American Images of Middle East Peoples: Impact of the High School.* Middle East Studies Association of North America, 1977.

—*The Arabs in the Mind of America.* Amana Books, 1988.

Television Coverage of the Middle East, ed. by William C. Adams. Ablex Publishing, 1981.

Terry, Janice T. *Mistaken Identity: Arab Stereotypes in Popular Writing.* American-Arab Affairs Council, 1985.

Tucker, Judith. *Women in Nineteenth Century Egypt.* Cambridge University Press, 1985.

Warnock, Kitty. *Land before Honour: Palestinian Women in the Occupied Territories*. Macmillan, 1990.

The World of Islam, Images and Echoes: A Critical Guide to Films and Recordings, ed. by Ellen Fairbanks-Bodman. American Council of Learned Societies, 1980.

Organizations With an Arab-American/Arab-Canadian Focus

Feminist Arab-American Network (FAN)
PO Box 38-1843
Cambridge MA 02238

Arab Canadian Women's Network
106 Duplex Ave.
Toronto Ontario M5P 2A7
Canada

> A member of the National Action Committee on the Status of Women.

Union of Palestinian Women's Associations in North America (UPWA)
PO Box 29110
Chicago IL 60629
(312) 436 6060

> UPWA's publication, *The Voice of Arab Women*, can be reached via: PO Box 1655, Dearborn MI 48121.

Arab Women Solidarity Association, North America
PO Box 95760
Seattle WA 98145
(206) 322-1360

> AWSA, North America formed in 1994 to respond to the issues facing Arab-American women, and to create solidarity among Arab women in North America, the Arab region, and internationally.

The Institute for Arab Women's Studies
1900 18th St. NW
Washington DC 20009
(202) 667 4540

> This organization produces studies on Arab feminism in general and Palestinian feminism in particular. See their publications: Suha Sabbagh, *Sex, Lies and Stereotypes: The Image of Arabs in American Popular Fiction,* and Suha Sabbagh and Ghada Talhami (e.), *Images and Reality: Palestinians Under Occupation in the Diaspora.*

Association for Middle East Women's Studies (AMEWS)
For membership and newsletter subscription information, write:
Nancy Kittner, Secretary/Treasurer, AMEWS
Centerville Rd.
East Wallingford VT 05742

American-Arab Anti-Discrimination Committee
4201 Connecticut Ave. NW Suite 500
Washington DC 20008
(202) 244 2990

> ADC is a national advocacy group for Arab-Americans and provides educational materials. Its publication, *ADC Times*, is published 10 times a year.

Arab, Arab-Canadian, Arab-American Lesbian Network (AALN)
PO Box 1504
Lawrence KS 66044

> Building support, resources, and friendships.

Arab Lesbian, Gay, and Bisexual Network
PO Box 460526
San Francisco CA 94114

National Association of Arab-Americans (NAAA)
1212 New York Ave, NW, Ste. 300
Washington, DC 20005
(202)842-1840

Radius of Arab-American Writers Ink (RAWI)
c/o Barbara Nimri Aziz
160 6th Ave.
New York NY 10013

About the Contributors

Azizah al-Hibri was born and educated in Beirut, Lebanon. She came to the United States in 1966 to pursue her graduate studies, and became a citizen many years later. She is presently a professor of law at the University of Richmond Law School. She has published many articles in feminist theory and is founding editor of *Hypatia*.

Lamea Abbas Amara is an Iraqi poet who has pursued a distinguished literary and diplomatic career. Seven collections of her poetry have been published in Arabic. She currently lives in La Mesa, California, where she is the editor of *Mandaee*, a bilingual cultural magazine.

Marti Farha Ammar has lectured widely on the current political situation in the Middle East, and has completed extensive studies of Arabic and translation. A world traveler and political activist, she is president of Save Lebanon, Inc., which provides humanitarian relief for Palestinian and Lebanese victims of the Lebanese civil war.

Barbara Nimri Aziz is a New York-based anthropologist and journalist who regularly writes from the Middle East. She is completing a book on the Arab experience of the war against Iraq. She is also producer and host of *Tahrir: Voices of the Arab World*, broadcast over Pacifica-WBAI radio in New York.

Martha Ani Boudakian is an activist and aspiring midwife. She is co-founder of an organization of Armenian feminists that may choose not to name itself. She currently lives in Boston and plans to return to the woods someday.

Ellen Mansoor Collier is a Houston-based freelance writer and editor who writes for a variety of magazines. A former magazine editor, she has a Bachelor of Journalism degree from the University of Texas at Austin.

Leila Diab is a freelance writer living in Palos Hill, Illinois. She has a B.A. in sociology and an M.A. in urban teaching. She is the public relations chairperson of the Union of Palestinian-American Women, and is actively involved in working for Palestinians' rights and women's rights.

Nada Elia grew up in Beirut, Lebanon. She received a B.A. from Beirut University College and an M.A. from the American University of Beirut, where she also lectured in the Cultural Studies Department. From 1983 to 1987, she worked as a journalist covering the Lebanese civil war. She has a doctorate in Comparative Literature from Purdue University.

Mona Fayad teaches English and Comparative Literature at Salem State College, Salem, Massachusetts. She has published a number of articles on Arab women writers and is currently working on a book about Arab women and nationalism. She is also writing a novel set in Syria.

Lilith Finkler is the daughter of a Polish father and Libyan mother, both Jews. She is a bisexual, biracial Gemini, straddling the borders of many worlds. As a survivor of the psychiatric industry, she is proud to reclaim the word "lunatic."

Bookda Gheisar lives in Seattle, Washington and is in practice as a feminist therapist. She has been previously published in Loss of the Ground Note: Women Writing on Their Mothers' Death.

Carol Haddad is a second-generation American of Lebanese and Syrian ancestry. She grew up in metropolitan Detroit and, after living in various parts of the United States and England, has returned to her home state, which she only partially considers home. She makes her living as an academic researcher and consultant.

Laila Halaby is an Arab-American who graduated from Washington University in 1988. She has just finished her Masters at UCLA in the Department of Near Eastern Languages and Cultures, and is currently working on a collection of Palestinian folktales which she would like to make available for children.

Marsha J. Hamilton is a librarian and an assistant professor at the Ohio State University Libraries where she served for eight years as Middle East Librarian. She is the author of *The Middle East and North Africa on Film: An Annotated Filmography,* and is a frequent lecturer on popular cultural images of peoples of the Middle East and North Africa, and cross-cultural communication. Ms. Hamilton co-produced *SALAAM,* a radio program of Middle Eastern music and culture, and served as a consultant on *Arabs in America,* a videotape on Arab immigration to the United States.

Trisha F. Harper is a poet whose work has been performed at the Smithsonian Institute, and has been anthologized in *Women for All Seasons* (Los Angeles Women's Building, 1987).

Happy/L.A. Hyder is a self-taught/exploring artist and dancer who is most happy when caught up in the creative process. Now in the second year of a wonderful relationship with Sylvia Palma, horizons are wide and possibilities endless. She dedicates her piece to her mother, Minnie E. Hyder, who always encouraged her in her artwork.

Adele Ne Jame lives and teaches creative writing in Honolulu, Hawaii. She held the position of Artist-in-Residence at the University of Wisconsin-Madison for the 1989-1990 academic year and received a National Endowment for the Arts award in 1990. Her poems have been published in various journals such as Nimrod, Ploughshares, The Blue Mesa Review, and *Manoa.* Her newest book of poems, *Fieldwork,* is forthcoming from Floating Island Publications.

Eileen Kaady has been writing poetry and articles reflecting her Arab-American roots for over fifteen years. Her poem, *Send a Cooling Breeze to Soothe the Soul of Lebanon,* was published in *Women of Color News* in 1985.

Joanna Kadi is a writer and editor. Her essays and short fiction have appeared in *Colors, Working Class Women in the Academy: Laborers in the Knowledge Factory, Sojourner: The Women's Forum, Sinister Wisdom,* and *Hurricane Alice.* Kadi is currently working on her first novel.

Pauline Kaldas was born in Egypt and immigrated to the United States in 1969. From 1990 to 1993, she lived in Egypt and taught at The American University in Cairo. She is currently working on her Ph.D. in English at SUNY Binghamton. The poems published here first appeared in lift magazine; her work has also appeared in *The Michigan Quarterly Review.*

Jennifer Khawaja is a film and video producer and community activist. Her article on grassroots video production, entitled *Process Video: Self-Reference and Social Change,* has been published in Canada and the U.S. She is presently working on a documentary film about issues facing Arab women living in North America as well as a feature-length drama about the lives of five women who come together as they explore their sexual and cultural identities.

Zana Macki is the former Regional Coordinator of the American-Arab Anti-Discrimination Committee (ADC) Greater Detroit Chapter. She holds degrees in English and Mass Communications from Wayne State University. She is first-generation Lebanese-American, living in Dearborn, Michigan.

L. J. Mahoul's essay is dedicated to her grandmother, who recently passed away, in loving memory of a great woman who touched so many lives yet whose own special life was barely known.

Lisa Suhair Majaj is a Palestinian-American currently writing a dissertation on Arab-American literature for the University of Michigan. Her poetry has appeared in the *Worcester Review, Woman of Power, Mr. Cogito,* and in other publications. She has an essay on Arab-American literature forthcoming in an anthology entitled *The Uses of Memory.*

Anne J. M. Mamary is a middle-class, christian-cultured dyke of Pennsylvania Dutch and Syrian ancestry. Currently she is a graduate student in feminist philosophy at the State University of New York at Binghamton. She lives with Java, a fabulous cat, and is lucky enough to have a lesbian cousin.

Leila Marshy is of Palestinian origin and a Montreal-based scriptwriter and film editor. She will soon be directing her first film and having her first child. Hopefully one won't pre-empt the other.

Mona Marshy is a Canadian of half-Palestinian origin. She recently returned from four months in the West Bank and Gaza Strip, to complete a master's thesis on the Palestinian women's movement for the Department of Geography at Carleton University.

D. H. Melhem, a native New Yorker, is the daughter of immigrants of Syro-Lebanese and Greek extraction who settled in Brooklyn. She is the author of three books of poetry, Notes on 94th Street, Rest in Love, and *Children of the House Afire.* She also wrote *Gwendolyn Brooks: Poetry and the Heroic Voice* and *Heroism in the New Black Poetry.* The latter study won an American Book Award (1991). Her first novel, *Blight,* was published by Riverrun Press in 1994. Dr. Melhem is at work on a musical drama based on her New York poems.

May Mansoor Munn is a Palestinian, Jerusalem-born, of Quaker faith. Although she taught school for many years, writing has been essential to her life—even when she was too busy to write. She writes because of a need to communicate a certain truth she has experienced. She is married to Albert Munn and has two wonderful children, Ellen Mansoor Collier, a writer and contributor to this book, and Jeff Mansoor, a graphic artist.

Naomi Shihab Nye has published three books of poems, *Different Ways to Pray, Hugging the Jukebox,* and *Yellow Glove.* She has edited an international collection of poems for young readers called *This Same Sky* and has recently published a picture book, *Sitti's Secrets*, from Four Winds Press. Her forthcoming book is *Red Suitcase*.

Marilynn Rashid lives and teaches Spanish in Detroit. Her essays, translations and poems have appeared in *The International Poetry Review, Fifth Estate, Short Story International, The Wayne Review* and elsewhere.

Pearl Davies Saad is a writer and painter living in the San Francisco Bay Area.

Marjorie Gellhorn Sa'adah, M.A., is an ethicist working as the executive director of Homeless Health Care Los Angeles. She is happy to have been named after her grandmother, Marjorie.

Doris Safie (of Palestinian origin) lives in New Hampshire where she works as a proofreader of Spanish legal texts and freelances as a writer and editor. Her most recent creative efforts appeared in the Spring 1991 issue of Paintbrush. She is also co-editor of *FACTS: The Palestinian Uprising,* published by the AAUG Press.

Therese Saliba teaches English at the University of Washington, Seattle, where she is completing her dissertation, "Saving Brown Women: Gender, Culture, and the Politics of Imperialism." She is also involved in peace and justice issues in the United States and the Middle East.

Margaret Salome is working on a Ph.D. in Romance linguistics. She spent her formative years in Miami and Montreal, learning Spanish, some Hebrew and a little French, and now lives in Seattle with a cat named Motec.

Mary Salome is an apprentice producer and engineer at KPFA, listener-sponsored radio in Berkeley, and an attendant for disabled people. She has had a short piece published in Hysteria, a student feminist magazine in Santa Cruz.

Linda Sawaya is a Lebanese artist with roots in the Los Angeles Arabic community. She has created covers for *My Grandmother's Cactus, Khalil Gibran, Beyond the Storm, Everyday Life in the Muslim Middle East,* among other titles. Her first two illustrated children's book are in publication Fall 1995. Sawaya lives and works in Portland, Oregon.

Michelle Sharif received her B.A. in Political Science from UC-Davis and her M.A. in Arab Studies from Georgetown University. While living in Jordan, she worked in the Palestinian refugee camps writing articles for the United Nations Relief and Works Agency's (UNRWA) magazine.

Linda Simon, an activist in the Arab-American community, has lived and worked in the Middle East and North Africa. She is writing a book about Camp Hammond, a summer camp in Massachusetts for Arab-American children.

"Zabelle" chose her name in honor of a thirteenth-century Armenian queen as well as two other Armenian literary women, Zabelle Khanjian Asadour ("Sybille," 1863-1934) and Zabelle Hovannisian Yessayan (1878-1937). Her article was first published in Ararat quarterly's special issue on Armenian feminism (Autumn 1988), edited by Arlene Avakian.

Hoda M. Zaki is Associate Professor of Political Science and Director of African American Studies at Hood College in Frederick, Maryland. Her publications include *Phoenix Renewed: The Survival and Mutation of Utopian Thought in North American Science Fiction, 1965-1982* (1988; Borgo Press, 1993) and articles on feminist and African-American science fiction.

Lorene Zarou-Zouzounis is a Palestinian-American, born in Ramallah, Palestine. She emigrated to the United States in 1964 with her family. She studies Creative Writing at San Francisco State University and has self-published a chapbook of poems entitled *Inquire Within.* Her poetry has appeared in various magazines around the country.

Permissions

Grateful acknowledgments to the following individuals and publishers, who allowed us to include their works in this collection:

Ellen Mansoor Collier's essay, "Arab-Americans: Living with Pride and Prejudice," was originally published in *Glamour,* and an updated version was published in the Peace Education Foundation's magazine.

A longer version of Marsha Hamilton's essay, "The Image of Arabs in the Sources of U.S. Culture," under the title "The Image of Arabs in Sources of American Culture," first appeared in *CHOICE* Magazine, April 1991.

Adele Ne Jame's poem, "A Blessing," was first published in *Denver Quarterly,*.

Joanna Kadi's essay, "Five Steps to Creating Culture," originally appeared in *Colors* magazine, Minneapolis, Minnesota, July 1993.

Pauline Kaldas' poems, "Exotic" and "ABC," originally appeared in *lift* magazine.

Lisa Suhair Majaj's poem, "Recognized Futures," is reprinted by permission of the author and Viking Penguin. The poem was first published in *Unsettling America: Race and Ethnicity in Contemporary American Poetry.* Edited by Maria Mazzioti Gillan and Jennifer Gillan, 1993.

D. H. Melhem's poem, "say french," was originally published in *Rest in Love,* copyright 1975, 1978 by D. H. Melhem. (New York: Dovetail Press.) Reprinted by permission of the author.

A longer version of Therese Saliba's essay, "Military Presence and Absences: Arab Women and the Persian Gulf War," was originally published in *Seeing Through the Media: The Persian Gulf War,* edited by Susan Jeffords and Lauren Rabinovitz. Copyright 1994 by Rutgers University Press.

May Mansoor Munn's essay, "Homecoming," originally appeared in *Friends Journal* and *Texas Magazine.*

Zabelle's essay, "Armenian/Lesbian: Telling Our Stories," is reprinted with the permission of *Ararat.*

Index

About the Editor

Joanna Kadi is a writer and editor. She has worked as a grassroots community organizer on a diverse range of issues including Palestinian self-determination and ending violence against women. Her essays and short fiction have appeared in *Colors, Working Class Women in the Academy: Laborers in the Knowledge Factory, Sojourner: The Women's Forum, Sinister Wisdom*, and *Hurricane Alice*. Kadi is currently working on her first novel.

About South End Press

South End Press is a non-profit, collectively run book publisher with over 180 titles in print. Since our founding in 1977, we have tried to meet the needs of readers who are exploring, or are already committed to, the politics of radical social change.

Our goal is to publish books that encourage critical thinking and constructive action on the key political, cultural, social, economic and ecological issues shaping life in the United States and in the world. In this way, we hope to give expression to a wide diversity of democratic social movements and to provide an alternative to the products of corporate publishing.

Through the Institute for Social and Cultural Change, South End Press works with other political media projects—*Z Magazine;* Speak Out!, a speakers bureau; the New Liberation News Service and the Publishers Support Project—to expand access to information and critical analysis.

Other titles from South End Press include:

Sisters of the Yam: Black Women and Self-Recovery, bell hooks
The Last Generation: Prose and Poetry, Cherríe Moraga
Reproductive Rights and Wrongs: The Global Politics of Population Control, Betsy Hartmann
Mujeres, Sida Y Activismo: The Spanish Edition of Women, AIDS, and Activism, The ACT UP/NY Women & AIDS Book Group
Hear My Testimony: Maria Teresa Tula, Human Rights Activist of El Salvador, Translated and edited by Lynn Stephen
Mediations: Forays Into the Culture and Gender Wars, Elayne Rapping
Memoir of a Race Traitor, Mab Segrest

The State of Asian America: Activism and Resistance in the 1990s, edited and introduced by Karin Aguilar-San Juan

The State of Native America: Genocide, Colonization, and Resistance, M. Annette Jaimes

Unsettling Relations: The University as a Site of Feminist Struggles, Himani Bannerji, Linda Carty, Kari Dehli, Susan Heald, and Kate McKenna

On Call: Political Essays, June Jordan

Yearning: Race, Gender and Cultural Politics, bell hooks

Black Looks: Race and Representation, bell hooks

A Dream Compels Us: Voices of Slavadoran Women, New American Press with a preface by Grace Paley

Abortion Without Apology: Radical History for the 1990s, Ninia Baehr

Ain't I a Woman: Black Woman and Feminism, bell hooks

Beauty Secrets: Women and the Politics of Appearance, Wendy Chapkis

Common Differences: Conflicts in Black and White Feminist Perspectives, Gloria Joseph and Jill Lewis

Feminist Theory: From Margin to Center, bell hooks

From Abortion to Reproductive Freedom: Transforming a Movement, edited by Marlene Gerber Fried

Loving In the War Years, Cherríe Moraga

Poverty in the American Dream: Women and Children First, Karin Stallard, Barbara Ehrenreich, and Holly Sklar

Race, Gender and Work: A Multicultural Economic History of Women in the United States, Teresa Amott and Julie Matthaei

Regulating the Lives of Women: Social Welfare Policy from Colonial Times to the Present, Mimi Abramovitz

Talking Back: Thinking Feminist, Thinking Black, bell hooks

Walking To The Edge: Essays of Resistance, Margaret Randall

Women, AIDS, and Activism, ACT UP/NY Women and AIDS Book Group

Interested In South End Press?

Buy South End Press titles at your local independent bookstore or order directly from publisher. Call Toll-free 1-800-533-8478.